Fashion & War in Popular Culture

Fashion & War in Popular Culture

Denise N. Rall

intellect Bristol, UK / Chicago, USA

First published in the UK in 2014 by
Intellect, The Mill, Parnall Road, Fishponds, Bristol, BS16 3JG, UK

First published in the USA in 2014 by
Intellect, The University of Chicago Press, 1427 E. 60th Street,
Chicago, IL 60637, USA

A catalogue record for this book is available from the
British Library.

Copy-editing: Susanne Hillen
Cover design: Stephanie Sarlos
Cover image: © Stokette, image 111484658, Shutterstock, Inc.
Production manager: Bethan Ball
Typesetting: Contentra Technologies

Print ISBN: 978-1-84150-751-4
ePDF ISBN: 978-1-78320-294-2
ePub ISBN: 978-1-78320-293-5

Printed and bound by Hobbs the Printers Ltd, UK

Table of Contents

Acknowledgements   vii

Introduction   1

Contextualizing fashion and war within popular culture   3
Jennifer Craik

Overview   9
Denise N. Rall

Section I: The military in popular culture   19

Chapter 1: Representation of female wartime bravery in Australia's
Wanda the War Girl and *Jane at War* from the UK   21
Jane Chapman

Chapter 2: Fashionable fascism: Cinematic images of the Nazi
before and after 9/11   35
Kylee M. Hartman-Warren

Chapter 3: Branding the muscled male body as military costume   57
Heather Smith and Richard Gehrmann

Section II: Fashion and the military   73

Chapter 4: In the service of clothes: Elsa Schiaparelli and the war experience   75
Annita Boyd

Chapter 5: The discipline of appearance: Military style
and Australian flight hostess uniforms 1930-1964   91
Prudence Black

Chapter 6: Models, medals, and the use of military emblems in fashion   107
Amanda Laugesen

**Section III: Framing youth fashion, textile artworks and postcolonial
               costume in the context of conflict**   **123**

Chapter 7: Battle dressed – clothing the criminal, or the horror
               of the 'hoodie' in Britain   125
Joanne Turney

Chapter 8: Dutch wax and display: London and the art of Yinka Shonibare   139
Davinia Gregory

Chapter 9: Costume and conquest: Introducing a proximity framework
               for post-war impacts on textile and fashion   157
Denise N. Rall

Afterword: The military in contemporary fashion   175
Denise N. Rall

Contributors   181

Acknowledgements

I would like to thank the Popular Culture Association of Australia and New Zealand (PopCAANZ) for making me welcome at their inaugural conference in Sydney in 2010, and for politely listening to my very much 'under development' ideas regarding changes in fashion following the Spanish conquest of Peru. Without the Association, I would not have made the valuable contacts that led to my brilliant list of contributors. Established scholars Vicki Karaminas, Prudence Black and Jo Turney provided leadership from behind the scenes. I especially thank Professor Jennifer Craik, who kindly agreed to introduce the volume.

Further, my contacts at Intellect were no less valuable, with initial enthusiasm from James Campbell, followed by the very hard work and perseverance of production manager Bethan Ball. All of my suggestions (and objections) were heard with great forbearance. I thank Beth especially for the patience and cheerful guidance that she provided throughout the process. Any remaining errors are strictly my own.

As always, I thank my family, Associate Professor J. Doland Nichols, Fran and Louis Rall, and Alyse Rall Benjamin. All of them are writers, variously: poets, scientific authors, and novelists of fantasy fiction. I would be a much poorer scholar without all of their help. I also thank the School of Arts and Social Sciences, Southern Cross University, for providing an adjunct appointment at a critical time in the writing process. Recently, I met Professor Emerita Beverly Gordon, from my former home institution: the University of Wisconsin-Madison. It was inspiring to see her work in the gorgeous volume: *Wearing Propaganda: Textiles on the Home Front in Japan, Britain, and the United States* (Yale University Press, 2005). The many connections between dress, textiles and war are not unique to this volume.

Finally, I thank my Costume instructors, Jean Ward and Glenda Pierce. I learned much about what it takes to make a garment work. From there, I could take costume forward into the conflicting world of war, and its manifestations in popular culture.

Denise N. Rall

Introduction

Contextualizing fashion and war within popular culture

Jennifer Craik

Fashion and war may seem like odd bedfellows and yet they are closely linked historically and culturally. This exciting volume addresses the relationship between fashion and war in popular culture. It explores diverse issues associated with the ways in which war, colonial occupation, cultural conquest and military dress have influenced and been influenced by fashion and codes of conduct associated with how we dress ourselves.

The pervasiveness of military uniforms in fashion is but one manifestation of this process. Military uniforms, in particular, offer fashion qualities of spectacle, order, repetition and carefully contrived lines and silhouettes while evoking images of discipline, civility and heroism (Craik 2005). The details of military uniforms have appeared again and again in the fashions of the past, leading Diana Vreeland to call uniforms 'the sportswear of the nineteenth century' (Answers.com 2000). The powerful signs and symbols can be readily appropriated selectively in the pursuit of fashion and popular culture. As Black argues: 'The uniform is the clothing of the modern disciplinary society' (see Black, Chapter 5, in this volume). This is one theme of this collection.

However, *Fashion and War in Popular Culture* covers more than that. The background to the volume is the complex interplay between war, colonialism, imperialism, postcolonialism and postmodernism. Histories of the cultural conquest of other cultures usually only refer to matters of dress, costume and fashion as an aside – an ephemeral symbol of the process of victory, defeat or pacification. The reality is that fashion is not only the most visible indicator of those processes but a remarkably agile signifier of the twists and turns – and nuances – of cultural conquest. Indeed, it is impossible to understand – or 'read' – fashion without knowledge of the context of its appearance. Arguably, history matters more to the understanding of fashion than to other disciplines.

Fashion is the body writ large as a social body that announces its location in time and space. It is also a communicative device that speaks to observers and demands a response and connection. My favourite story about fashion and the body is anthropologist Claude Lévi-Strauss' account of how the South American Caduveo Indians appropriated the Spanish Baroque motifs of stripes, spirals and whorls in their body decoration and art. He writes:

After the Indians saw a European warship for the first time, when the *Maracanha* sailed up the Paraguay in 1857, the sailors noticed the next day that their bodies were covered with anchor-shaped motifs; one Indian even had an officer's uniform painted in great detail all over his torso – with buttons and stripes, and the sword-belt over the coat-tails (Lévi-Strauss 1976: 243).

Whether this was a case of imitation or coincidence, the example of the painted 'officer' illustrates that the Indians recognized the significance of the details of the uniform as markers of identity, status and communication which they sought to replicate through body decoration. Lévi-Strauss goes on to explain how Caduveo art reproduces dualisms that underpin their social organization by creating an aesthetic map of social codes and rules. For a pre-literate society, this provided an accessible way of recoding and transmitting the tenets of culture – akin to Australian Aboriginal dreamtime myths and paintings, Chinese dragon robes of the ruling dynasty, or the knotted cords (*khipu* or *quipu*) used for record-keeping by the Inkas (see Rall, Chapter 9, in this volume). Is this really any different from the use of military insignia (e.g. epaulettes, brass buttons, khaki or camouflage) in contemporary fashion? Or, even without clothing, contemporary male soldiers present a hyper-masculine and muscled body that in itself becomes a type of uniform (see Smith & Gehrmann, Chapter 3, this volume).We are dressing our bodies to convey precise messages about who we are, where we come from, to whom and where we belong, and what we believe in.

To appreciate the symbolism of fashion, it is necessary to appreciate the complex interplay of influences that shape it. Karen Tranberg Hansen (2010: 155) has differentiated colonialism (rule by an external power) from imperialism (dominating influence over another culture) and the ways in which 'dress became an important boundary-marking mechanism' both for the external power and subjugated people (Tranberg Hansen 2010: 156). The former imposes dress codes and western garments which are adopted and adapted to varying degrees though often intermixed with local dress to create new modes of dress. In other words, even where a dress code appears to have been imposed successfully, there are different meanings attached to the clothes by the colonizers and the colonized that reflect the contestation of the rules:

> Because the meanings of the dressed body everywhere are ambiguous, the colonial encounter enabled local people to take pride in long-held aesthetics expressed in new dress media and forms. It enabled the creation of styles of "national dress" that as invented traditions have served as cultural assertions for shifting claims to political voice and representation between the late colonial period and the present (Tranberg Hansen 2010: 159).

Perhaps the best example she gives is the adoption of a Prussian-style military uniform with a traditional high Chinese collar by the Chinese in the late 19th century. Intended as a 'modern' but 'not too Western' school uniform, it later became politicized as the Sun Yat-sen suit and after the Cultural Revolution, as the Mao Zedong suit – now the sartorial epitome of pre-Deng Xiaoping China (Tranberg Hansen 2010: 158). This example is also instructive in showing the prevalence of cultural borrowing – or hybridity – of fashion in poaching diverse styles from different places and times and re-working them to suit new agendas and sartorial circumstances.

Fashion today borrows from different cultures, different pasts, different futures and different identities in the ultimate pastiche of body dressing 'in a perpetual state of flux' (Rovine 2005: 227). Popular culture occurs locally but draws on global trends too. It is hard to pigeonhole people as intrinsically representative of just one culture or locality. As the chapter about the expat Nigerian artist shows, having lived in the United Kingdom for 30 years, Yinka Shonibare regards himself as a Londoner while art critics try to position him as an African postcolonial migrant. He sees himself as a 'cultural hybrid' and his work as 'resistance against stereotype and enforced identity' (see Gregory, Chapter 8, in this volume). In London, Shonibare revels in its 'vindaloo Britishness'. 'It's a mixed up thing … This purity notion is nonsense, and I cherish that.' (Shonibare quoted by Cooke 2010, as above). His notion of cultural artefacts is that of a meshing of cultures, influences and places in a mish-mash of interdependence. As he puts it:

> We all pinch from one another. We take what we like, and in doing so, we are, whether we like it or not joined together in one great and vibrant web (Shonibare quoted by Cooke 2010).

All the authors and chapters in this volume epitomize this play of cultural hybridity framed within the context of the links between fashion and war and the ways in which they have shaped many aspects of popular culture. Rall's concluding micro, meso and macro analysis illustrates different levels of proximity or connectedness between clothes and wearers which shapes how individuals, cultural institutions and globalized fashion trends wear social relations through clothing that creates multiple hierarchies of symbolism and meanings. The paradox is that although – as Rall argues – 'war, textiles and fashion are incontrovertibly linked' (see Rall, Chapter 9, in this volume), commentators frequently only recognize the superficial connections – such as details of military paraphernalia found in fashion or startling fashion images captured during war or cultural conquest.

As the chapters here show, clothing and fashion are inevitably political and politicized whether through the stylized representation of Nazis in post-9/11 Hollywood films; the 'threat' posed by young men in hoodies; Schiaparelli's uncompromising wartime-shaped couture; the military embodiment of air stewards' uniforms; controversial reactions to the use of military medals in fashion; expat artists' cultural commentaries; or textile tales that are woven out of colonial and postcolonial encounters. These topics eloquently open up a revitalized field of studies in fashion and popular culture offering new perspectives and developing diverse analytic approaches.

In particular, it is difficult to argue that western ways and consumerism is a one-way trend from north to south but rather 'western goods are often absorbed, refashioned, and reinterpreted in local cultural systems, so that what looks like imitation or copying is really much more complex' (Wilk 1998). Rather, the spread of cultural diversification and use of western consumer goods signals

> local difference rather than a means of emulating a metropolitan standard. The implication is that the adoption of Western goods and styles will be selective, gradual, and predictable only at a local level (Wilk 1998: 325).

Understanding the complex forces shaping fashion, textile and clothing behaviour thus requires 'increasing sophistication and serious political debate of the consequences of mass consumerism' (Wilk 1998: 327). War may be the most visible symbol of globalization but cultural hybridity and interdependence are its constant markers. Until fashion is taken seriously as a cultural form and institution (see Hollander 1992: 27), the centrality of clothing in creating identities and making statements through garments and styles will remain under-appreciated and the true significance of the place of war and fashion in popular culture obscured.

References

Answers.com. (2000). 'Military Influences on Fashion', *Oxford Companion to US Military History*. http://www.answers.com/topic/military-influences-on-fashion. Accessed 19 July 2013.

Craik, J. (2005). *Uniforms Exposed: From Conformity to Transgression*. Oxford: Berg.

Hollander, A. (1992). 'The Modernization of Fashion', *Design Quarterly*, 154, pp. 27–33.

Lévi-Strauss, C. (1975). 'A Native Community and its Life-Style', in *Tristes Tropiques*, pp. 229–56. Harmondsworth, Middlesex: Penguin Books.

Rovine, V. (2005). 'Working the Edge: XULY.Bët's Recycled Clothing', in H. Clark and A. Palmer, (eds), *Old Clothes, New Looks: Second Hand Fashion*, pp. 215–27. Oxford: Berg.

Tranberg Hansen, K. (2010). 'Colonialism and Imperialism', in V. Steele (ed.), *The Berg Companion to Fashion*, pp. 155–59. Oxford: Berg.

Wilk, R. (1998). 'Emulation, Imitation, and Global Consumption', *Organization and Environment*, 11: 3, pp. 314–33.

Overview

Denise N. Rall

Changes in regime have often demanded changes in costume, and this volume explores war and its impact on textiles, clothing and fashion from a variety of perspectives. The first two sections focus on studies of popular culture that explore the various shapes of military impact on costume during and after the First and Second World Wars (WWI and WWII), as well as those from conflicts in Vietnam, Iraq and Afghanistan. The third section considers the far-reaching implications of other types of conflicts, such as the recent youth revolts in Britain. Lastly, the book considers the postcolonial effects of conflict, trade and religion on the textiles and clothing of indigenous peoples in Africa and South America. As noted throughout, these effects are rarely straightforward. Graeme Were makes this clear in his chapter on Pacific islanders, specifically, the Melanesians:

> A wealth of historical records, museum collections and photographic evidence suggests that in fact some Melanesians selectively sought out printed garments of various types ... [so] Melanesians were actually *operating strategically* in their uptake of European dress ... rather than adher[ing] to the missionary stipulation of dressing the body (Were 2005, emphasis added: 159–60).

It is these *strategic responses* of indigenous practices in regards to fashion and clothing following the impacts of war, commerce and/or religious enterprises that are teased out in Section III. Often, post-intervention alterations or restrictions in clothing or textile may appear as arbitrary, but they always serve some purpose integral to the dominion of one culture over another. These forced alterations in clothing can pass into folklore as myths, but often the archaeological or historical records of the day provide factual evidence. Details of clothing that reflects military or colonial interventions can be found in Section III (Chapter 9) and in the Introduction.

Alteration in costume may be deliberate or accidental, but it always comes with a price: a supersession of one set of traditions and beliefs with another. As clothing forms a primary expressive indicator of culture, this interruption in local practice – whether due to military conquest, internal conflict, religious intervention, or economic trade – becomes a meaningful indicator of subservience. The effect of conquest on costume contains multiple strands of meaning often linked to discussions of the history of fashion (see Hollander 1993; Vincent 2009) or as part of a postcolonial exercise (see Küchler & Miller 2005). Other authors, such as feminist and historian Cynthia Cockburn (2007) and Helena Carreiras (2006; 2008), have articulated the extent of military intervention and its impact on the lives of women. This collection seeks to explicate some of the many strands of war, and how it infringes on fashion and textile through the lens of popular culture in Anglo-American-European traditions – always bearing in mind, that these 'traditions' wear on their backs the sequestration and embodiment of many other cultures. Here, scholars and critics from a wide range of backgrounds offer descriptive case studies, analyses and/or theoretical standpoints to locate illustrative examples of how conflict and its engagement with textile and fashion impacts on a variety of artistic enterprises. These questions come to the fore:

Where and how has the military view of the world influenced, or even dictated, images of body and dress in popular culture?

Where and how has the aesthetics of war appeared in high fashion?

How has military invasion, global trade and religious conversion changed the very fabric of textile and the meanings of native costume throughout history?

Is there a framework that will help explain the relationships between society, textiles and fashion after colonialism?

Section I: The military in popular culture

In this section, explorations of how war and the military has influenced the 'look' of popular culture lays the foundation for the later chapters that consider how war and military dress have influenced trends in fashion, clothing and textile art. These chapters provoke current thinking on the aesthetics of clothing and the military from three very different vantage points. The first chapter reviews the images of women from within the cultural record of WWII comic strips in Australia and the United Kingdom (UK). The second chapter jumps to the 21st century, and the portrayal of Nazis in both pre- and post-September 11, 2001 (hereafter, post-9/11) Hollywood films. The post-9/11 imagery and costuming are then compared with filmic representations of Nazis before the 9/11 attacks in the United States (US). The third chapter considers the changes in Australian male soldiers and their physiques in the early 21st century, and how these changes comprise a 'new brand' of soldier. These three explorations of the imagery of war in the media and on soldiers' bodies help to frame discussion points that will be further developed in Section II.

Representations of female wartime bravery in Australia's *Wanda the War Girl* and *Jane at War* from the UK

Jane Chapman opens this section with a detailed examination of the images of women in two WWII comic strips: *Wanda the War Girl* from the (Sydney) *Sunday Telegraph* and *Jane at War* from the UK's *Daily Mirror*. There are essential differences in how the two heroines respond to the animated dangers of wartime, as drawn by, respectively, Kath O'Brien and Norman Pett. As Chapman reveals, both characters portray typical 1940s values, but in different ways: the female character of Wanda was powerful and productive in the largely masculine wartime arena, whereas Jane was brave and well intentioned, but accident-prone, that is, she regularly lost her clothes. For both characters, fashion provided 'pin-up' value. These fictionalized portrayals were exaggerated for dramatic effect, but, on a deeper level, they drew attention to how women throughout Australia, the UK and the US acted for the Allied war effort. With hindsight, it is clear that the fact of women's enhanced responsibilities during wartime would ultimately prove useful, in the debate for equality between the sexes, for bettering women's position. In Wanda and Jane's depictions of wartime bravery, their efforts became a valid cultural record of the period. The presence of women in wartime, however fictionalized, could be viewed as a move that would further collapse the 19th-century notion that 'women's place is in the home'.

Fashionable fascism: Cinematic images of the Nazi before and after 9/11

A very different look at wartime imagery is developed by Kylee M. Hartman-Warren, who outlines the bifurcation in the portrayal of Nazi soldiers in pre- and post-9/11 Hollywood films. As Hartman-Warren notes, images of soldiers from Germany's National Socialist Party (the Nazis) have increased in numbers in both popular cinema and popular culture since the 9/11 attacks on the US. Further, the rise of Hollywood's 'new Nazi' demonstrates that the process of 'Nazisploitation' has promoted the Nazi aesthetic in high fashion, architecture, mass media, and on the Internet. The penetration of Nazi aesthetic in film has reconstructed the stock Hollywood images of WWII with overtones of humour, notions of chic, and the employment of a reflective type of satire that has become popular following the events of 9/11.

Branding the muscled male body as military costume

The third chapter in this section, from Richard Gehrmann and Heather Smith, brings an entirely new issue to the forefront: that of the muscled male body as military costume. This new 'brand' of the muscular and masculine soldier has been shaped by a body-obsessed popular culture and, in the Australian case, differs markedly from earlier wartime representations of the Australian manly body. This chapter considers selected images of the changing male military body throughout the 20th century, contrasting these with the heroic male body promoted in Australia's pictorial past. A new type of soldier's body has become important in contemporary film and popular media, following on from current conflicts in Afghanistan and Iraq.

The first section of this volume highlights the breadth of military imagery that persists from the two world wars, and how these influences pervaded popular culture in the last century as well as today. War is not forgotten, either by the entertainment media or by manufacturers of mainstream clothing. The Anglo-European cultural resonances of courage and discipline in wartime became increasingly infiltrated by what may be called an ironic stance about fashion and femininity, as well as issues of masculinity and combat. These debates are explored further in Section II.

Section II: Fashion and the military

The second section of this volume further details the processes of fashion: its construction, its promulgation, and its increasing contextualisation within the spheres of modernity and femininity as they evolved and changed during WWI and WWII, as well as Cold War and contemporary conflicts.

In the service of clothes: Elsa Schiaparelli and the war experience

In Chapter 4, Annita Boyd offers a detailed historical case study in the story of Elsa Schiaparelli, or Schiap, as she became known, one of the fashion industry's most iconic personages. From her famous 21 Place Vendôme atelier in Paris, Schiaparelli was able to flourish and fulfil her destiny as a true haute couturier. In particular, Boyd argues, her 'look' – 'sharp, "hard chic", rather masculine, fitted look of padded shoulders, nipped-in waist and narrow hips' – became synonymous with global stars, such as Katherine Hepburn, Greta Garbo and Joan Crawford. First, Schiap's 'look' complemented the body shape and facial structure of these famous actors, and secondly, it was a style designed to enhance the fit and healthy body of the New Woman who could now compete in the public masculine domain. Finally, Schiap's war work while driving an ambulance in the 1940s seems to have given her a perspective on 'the uniform' that did not appeal to younger women (especially American women) after the war was over. Here, considerations of nostalgia, longing, and the new prosperity offered by synthetic fabrics, illustrated in the über-femininity of Dior and Chanel, signalled a reactionary movement in fashion that left Schiap to make her living by designing nurses' uniforms during the 1960s.

The discipline of appearance: Military style and Australian flight hostess uniforms 1930–1964

Prudence Black, in Chapter 5, describes how military uniforms influenced the style of the civilian uniforms of Australian flight hostesses from the 1930s through to the early 1960s. Not only aircraft, but also uniforms changed as a response to the two major world wars. Uniforms, historically, articulated the human body in relation to the requirements of war. Black demonstrates how flight hostesses are linked, via their uniforms, to the aeroplane-machine in precisely the same way. As a technology, uniforms shape and code the body in such a way that they become a unit that belongs to a collective whole. The flight hostess uniform, worn since the 1930s, is a technology that articulates a line of command and disciplines the body both physically and aesthetically. Uniforms, as the visible signifiers of the line of command, also represent subjection to regulated behaviour, so that the flight hostesses' appearance also articulates a code of behaviour. This study elucidates an important moment in the construction of the flight hostess uniform in Australia as well as the ways in which the discipline of the uniform imposes an external power on the body.

Models, medals, and the use of military emblems in fashion

In Chapter 6, the final chapter in Section II, Amanda Laugesen details two significant events in the fashion industry: the use of military medals and other uniform insignia, one in New Zealand, and the second in the US. During a fashion show offered by the designer Kate Sylvester, the inclusion of war medals – all of them facsimiles of real service medals – provoked a great controversy, in which representatives of the Australian Returned and Services League (RSL), the predominant veterans' organization in Australia and a prominent voice in public affairs, immediately stated their objections as soon as photographs of the fashion show hit the newspapers. This public outcry was similar, Laugesen notes, to a previous controversy in the US, where choreographer and judge Mia Michaels, on the popular television dance competition, *So You Think You Can Dance*, wore a United States Marines dress blouse, with the Marine emblems displayed upside down. The incident created a flurry of outrage, mostly expressed on the Internet. In citing these two examples, Laugesan demonstrates how fashion and the military function within discrete symbolic spheres, maintaining contradictory but similar codes of conduct.

Section III: Framing youth fashion, textile artworks and postcolonial costume in the context of conflict

This final section speaks to contemporary concerns. Beyond the complex web of interactions between fashion and war in the sphere of popular culture and fashion lies a further sphere of representation that links both fashion and war to more abstract notions of how post-conquest cultures rebel against dominant colonial paradigms. This section begins with a study of British contemporary youth and their adoption of the hoodie as a statement of revolt. Next, an exploration of contemporary textile art from the Nigerian-British artist Yinka Shonibare addresses vexatious issues about how London as a city deals with issues of 'blackness' and slavery in its postcolonial past. Finally, the section concludes by offering two case studies in postcolonial intervention in textile and fashion, along with a proximity framework that will help explicate the interrelationships between textile, clothing and military conquest.

Battle dressed – clothing the criminal, or the horror of the 'hoodie' in Britain

In Chapter 7, Joanne Turney examines the increasing criminalization of the hoodie in Britain by asking the question: does clothing mediate behaviour and can wearing a 'coded' garment elicit specific responses from those around us? Turney explores more specifically how mainstream popular culture currently assigns meaning to clothing. In current UK fashion, those adopting the 'uniform' of the black hoodie might not have criminal intentions, but might want to express their rebellion against society generally, therefore the garment becomes symbolic of countercultural sympathies. Turney's chapter adroitly assesses the 'moral panic' and 'media furore' that has developed in Britain from the wearing of a 'seemingly innocuous piece of clothing; the hoodie.'

Dutch wax and display: London and the art of Yinka Shonibare

Davinia Gregory, in Chapter 8, details her personal journey and engagement with new British criticism and postcolonial critique that brought her in meaningful proximity to the Nigerian-born installation and graphic artist, Yinka Shonibare, MBE. As she describes, Shonibare's work came to the fore alongside the Young British Artists movement, and had significant impact on London's cultural fabric in the early 2000s. This chapter builds a historiography of the cultural theory surrounding Shonibare's artworks, particularly his sculptures, grouped here under the nickname the 'Headless Colonials.' Gregory explores his reasons for employing the iconic Dutch wax batik textiles in his work. Further, she reconsiders how the work of Shonibare, as well as other works of Britain's so-called Young British Artists continues the 'endless battle' for seamless, frictionless multiculturalism and pluralism in London. As cultural conflict waxes and wanes in early 21st-century London, Shonibare's work is somewhere present at each juncture to encourage commentary and critique.

Costume and conquest: Introducing a proximity framework for post-war impacts on textile and fashion

This collection concludes with my own contribution, Chapter 9, in which I outline two case studies, and then build a theoretical framework in order to analyse how post-military encounters have shaped fashion and textile. The chapter begins by assessing the impact of

Spanish *conquistadors* on the textiles of the Inkan empire. The impacts of conquest force a postcolonial standpoint, as both the military invasion and the subsequent 'education' of the indigenous populace by the Roman Catholic missionaries changed the meanings and values of woven artefacts in Peru. A second brief case study follows the high-fashion brand XULY.Bët from the African designer Lamine Badian Kouyaté. His brand sought to relocate colonial aspects of European dominion in Africa (in particular, Senegal) by 'decolonizing' fashion. He removed fashion from its haute couture status by recycling elements of clothing from the scrapheaps.

The chapter concludes with the outline of a theoretical framework, one inherited from ecological economic theory and now widely used in applied sociology, which considers textile from the point of view of a tiered analysis. The micro- meso- and macro- framework forms a proximity analysis which offers a way to measure the distance between the social 'fabric' of a community and the production of textiles and fashion. These measures of proximity can be applied cross-culturally to differentiate between pre- and post-military, as well as postcolonial incursions into various societies, both ancient and contemporary.

Afterword: The military in contemporary fashion

The Afterword highlights a number of recent activities in the world of fashion that promote, utilize and/or critique war. Fashion magazines, for example, continue to offer multiple page spreads on how to put together a high-fashion military look, under categories such as 'Boot camp', 'Tactical response' and 'Jungle warfare', with the exhortation that donning a camouflaged T-shirt under a black blazer will provide a quick update to the latest fashionable 'look'. In contrast, two high-fashion jewellery designers have chosen to work with metals recovered from AK-47 automatic rifles seized from war zones in the African Republic of Congo.

The book concludes by suggesting that there are many linkages between war, textiles and fashion, with the recognition that there is much to explore. It remains a project for future researchers, artists and fashion designers to not ignore the painful existence of war and military activities, but to elucidate, and thereby challenge, these relationships as they continue to appear in fashion and popular culture.

References

Carreiras, H. (ed.) (2006). *Gender and the Military: Women in the Armed Forces of Western Democracies.* London: Routledge.

Carreiras, H. & Kuemmel, G. (eds) (2008). *Women in the Military and in Armed Conflict.* The Netherlands: Springer.

Cockburn, C. (ed.) (2007). *From Where We Stand: War, Women's Activism and Feminist Analysis.* London: Zed Books.

Hollander, A. (1993). *Seeing Through Clothes.* New York: Viking Press.

Küchler, S. & Miller, D. (eds) (2005). *Clothing as Material Culture.* Oxford: Berg.

Vincent, S. J. (2009). *The Anatomy of Fashion: Dressing the Body from the Renaissance to Today.* Oxford: Berg.

Were, G. (2005). 'Pattern, efficacy and enterprise: on the fabrication of connections in Melanesia', in S. Küchler & D. Miller (eds), *Clothing as Material Culture,* pp. 159–74. Oxford: Berg.

Section I

The military in popular culture

Chapter 1

Representation of female wartime bravery in Australia's
Wanda the War Girl and *Jane at War* from the UK

Jane Chapman

Introduction

During the Second World War (WWII), one of life's simple pleasures was to read the lift-out comics sections in the Sunday newspapers. Ruth Marchant James, a resident of Cottesloe in Perth, recalls that she could not wait to consume *Wanda the War Girl*, an Australian comic strip first published in the (Sydney) *Sunday Telegraph* in 1943, and later collected into two comic books (2007). A school history textbook about the period claims that Wanda was the first wartime Australian female icon: servicemen painted her picture on their tanks and planes and she was said to be Australia's favourite pin-up (Ciddor 1998: 23). She escaped from espionage dangers involving German and Japanese armed forces, and her foolhardy exploits were often drawn from contemporary newspaper stories. After the war, her adventures morphed into detective-style escapades, and the glamorous, well-dressed heroine embarked upon dangerous exploits until the strip was abruptly terminated mid-adventure in 1951 (NLA 1984). Unfortunately, the locally produced comic could not compete with American imports.

Wanda the War Girl appealed to adults and was said to be more popular with children than *Superman* (Ciddor 1998: 23). Not only was Wanda beautiful and feminine, she was also a tough independent woman. Creator Kath O'Brien's intention was 'to give credit to Australian service girls for the marvelous job they are doing'. O'Brien recognized the changing social status and working lives of women. The overall effect of the strip was refreshingly different to the generally negative depiction of the sexualized woman in Australian war comics (Laurie 1999: 121). O'Brien was influenced by *Black Fury*, an early wartime comic in the *Telegraph* (drawn by another woman, American Tarpé Mills), and by Norman Pett's extremely successful *Jane*, who appeared in Britain's *Daily Mirror*. According to John Ryan, O'Brien's illustrative style is one of the most original and individual styles to appear in Australian comics, and is reminiscent of the work of William Dobell (1979: 53). Eventually, the strips were collected into comic books published by Consolidated Press first as *The War Comic* and then as the first and the fourth in the *Supercomic Series* (1947–1950s) – the only original local products out of 66 US reprints (NLA MS 6514). After the war, O'Brien increasingly based her stories (written in conjunction with journalist C. W. Brien) on the novels of Ashton Woolfe, a self-promoting former employee of the French security services; she combined his (embellished) real-life accounts with items from newspapers.

Figure 1.

Wanda the War Girl was 'one of the first comics to reflect a female point of view [and was] reflective of its period' (Ryan 1979: 53). This chapter argues that *Wanda the War Girl* was a fresh type of female representation that differs from others during the period in both form and in substance. *Wanda* extended the scope and range of female comic-strip characters but she was also a sexually provocative pin-up who undoubtedly aided wartime propaganda.

Jane at War was even more sexually provocative, but this too was in furtherance of the war effort. She was a different type of female to Wanda: just as patriotic and brave, but a character whose good intentions were invariably accident-prone. When Jane, who worked as a spy, got into difficulty, her clothes were always central to the storyline because the scrape would entail her losing most of them. Thus fashion played an important part in the essential pin-up Zeitgeist. Clothes had to be fashionable, feminine, and carefully styled to display the character's perfect figure and shapely curves, and, in contrast to Wanda, whose image was powerful, Jane's underwear was the most essential part of her wardrobe. Jane's creator Norman Pett was under much pressure to produce speedily and regularly for the British national tabloid the *Daily Mirror*. On one occasion he missed his deadline and had his contract suspended. After he had reached an agreement with the management, Jane returned and told her fans that she had been away because she had lost her pants. The newspaper office was then inundated with parcels from readers containing replacement undies, including one with a touching note from a 13-year-old girl, 'Dear Jane, Perhaps these will help you out' (Saunders 2004: 24). Unlike Wanda, who was created from O'Brien's imagination, Pett's drawings were constructed around regular poses by a real-life model, Christabel Leighton-Porter, who also gave stage shows for the troops during the war. She became a celebrity in her own right, but always posing as Jane, accompanied by a real dog ('Fritzi'), identical to the comic-strip canine.

Context

It is generally accepted that if there had not been a war there would never have been an Australian comic-book industry (Gordon 1998: 10).[1] This was due mainly to import licensing regulations and economic sanctions that restricted American imports during WWII: by 1948, the industry had grown to such an extent that there were 38 local and imported (mainly British) comic titles available each week (Stone 1994: 72; Ryan 1979: 197). However, when import restrictions were lifted, American products flooded the market again to such an extent that in the post-war period 80 per cent of comics circulating originated in the United States (Lent 1999: 22). Despite the heavy competition – or maybe because of it – the popular characters produced in local comics have a social significance as part of the nation's cultural heritage.

Wanda the War Girl provided a newly progressive depiction of women, and as such, it mirrored both wartime representations and a new social trend that saw women leave the home in order to serve the war effort. Female Australian comic-book artists such as O'Brien shared a 'strong commitment to giving a more balanced view of women in comics' (Ungar, in Shiell (ed.) 1998: 79). This point is best explored by looking briefly at female representation before WWII.

In US comics history, the pre-WWII period is referred to as 'The Early Industrial Age' (Lopes 2009). This primitive label is reflected in the content of other Australian visual archives of the period such as cartoons where female depictions are somewhat unenlightened. John Foster points to sexism by omission and provides examples where no women appear at all, even as protagonists or assistants (1990: 18). In *Bluey and Curley*, when women do appear, they are 'domestic tyrants who will not allow their male partners any pleasure or they are silly and frivolous' (Ungar 1998: 70). Popular strips aimed at the adult market such as *Bluey and Curley* and *Wally and the Major* were set in male-dominated worlds, where female characters were often nameless – 'Mum', 'Mrs Curley', 'Mrs Bluey' – and who never seemed to leave the house.[2] Comics theorists McAllister et al. point out that portrayals of life are not neutral or random (2001: 5): it is not coincidental, therefore, that when women were featured working, it was usually in jobs offering little opportunity for adventure. Most often, women appeared as honeytraps or as harridans (Minell 2003).

As Foster points out, 95 per cent of those who created comics were male and it was always assumed (during the wartime period at least; this changed in the post-war years) that 90 per cent of the readers were too. The adventure genre dominated and bravery centred on missions to create 'peace and order out of the chaos produced by the forces of evil' (Foster 1999: 145). Women's roles were as damsels in distress, helpmates for the male protagonist, or victims. Historians of comics acknowledge that in wartime comics, women were usually depicted as civilian casualties, grieving relatives, and/or the victims of rape, pillage, looting or starvation (Stromberg 2010: 50). Up until 1939 women were not usually shown as members of the armed services, and WWII was the first time that Australian women were depicted in such roles. *Wanda the War Girl* reflected this change; as Joseph Witek suggests, 'Art has a psychological need to hear and render the truth' (1989: 114). This aspect of representation can also be seen in the US comics industry, where female characters assumed service roles in addition to becoming costumed superheroes (Robbins 1996).

Of course, stereotyping of women either as harridans or as honeytraps was not unique to Australia. Worldwide, the majority of characters depicted in comics have been male and the corollary of this seems to have been that most female characters have been categorized as virgin, mother, or crone (Stromberg 2010: 50). Women's roles may, in fact, be further reduced to just two categories: either maiden/vamp or mother/old hag. The former are depicted as busty, physically exaggerated objects of desire – worthy only of rescue or 'merely a beautiful token to be at the side of the male main character' (Stromberg 2010: 136). Conversely, the mother/hag is usually ugly and dominates her overly domesticated husband.

Social realism

Roger Sabin has noted that American superheroes became patriotic figures fighting for their country – 'unashamed morale-boosters' – so why should a woman not also fulfill this function (1996: 146)? Unlike her American contemporary 'Miss Lace' in *Male Call*, Wanda did not just hang around the army bases like a 'perpetual maybe' (Stromberg 2010: 51) – that is, a female who may be sexually available. Wanda was a proactive adventuress/spy for the war effort, with the result that her representation was less patronizing than that of previous female characters.

Witek acknowledges that there is a recent tendency to connect 'the textual specificities of the comic form to the embeddedness (*sic*) of comics in social, cultural, and economic systems' (1999: 4). Certainly, war comics of a more masculine type published in the post-war period tended to have high levels of factuality and were often based on true stories. All the same, it is clearly not possible to obtain a rounded picture of the war period from comics. The social history of Australia, as it relates to women, has its limitations. The society that spawned comics in this period has since changed radically of course, and while, according to Foster, 'no rounded view of the history is possible, however, simply because of the natures of both the medium and its readers' (1999: 150–51), it is also true that comics provide 'pieces of the mirror' that can be assembled (1990: 22). Wanda's wartime bravery reflects the new social and political realities that heralded a change in the attitude towards women.[3] McAllister, Sewell and Gordon stress that ideology is strongly connected to issues of social power and Wanda, in this respect, is often ideologically contradictory (2001: 2–3). Yet, despite such limitations and contradictions, this particular strip has value as a social document because of its acknowledgement of the important role of the active servicewoman.

Pin-ups

It is true that Wanda was a voyeur's delight, for her clothes were constantly torn – the better to display her long, shapely legs and impressive bosom. While she was more modest than her risqué English wartime equivalent, Jane, Wanda retained the suggestion of sex, albeit unspoken. It is worth noting that *Wanda the War Girl* was drawn by a female artist, and while she competed with Moira Bertram's Jo (*Jo and her Magic Cape*), Tarpé Mills' *Miss Fury*, and Dale Messick's *Brenda Starr*, it was Wanda who became the most widely displayed Australian pin-up. The comic character Jane was also a huge success as a pin-up (Saunders 2004); and Wanda, like Jane, was a 'truly national phenomenon and was seen as boosting the morale of the men in military service' (Stromberg 2010: 50–51). Jane was credited as having helped the British troops to travel six miles into German-occupied France in just one day, following D-Day, when she finally shed *all*, rather than just some, of her clothes (Saunders 2004: 90–114): in fact, scholars have acknowledged that the pin-up can channel sexual energy by transforming it into a weapon as military energy (Kakoudaki 2004: 231). Both Wanda and Jane are the result of propaganda campaigns that encouraged men to idolize a particular sort of woman – the attractive servicewoman (Westbrook 1990: 587). In the face of a global conflict of unprecedented reach, governments needed to recruit women for the war effort which meant that the expansion of the role of women was inevitable. What was new in representational terms was that these 'new' women were sexy, powerful, brave and productive.

There were three main taboo subjects during the 1940s and 1950s for Australian comics: sex, violence and bad language. Kissing and passionate embraces in romance comics were permitted but 'there was seldom any physical contact between the genders' (Foster 1999: 145). Casual sex was considered risky, both to health and to national security. Indeed, in relation to the representation of women in the illustrative archives held by the National Archives of Australia, Minell comments:

> If they were not traitorous, disease-ridden "femmes fatales", they were scattily-minded naïve young things who seemed to be more of a hindrance to the war effort than a help.

It would be interesting to know how successful the foolhardy exploits of *Wanda the War Girl* were as an aid to female recruitment for the services! (2003: 22).

Other female characters

Much of Wanda's female competition was not quite as socially realistic. In January 1945 the *Daily Mirror* introduced another Australian cartoon strip by 16-year-old Moira Bertram, *Jo and her Magic Cape*: dark-haired Jo was beautiful and used her magic cape to help her boyfriend – an American pilot named Serge – to outwit gangsters, as well as the Japanese. The magic cape was a common trope – a comic-strip fictional device to speed up the narrative and herald action – but its fantastic nature detracted from Jo's innate bravery and credibility. The strip ran for a few months before moving into comic books. Another local artist, Syd Miller (of *Chesty Bond* fame), in 1945 created a female character called *Sandra* for the *Melbourne Herald*. Although Sandra also appeared in England and elsewhere, Miller, according to John Ryan, found that a female character limited the type of stories he could present. Sandra was axed the following year to be replaced by the inimitable *Rod Craig*, an adventure strip that was adapted as a radio serial (Ryan 1979: 54). Comic creators believed that their male readership would not tolerate too many female characters because such characters slowed down the action. The relative scarcity of female characters meant that those who did appear were not only more likely to occupy traditional roles, such as mother or wife, but would be open to stereotyping. Martin Barker argues a form of mitigation against allegations of stereotyping, however, by stating that the comic form has an equalizing effect. This, he argues, should point theorists towards a slightly different line of enquiry:

> It makes no difference whether it is a stereotype of a plumber, a tax inspector, a policeman, a black person, a demented pig or a coward. For purposes of the strip, all are equalized. Therefore they are not just "stereotypes", they are much more; they are *types for the purposes of the formula of the stories* (Barker 1989: 116).

Notwithstanding, there must be a relativist case to argue: 'types' of women impact upon cultural understanding of a far larger proportion of a country's population than do those of plumbers. Clearly, the issue of representation within the comics form is a complex one: contemporary scholarship is particularly sensitive to ways in which visual representation on the 'Other' is historically determined. W. J. T. Mitchell, for instance, discusses how 'the relative position of visual and verbal representation is … never simply a formal issue or a question to be settled by scientific semiotics' (Worcester and Heer 2009: 116). In comics and graphic art the danger of negative caricature is very real, and reductive iconography can have a dehumanizing effect when it is presented in the form of deformed features (big bust, fat body, heavy wrinkles, etc.). Character types need to be easily recognized – unique identity tends not to be celebrated.

One problem from the standpoint of historical female representation is the lack of a range of formulas involving women, exacerbated by a propensity to copy American formats and types when the originals were not available: such as the case with local comic artist Dan Russell's 1942 creation of reporter *Wanda Dare*, an imitation of *Brenda Starr*. In this, admittedly limited, context, *Wanda the War Girl* appears relatively progressive, especially in the light of other problems associated with the comics form and the impact of such problems on the representation of gender. The complex way in which words and pictures are combined can allow for a range of meaning but comic-strip space is constrained (Walker 1994: 9), and such limitations may encourage creators to resort to Barker's types for the formula of the story. The spatial limitations of the form help to produce certain conventions such as visual shorthand, a reliance on standard character types, and formulaic plots. As McCloud argues, comics are uniquely placed to explore the space between reality and representation because the visuals operate mainly as iconic translations and this is reinforced by the narrative structure ([1993] 1994: 24–25). Narrative speed and concision is often helped by the fact that comics can change point of view easily (Carrier 2000: 55), something that can be both a strength and a weakness of the form.

Reading *Wanda the War Girl*

Wanda is significant because she was a new 'type' of character: a tough adventuress who makes an active contribution to the war effort. In the *Sunday Telegraph* on 2 January 1944, Wanda – suitably attired in sexy jungle gear – is taking the lead by suggesting that her associate Jim and their helper take a store of Japanese rifles. Although she keeps watch while the two men do the business, she still runs fast and is always at the centre of the action. She shoots a rifle and provides insightful narrative comments while all three are firing at the enemy. In February 1944 Wanda proves once more that she can always keep up with the men, and climb dangerous rock faces too, while simultaneously displaying her gorgeous legs. She insists on going ahead with Jim to do a 'recce'. Similarly, in the next episode she contributes to forward planning and strategic thinking. She makes useful suggestions on tactics as the team progress by proposing that their captured Japanese prisoner could open the cave door: 'make him do his Buddha opening act'. This works, and they open a hidden cave full of wretched prisoners, for whom Wanda shows feminine compassion: 'better release these poor old fellows now, hadn't we?' Then she places a bomb in the Japanese radio device (she is technical as well), and makes a run for it, with pistol in hand, still looking shapely.

On 5 March 1944 we see the other Aussie troops respectfully accepting her as an equal: she shakes hands with them to say thanks, tells them to take care and says goodbye – the 'matey' thing to do. One of them replies, 'we'll be ok, Wanda. We've got to rejoin our cobbers'. Then, as Jim flies the captured plane away, Wanda operates the radio controls, sending a Morse code message: 'Jap radio station gone sky high. Reporting HQRS today.

Flying Jap plane. Will signal approach. Wanda'. What amazing capability, control and technical expertise: good entertainment, but also positive encouragement for readers!

Reading post-war *Wanda* and *Jane*

Despite the improbabilities, and the inconsistencies with regard to gender, *Wanda the War Girl* and her post-war incarnation nonetheless provided a step forward for female representation. Published in April 1948, the post-war comic book *Wanda in India* becomes too fanciful, however. Page one reveals that the Japanese are planning a takeover of India: this of course is in the wake of Hiroshima and Nagasaki. By page four the exotic foreign clothes have become a bit theatrical. Admittedly, the fictional kingdom of Dapur was located on the Afghan/India border at around the time of the creation of Pakistan, but Wanda here looks like a belly dancer or an advert for Turkish delight. Local women are similarly dressed, half-naked in bikini tops and see-through harem trousers. Dramatic stylization has its own equivalent literary shorthand that defines nationality. Thus, Wanda, disguised as a servant boy (!), comes across a British agent, also in disguise and wearing a turban. Wanda tells him that a Japanese air squadron is hidden in the hills, and he responds, 'Oh topping! We'll arrange for a bally surprise for the jolly old nips on their next visit, what!' The story ends with the local prince swearing allegiance to the allied cause – danger over and mission accomplished. Wanda and her sidekick Jim move on to China to fight 'pro-Jap agents'.

This time Wanda is back in her sexy short shorts, but somehow her progressive wartime style has given way to the American Cold War superhero image, and realism is sacrificed en route. She is rescued by Jim and a British secret service officer (called Lord Nicholas) after Chinese bandits, looking somewhat dated in 'coolie' hats, have captured her while she was changing into native clothes (always the best time to get Wanda). Although the visual representation of the Chinese, for instance, looks outmoded to us, the concerns of these post-war Wanda comic books very much reflect those of the contemporary Cold War period – irrational as these may seem to today's readers.

This is especially true of the second Wanda comic-book publication entitled *Wanda Smashes the Black Market*. At a time when there was rationing, shortages and hardship almost worldwide, the existence of a black market posed a major problem for post-war economic reconstruction, in addition to provoking feelings of injustice and anger amongst people who were at the sharp end of profiteering and coupon systems.[4] This kind of content is also an example of how the comic strip and book, as an American form, was customized for local cultural, moral and political purposes. As Possamai indicates, 'Within this new post-WWII space local creators took an exotic art American form and, during a period of relative isolation from the industry, transformed it into something expressive of the identity of its Australian creators and readers'. Yet, by the late 1950s, the honeymoon was over and, in the face of economic competition from US imports, television and local censorship, the local industry declined (Possamai 2003: 113). American comics were criticized by anti-comics campaigners as 'un-Australian in speech and style' (Lent 1999: 25) but, as this was not accompanied by any form of cultural protection for home-grown alternatives, Australian comics effectively disappeared in the 1950s.

Jane's propensity to shed clothes provides clear, if ironic, evidence of the central role that fashion played as the visual instrument of her naïve eroticism. It also prompted an ongoing storyline with plenty of scope for support ephemera, such as books, posters, calendars and the publication *Jane's Journal*. A final-page cartoon in the1946 edition by Rylee Publications epitomizes the post-war image. Jane is leaving her house for work (with Fritzi, as ever), striding out through the front gate purposefully, with an umbrella in one hand and a purse in the other, sporting a smart hat and a stylish pencil-shaped jacket that displays her waist and is bordered by a business-like crisp white collar. She also wears high heels and silk stockings. However, the frill of her underwear is visible below the bottom of her jacket, and leads on to frilly suspenders. The caption reads, 'I can't help feeling I've forgotten something'. This kind of formula kept Pett busy with Jane from 1932 to 1948 and was then continued by Pett's assistant Mike Hubbard through to 1959 (Saunders 2004: 164). There were also two *Jane* cinema films and a 1982 BBC Television series, while Christabel Leighton-Porter, in the role of Jane, continued to make charity appeals and other public appearances until 1980. Yet it was the comic-strip wartime heroine with a big-hearted and a generous spirit that became known as the armed forces' secret weapon. In this role, her clothes – and their regular disappearance, modestly portrayed – captured the imagination of the time, providing an iconic symbolism that served to simultaneously inspire and amuse wartime populations worldwide.

Conclusion

Wanda the War Girl – an iconic phenomenon that is part of Australia's heritage – broke the mould by overcoming the limitations in the representation of women. O'Brien's new type of female character also clearly delighted readers. In her role as pin-up, Wanda supported Australian troops in their war effort, and her bravery, which bordered on recklessness, was a deliberate exaggeration in pursuit of that aim. Although the strip's valorization of female bravery served the needs of wartime propaganda, it was significant in other ways, too. It bridged the gap between child and adult readerships and thus demonstrated the flexibility and artistic potential of comics as a popular form. Wanda represented female liberation through conscription to the war-machine; and, reflecting the change in the role of women (and the contemporary widespread support of that change), the female characters in *Wanda the War Girl* were treated as equal to men. In *Wanda*, O'Brien created not only a new space for women, but did so through popular entertainment. The moral message was both hugely successful and useful to a society in transition. *Wanda* provides an important record of gendered values at a turning point in history, when attitudes towards women, and their contribution to society, were undergoing fundamental change.

Acknowledgements

Thanks are due to the Arts and Humanities Research Council (AHRC), United Kingdom, for their funding of the project 'Comics and the World Wars – a cultural record'; to Macquarie University, where the author is an adjunct professor, and to the editor and editorial team.

References

Barker, M. (1989). *Comics: Ideology, Power and the Critics*. Manchester: Manchester University Press.

Carrier, D. (2000). *The Aesthetics of Comics*. University Park, PA: Pennsylvania State University Press.

Ciddor, A. (1998). *Australia in the Twentieth Century*. South Yarra: Macmillan Education Australia.

Collingham, L. (2011). *The Taste of War*. London: Allen Lane.

Foster, J. (1990). 'The image of Australia and Australians in locally-produced comics', *Papers: Explorations into Children's Literature*, 1, pp. 11–23.

———— (1999). 'The slow death of a monochromatic world: The social history of Australia as seen through its children's comic books', *Journal of Popular Culture*, 33: 1, pp. 139–52.

Gordon, I. (1998). 'From the bulletin to comics: Comic art in Australia 1890–1950', in A. Shiell (ed.), *Bonzer: Australian Comics 1900–1990s*, pp. 1–14. Victoria: Elgua Media.

Hamilton, M. (2006). 'I found a lovely photo of you and just thought I would drop you a few lines: Australian servicemen, mateship, and the World War II pin-up girl', *Eras*, 8th ed., November, http://www.arts.monasg.edu.au/eras. Accessed 11 October 2010.

———— (2009). *Our Girls: Aussie Pin-Ups of the 40s and 50s*. South Melbourne, Vic.: Arcade Publications.

Higonnet, M. R. et al. (eds) (1987). *Behind the Lines: Gender and the Two World Wars*. New Haven and London: Yale University Press.

James, R. Marchant (2007). *Cottesloe: A Town of Distinction*. Town of Cottesloe.

Kakoudaki, D. (2004). 'Pinup: The American secret weapon in World War II', in Linda Williams (ed.), *Porn Studies*. Durham: Duke University Press.

Laurie, R. (1999). 'Masculinities and war comics', *Journal of Australian Studies*, 60, pp. 114–21.

Lent, J. A. (1999). 'The comics debate internationally', in *Pulp Demons: International Dimensions of the Postwar Anti-Comics Campaign*, pp. 9–41. Cranbury, NJ: Associated University Presses.

Lopes, P. (2009). *Demanding Respect: The Evolution of the American Comic Book*. Philadelphia: Temple University Press.

McAllister, M. P., Sewell, E. H. Jr and Gordon, I. (eds) (2001). 'Introducing comics and ideology', in *Comics & Ideology*, pp. 1–14. New York: Peter Lang.

McCloud, S. ([1993] 1994). *Understanding Comics*. New York: Harper Collins.

Minell, M. (2003). *A Nation's Imagination: Australia's Copyright Records, 1854–1968*. Canberra: National Archives of Australia.

Mitchell, W. J. T. (2009). 'Beyond comparison', in Worcester and Heer (eds), *Comics Studies Reader*, pp. 116–23. Jackson: University Press of Mississippi.

National Library of Australia (NLA) (1984). *The John Ryan Collection*, MS 6514, boxes 56, 58, 59, 60, 63, 64, M128495/232, M126495/70.

Okita, Saburo (ed.) (1992). *Post-War Reconstruction of the Japanese Economy*. Tokyo: University of Tokyo Press.

Possamai, A. (2003). 'The social construction of comic books as a (non) recognised form of art in Australia', *Form/Work*, 6, pp. 109–21.

Robbins, Trina (1996). *The Great Women Superheroes*. Ann Arbor: University of Michigan Press.

Ryan, J. (1979). *Panel to Panel: A History of Australian Comics*. New South Wales: Cassell Australia Ltd.

Sabin, R. (1996). *Comics, Comix & Graphic Novels*. London: Phaidon.

Saunders, A. (2004). *Jane: A Pin Up at War*. Barnsley, South Yorkshire: Leo Cooper.

Steege, P. (2007). *Black Market, Cold War*. Pennsylvania: Villanova University Press.

Stone, R. (1994). 'Achieving fandom: John Ryan and Australian comics in the National Library of Australia', in Toby Burrows and Grant Stone (eds), *Australian & New Zealand Journal of Serials Librarianship*, 4.

Stromberg, F. (2010). *Comic Art Propaganda: A Graphic History*. Lewes, East Sussex: Ilex.

Ungar, I. (1998). *Bonzer: Australian comics 1900–1990s*, in A. Shiell (ed.), Victoria: Elgua Media, pp. 69–80.

Varnum, R. and Gibbons, C. T. (2001). *The Language of Comics: Word and Image*. Jackson, MS: University of Mississippi Press.

Versaci, R. (2007). *This Book Contains Graphic Language: Comics as Literature*. New York and London: Continuum.

Walker, L. (1994). 'The feminine condition: Cartoon images of women in *The New Yorker*', *Inks*, 1: 3, pp. 8–17.

Westbrook, R. B. (1990). 'I want a girl, just like the girl that married Harry James; American women and the problem of political obligation in World War II', *American Quarterly*, 42: 4, pp. 587–614.

Witek, J. (1989). *Comic Books as History: The Narrative Art of Jack Jackson, Art Spiegelman, and Harvey Pekar*. Jackson, MS: University of Mississippi Press.

——— (1999). 'Comics criticism in the United States: A brief historical survey', *International Journal of Comic Art*, 1: 1, pp. 4–16.

Notes

1. Throughout Europe and Latin America, and in Canada and Japan, comic books and comic strips are regarded as serious artistic and cultural productions. In the United States, however, comics have traditionally been considered a lowbrow medium (Varnum and Gibbons 2001).
2. Later this began to change, especially in Australian-drawn adventure strips that offered scope for female character development and participation. Sister Janet Grant (Royal Flying Doctor Service) was a key character in John Dixon's strip *Air Hawk and the Flying Doctor* (1959–86). I am grateful to one of the peer reviewers for this example.
3. For a historical analysis, see Higonnet et al. (1987).
4. For the impact internationally, see Collingham (2011), Okita (1992) and Steege (2007).

Chapter 2

Fashionable fascism: Cinematic images of the Nazi before and after 9/11

Kylee M. Hartman-Warren

Introduction

Nazi villains have terrorized the big screen since Fritz Lang's 1941 film *Man Hunt*. These early Nazis were depicted in desaturated films, as stern figures that were tyrannical, boorish, monstrous or faceless. After September 11 2001 (post-9/11), however, this cinematic villain adopts a new form. Like the 'bad guys' in comic books and fantasy films, the Nazis of post-9/11 movies such as *Inglourious Basterds* (Tarantino 2009), *Iron Sky* (Vuorensola 2012) and *Valkyrie* (Singer 2008) are smooth-talking, glamorous and sometimes heroic. The events of 9/11 changed cinema at large, and big-screen protagonists increasingly reflected new areas of tension. As Sanchez-Escalonilla reports, these include 'the conflict between national security and civil liberties, (and) the risk of xenophobia and entrenchment' (2010: 11). Has post-9/11 cinematic fascist aesthetics become seductive, or have directors sought to explore humanity trapped in today's anti-terrorism rhetoric? This chapter considers whether this 'seductive fascism' threatens a freethinking society, or whether it is popular culture's reaction to a post-9/11 world – where the Patriot Act, surveillance and random searches have become a part of the daily routine.

Iron Sky and the post-9/11 Nazi invasion

In April 2012, *Iron Sky* invaded cinemas across the world. Featuring an action-packed plot where Nazis return to Earth in 2018 as a US president fashioned after Sarah Palin prepares for re-election, this film involves every possible element of the post-9/11 science fiction blockbuster. It includes the 'traditional master plots of invasion and catastrophe in action, science fiction, and fantasy' (Sanchez-Escalonilla 2010: 11). Through humour and satire, *Iron Sky's* narrative introduces controversial issues that have arisen in a post-9/11 world. It incorporates a US command that 'will not negotiate with terrorists,' in addition to Nazi military personnel who are notorious for inspiring xenophobia and threatening civil liberties. *Iron Sky* also fits well within the action and the science fiction genre. Nazis launch a meteor *blitzkrieg* on New York City, which causes panic and military retaliation. The action of the film is set in the near future but the Nazis have employed older technologies to inhabit the moon and launch an attack on the Earth by controlling meteors. This idea that old technology could be sufficiently advanced without becoming sleek and 'modernized,' falls within the genre of speculative science fiction. Finally, *Iron Sky* addresses both patriotism and terrorism in a post-9/11 context. It boasts red, white and blue propaganda posters featuring the US president who pays homage to George W. Bush by naming the largest US space station after him. The Nazi attacks strike at New York City landmarks, which explode and crumble on to streets teeming with frightened pedestrians, mimicking the famous scenes of destruction broadcast by Fox News and CNN in the days following 9/11. In addition to possessing the qualities of a post-9/11 visual narrative, *Iron Sky* also deploys the figure of the Nazi in a way that is similar to other contemporary Nazi films released between 2008 and 2009. *Iron Sky*'s Nazis are sexy, and sharply dressed in pristine, ranked uniforms – and they are not always 'evil.' In fact, some of these 'Moon Nazis' have sympathetic qualities, and are simply ill-educated victims of a warmongering propaganda machine which promotes nationalistic pride, militant strength, and xenophobia. In this way, *Iron Sky* seems to parody the post-9/11 Hollywood action films as much as it does the Nazi regime of the Second World War (WWII) era (see Plate i).

A growing body of literature now exists on 9/11's impact on Hollywood's popular cinema. Sanchez-Escalonilla's observations focus on action and fantasy films, while Douglas Kellner's *Cinema Wars: Hollywood Film and Politics in the Bush-Cheney Era* outlines catastrophe and social apocalypse in science fiction, action, and fantasy films after 9/11 (2009). Kellner examines both conservative narratives that reaffirm the anti-terrorist patriotic message, and the fantasies and satires that subvert patriotic rhetoric and poke fun at the Bush-Cheney regime. *Reframing 9/11* is a collection of articles by scholars that discusses Superman, Batman and zombies alongside consumerism, military fetish, and the culture of fear (Birkenstein, Froula, & Randell 2010). Heller's *The Selling of 9/11*, meanwhile, focuses on the way in which popular culture has 'consumed' the tragedy of 9/11 through products of memory and through the 'stuff' that makes this tragedy marketable (2005). Heller offers that the habits of post-9/11 consumers may be compared to those that developed following tragedies such as the Holocaust. Consumerism here is critiqued as a trivializing response to tragedy, an impulse that can be examined in the context of film and popular culture's acceptance of the Nazi aesthetic within the post-9/11 world.

Science fiction, fantasy, action and catastrophe genre films discussed in literature on post-9/11 cinema all boast narratives featuring protagonists struggling in environments teeming with totalitarian threats and restrictions on civil liberties. Like *Iron Sky*, the Nazi films released since the World Trade Center's destruction share these themes, and in many cases can be categorized within at least one of these genres. Most of these films were released between 2008 and 2009, and their production tapered off with the release of *Iron Sky*. Films such as *The Reader* (Daldry), *The Boy in the Striped Pyjamas* (Herman), *Valkyrie* (Singer), *Good* (Amorim), *Defiance* (Zwick), and *The Spirit* (Miller) all saw their release in 2008; and *Inglourious Basterds* (Tarantino) and *Dead Snow* (Wirkola) were released in 2009. All of these titles depart from the classic A-list Holocaust film in both narrative and aesthetic design. They are 'Nazi' rather than Holocaust films, because the action centres around Nazi protagonists, antagonists, or in most cases, both. In addition, several of these films portray the Nazi in a hyper-stylized fashion: the soldiers are beautiful, sexy and charming, and they wear an exceptionally tailored version of the iconic uniform compared to that worn by the Nazi in many pre-9/11 mainstream Holocaust and WWII films. The newer Nazi films also lack the desaturated look which gave the pre-9/11 films a historic appearance. In the new films, civilian costumes are fashionable, the colour palettes are rich, and settings boast stylized or opulent spaces richly decorated with Nazi banners, art deco statues, mosaics featuring swastikas and elegant portraits of Nazi soldiers.

These films, with their colourful opulence, serve as eye candy, and the Nazis within them easily become items of fantasy, or even nostalgia. One might even argue that this opulence, together with the prolific use of the swastika and other regalia, as well as a kind of idealization, exploits the Nazi in a similar fashion to that seen in B-rated WWII films of the 1970s. In his introduction to *Nazisploitation! The Nazi Image in Low-Brow Cinema and Culture,* Daniel Magilow defines Nazisploitation films as those which 'relied more on sensationalistic tag lines and sexually provocative marketing' (2012: 2). Magilow describes other characteristics of these films, which include gory violence, sexualized caricatures, and frequent use of the iconic SS uniform in its most idealized state. He also suggests that there has been a renaissance in Nazisploitation, claiming, 'where Nazisploitation was once taboo, today its motifs and narrative conceits have permeated big budget studio productions and mainstream popular culture' (2012: 6). Many of these contemporary films, which fall within the category of Nazisploitation, also display post-9/11 themes. Like the action films described by Sanchez-Escalonilla (2010: 1–7), they feature totalitarian regimes that restrict civil liberties and promote xenophobia.

There are also films that, while not explicitly borrowing from Nazi military fashion, aesthetics and colour scheme, have a visual dynamic that is as polished and luxurious as that found in the post-9/11 Nazi films. These are discussed later in the chapter.

Scholars suggest that the revival of the super-villain in the Nazi uniform may be a reaction to the events of September 11 2001. In a post-9/11 world where the War on Terror seeks to destroy ambiguous targets with faceless identities, Dery explains, 'Hitler endures because he puts a human face on an evil so incomprehensibly monstrous it confounds psychological analysis or historical contextualization, inviting us to make sense of it in theological, even mythic, terms' (Dery 2012: 103). The author Craig This addresses this phenomenon in Marvel Comics' post-9/11 revival of *Captain America*, which features Nazis as the primary antagonists (2012: 220). This suggests that, in the wake of the 9/11 attacks:

> Marvel Comics turned to the Nazis as a way to boost morale. They brought back the Third Reich as a coherent enemy that its most "American" of heroes, Captain America, could defeat … in replacing al-Qaeda with the Nazis, [Marvel] created a villain for American comic book readers that could be seen, fought, and ultimately defeated (2012: 220).

Like the action, fantasy and science fiction films in the post-9/11 context discussed above, the majority of these new Nazi films offered the same kind of refurbishment of the catastrophic action film. Only this time, they arrived waving the Nazi banner.

The lasting power of the Nazi aesthetic

The Nazi aesthetic has influenced contemporary culture since the rise of the Third Reich. Seen across fashion, propaganda and architecture, it is defined by its streamlined elegance and employs sharp angles, symmetry and clean, tri-coloured schemes (Guenther 2004). Though simple, this aesthetic is both visually awe-inspiring and reflective of the National Socialist ideal that greatness and superiority derive from order, hard work and patriotism. Praised and condemned, the Nazi aesthetic has both seduced and terrified viewers over the last 70 years. In his introduction to *Aesthetics and World Politics*, Roland Bleiker states that:

> … aesthetic beauty could lead us astray, so to speak, seductively promoting and at the same time disguising a vision of the world that is inherently dangerous, perhaps even evil. The aesthetic seduction of Nazi Germany is ample testimony here, as exemplified, for instance, by some of its most prominent artistic defenders, from the novelist Louis-Fernand Celine, to the poet Ezra Pound and the film-maker Leni Riefenstahl. The remarkable artistic creations of the latter, such as *Triumph of the Will* or *Olympia,* helped the Nazi regime turn mere propaganda into a broader mythology that was instrumental in gaining popular support for a racist and militaristic state apparatus (2009: 10).

Bleiker further suggests that aesthetic beauty can seduce and manipulate people into an ideology associated with it. The Nazi aesthetic therefore became a key component in the Nazi war and propaganda machine, and this same aesthetic continues to weave its way into contemporary culture and cinema.

The rationalist architecture movement influenced key features of the Nazi aesthetic, also the Social realist style (found across a wide spectrum of film today) had a lasting impact on the Nazi propaganda machine. The iconic black, red and white colour scheme drawn from the Nazi flag and used in much of the National Socialist Party's military attire and regalia continues to be used to symbolize evil or forbidden seduction in film and popular culture. The Nazi uniform and associated regalia remains iconic, influential, and generally represents the taboo status of Nazism. The aesthetic was not entirely crushed at the end of WWII and returned to popular culture in the form of a taboo fetish during the Nazisploitation trend in the 1970s. However, at least in fashion, film and popular culture, it is an aesthetic whose reappearance has been largely uncriticized, and its shameless proliferation in post-9/11 culture is something that deserves scrutiny.

Heroic realism, which inspired Nazi art and propaganda, arrived during Germany's Great Depression, and focused on the plight of the working class. The Nazi propaganda machine blended the Social realist image of the patriotic worker with the heroic, and often portrayed heroic men as individuals who worked and fought for their nation. Leni Riefenstahl's movie, *Triumph of the Will* (1935) echoes this message by showing young chiselled 'Aryan' men working the land, and then appearing later in uniform, pledging to serve a Greater Germany.

As Susan Sontag states, '*Triumph of the Will* uses overpopulated wide shots of massed figures alternating with close-ups that isolate a single passion, a single perfect submission: in a temperate zone clean-cut people in uniforms group and regroup, as if they were seeking the perfect choreography to express their fealty' ([1975] 2002: 87). This idea of individuals working hard for their leader, to then submit en masse, often in uniform, not only features in Riefenstahl's work. This trope has entered cinematic narrative, where individuals join a movement under a leader in order to be heroic in the name of that leader. Films found within franchises such as *Star Wars* (Lucas 1977 to 2008), or *Harry Potter* (Yates 2007, 2010, 2011), feature similar group shots, of ordered people in vast spaces, all attending to leaders on pedestals, and landscape views of throne rooms or great halls from the elevated point of view of someone from the centre back.

Architecture was also integral to the fascist movement. Characterized by its open space, neoclassical style, smooth-edged lines and symmetrical composition, this architecture arose in both Germany and Italy in the 1930s and 1940s (This 2012). The exterior of these buildings were designed to dwarf and tower over individuals, their interiors were clean and often polished, and the use of light marble and colour were designed to give a sense of openness. Exterior and interior design was often spartan. At the same time, these buildings stood next to the older structures that predated the Nazi era, and Bavarian castles and towns continued to boast an old-world European charm. Both old and new architectures appear in several contemporary films.

Hitler's fascist regime also used provocative colours that continue to be used together, often to represent edgy fashion or evil caricatures such as vampires and super-villains. Nathan Maxwell Cann suggests that 'visually, black and white with red highlights is a very seductive colour scheme. The black and white create a visual contrast that is clean and orderly, while the provocative touches of red stimulate and awaken the senses. Success stories of this combo abound from typewriter ink to *Sin City* to the design of this very blog'[1]. These colour schemes continue to influence fashion, film costumes, and interior film sets when depicting authority or royalty.

The uniform itself provokes fascination, and has inspired experimental fashion since the sixties, when alternative progressives wore it as a sign of subversion. The Nazi SS uniform in particular draws attention to itself, partly because it is a uniform, and partly because of how it differentiated itself from other uniforms of its time. Susan Sontag identified this fascination with fascism during the first wave of Nazisploitation films: 'there is a general fantasy about uniforms. They suggest community, order, identity (through ranks, badges, medals, things which declare who the wearer is and what he has done: his worth is recognized), competence, legitimate authority, the legitimate exercise of violence' ([1975] 2002: 99). Sontag suggests that the Nazi uniform is an object of sexual fetish because an SS officer embodied the ideal fascist, someone who carried out their mission efficiently and dramatically by adhering to a stylized aesthetic dress code that commanded obedience. Sontag continues, 'the SS was designed as an elite military community that would be not only supremely violent, but also supremely beautiful' ([1975] 2002: 99). The SS uniform remains a seductive garment to film and popular culture. As an object of fetish, the Nazi uniform has long since departed from the underground of bondage, domination and sadomasochism (BDSM) clubs, and appears in edgy popular culture everywhere. It has inspired looks found in corporate fashion, military-inspired couture, and alternative gothic, industrial, dieselpunk and steampunk fashion movements (Gauzot 2011). It has influenced the costumes of villains such as those found in *Harry Potter, V for Vendetta* (Teigue 2006), and *Dr. Horrible's Sing-Along Blog*.[2] It has also inspired the look of fighter characters in films such as *Starship Troopers: Invasion* (Aramaki 2012), music videos such as Lady Gaga's *Alejandro* (2010), video games such as *Deus Ex,* and miniature games such as *Warhammer 40k*. Japan has a rising culture of cos-players who wear Nazi uniforms or have Nazi-themed weddings.[3] There is also a new wave of pornographic Nazi anime that currently populates the Internet on various sites[4], as well as pictorial Nazi porn on a card game called Barbarossa.[5]

It is not entirely surprising that modern fashion and fascism have influenced each other at a time of technical advancement. In an interview discussing his book on Italian fashion in the time of Mussolini, Mario Lupano stated, 'We wanted to look at uniformity as an aesthetic and the ways that order, rationality, and technical control became really important. There's a lot of totalitarianism in fashion: the big dreams and ambitions, the sense of new beginnings, the attempts to define an epoch'[6] (see also Lupano & Vaccari, 2009, *Fashion at the time of fascism: Italian modernist lifestyle, 1922–1943*). The imagery of war continues to resonate when one considers the ambitions of the established luxury fashion houses, their collections, and the 'stories' and 'campaigns' which define their seasons and tie each piece of their collections under central themes that are unified by both visual cues and narrative triggers.

Sontag's comments on culture's fascination with fascism were made at a time when progressive and alternative culture embraced Nazi aesthetics, themes and iconography. The second half of the 1970s gave rise to the brief era of Nazisploitation, which was mostly found in the taboo, underground, or rebellious cultures of that time. Taboo portrayals of the Nazi introduced the hyper-sexualized Nazi, or the Nazi character who used sex to dominate. Art-house films like *The Night Porter* (Cavani 1974) and *Salon Kitty* (Brass 1976) portrayed Nazis with seductively dominating qualities, whereas films like *Ilsa: She-Wolf of the SS* (Edmonds 1975), and punk, glam, and gothic rock bands, all brought Nazi symbolism and fashion sense to their image (see Plate ii).

The alternative music industry also started to exploit Nazi imagery. The English rock band Joy Division, for example, which formed in 1976 and is still cherished as iconic in the gothic music scene, took their band name from the term used for a unit of Jewish women who were forced to work in concentration camps as sex slaves. The singer Siouxsie Sioux notes in an interview she did with *Uncut*: 'The culture around then was Monty Python, Basil Fawlty, Freddie Star, the Producers – Springtime for Hitler. ... It was very much *Salon Kitty*. It was used as a glamour thing'[7] (Goddard 2005). In this interview, Siouxsie Sioux noted that the 'political correctness' around the mention of Nazis 'was very oppressive ... it was very Nazi.' Yet, while Sontag was able to discuss society's fascination with the fascist aesthetic in the halls of the universities, individuals like Siouxsie Sioux could not engage with the aesthetic without being criticized. At the time, donning Nazi-inspired attire was still taboo, and mainstream cinematic characters who did so were generally the 'bad guys.'

Cinematic portrayal of the Nazi before 9/11

Nazis have been invading the silver screen since the Third Reich's reign in Germany. In addition to being protagonists in Leni Riefenstahl's propaganda film *Triumph of the Will,* Nazis have served as villains in Fritz Lang's *Man Hunt,* and the famous classic, *Casablanca* (Curtiz 1942). They have presented themselves as the undisputed bad guys in every film genre since WWII, and their evil is so nefarious that they are relegated to the league of zombies and aliens – making them objects that can be slaughtered en masse, and without mercy. Broadly speaking, there were two categories of Nazi films: A-list films which featured a sensitively framed historical context and a moral message, and the taboo B-rated Nazisploitation films that often included sexualized themes and prompted controversy. The A-list films generally fell within the following categories: war romance, action and suspense, or the Holocaust film.

The war romance, usually imbued with a touch of glamour, unabashedly portrays the lover and their friends in stylish costumes in a narrative in which the protagonists fight for their love in a war-torn society. Nazis were not the focus of such films, but served as antagonists and, as such, lacked any real character development. While clearly figures of authority, Nazi dress in such roles is not bold in the manner of the uniforms in *Valkyrie* or *Inglourious Basterds*, for example. It is certainly the case that the film classic *Casablanca* depicts a glamorous aesthetic in the impeccably dressed Major Strasser. But Strasser is not a primary character and he is unable to use his presence to wield the authority his uniform might be expected to command. In the end, in common with many Nazi officers in films of this era, he is shot.

Marlon Brando's character Lt Christian Diestl in *The Young Lions* (Dmytryk 1958), by contrast, possesses inner and outer beauty. Diestl has ambivalent feelings about the war, and tries not to kill if he can avoid it. But, regardless of his inner conflict (and he is not always shown in Nazi uniform), he remains irredeemable simply on account of his status as a Nazi. He ends up shot, and dies in a mud puddle: Nazism, it is suggested, will never be forgiven.

Primary examples of Nazi action films predating 9/11 include *The Great Escape* (Sturges 1963), and the first two *Indiana Jones* films (Spielberg 1981, 1984). *The Great Escape* follows Allied soldiers as they attempt to escape a German-managed POW camp by digging tunnels that would lead them beyond the gates. With its famous upbeat theme tune and its witty banter, the film mingles comedic tropes and suspense. The real tragedy occurs when all but three of the escapees are killed by the Nazis, once again emphasizing the regime's brutality. This film is not glamorous, nor do the Nazis appear polished or attractive; with the exception of the German Kommandant von Luger, most of them lack character. Their sole purpose is to monitor, capture or kill the Allied escapees.

The Indiana Jones movies include similarly styled Nazis. They are the archetypal 'bad guys', who chase and attempt to kill Indiana Jones, or reach the precious artefacts before he does. They are fashioned as the primary antagonist in much the same way as those in *The Great Escape, Bedknobs and Broomsticks* (Stevenson 1971), or even *Casablanca*. A ringleader, who might have some identifiable personality, may be singled out but, for the most part, the audience does not get to know these characters. All the audience sees is how the protagonists are hunted by the Nazis.

The Holocaust film's understated costume design and cinematic style relied on realism and desaturated colour schemes. Films like *Schindler's List* (Spielberg 1993), *Life is Beautiful* (Benigni 1997) and *The Pianist* (Polanski 2002) capture the everyday interactions between Nazis and their victims, often with the didactic aim of enlisting the viewer's sympathy in order to make the point that such atrocities should never be allowed to happen again (Classen 2009). To win the approval of critic, viewer and Holocaust survivor alike, these films must address the subject in a historically sensitive manner but without sentimentality. This is a difficult balance to achieve. If the film is too sentimental, it threatens to both trade on and pervert a historical tragedy; if it is too emotionally restrained, it may fail to adequately engage the viewer thereby squandering the chance to reflect intelligently on humanity's capacity for atrocity.

These films establish a setting that is historically nostalgic. Their key antagonists, however, do not sustain the ideal fascist aesthetic throughout the film. *Schindler's List* initially presents the Nazis as glamorous – individuals to appease and admire. The film introduces Oskar Schindler as he dresses in fine attire, fixes his Nazi Party pen to his suit lapel, and strides into an elegant nightclub populated by the party elite. By the end of the night, they join him in posing for photographs that decorate his office throughout the rest of the film. From that point forward, the Nazis themselves degenerate. They may maintain their handsome uniforms, but they also become increasingly boorish and brutish. Amon Goeth epitomizes the worst of this behaviour in a scene where he wakes up hung-over, stumbles to his balcony, shoots a few Jewish prisoners, and pisses in a toilet. In effect, he degenerates from the Aryan ideal, through drinking, abusing women, fornicating, and mindlessly killing. His degradation causes the Nazi uniform to also degenerate, along with other aspects of the Nazi aesthetic.

The film *Life is Beautiful* follows the footsteps of an Italian-Jewish man, whose humour and romance help him endure life in the concentration camp. In 1945, Guido, his wife and his young son are taken to a concentration camp. Guido maintains to the boy that this is actually an elaborate game, where the contestants are competing for a tank. Even the most frightening aspects of camp life are absorbed into the fiction of the game, and Guido continues to play his part until he is marched off to be executed. The character of the Nazi camp doctor is distinctive, yet even he does not look as polished as the Nazis in *Valkyrie*, and nor does he help Guido survive or escape. The film proved controversial for its blend of comedy and tragedy rather than its portrayal of the Nazis; they remain faceless villains here, and are not romanticized. They maintain order and, in their ill-fitting uniforms, they lack the polish of Nazis portrayed in the post-9/11 films.

The Pianist examines the everyday trials of pianist Wladyslaw Szpilman, and his struggles to survive in the Warsaw Ghetto. He manages to avoid being sent to a death camp, and wanders through a tattered Poland, struggling to find the basic necessities of life. He finds an abandoned building with a piano, and here encounters Wehrmacht officer Wilm Hosenfeld, who asks Szpilman to play the piano. Hosenfeld consequently allows Szpilman to hide in the house, and brings him food. As the Germans lose the war, Hosenfeld leaves Szpilman with his greatcoat, and departs. The film's design has the rugged realism of wartime documentaries and a watered-down colour palette. With the exception of Hosenfeld in the key piano scene, the Nazis are shown as unglamorous in this film; their uniforms are not particularly well shaped, and they appear exhausted. Hosenfeld is a sacrificial character, and, like Brando's character in *The Young Lions,* he cannot be redeemed by his one humane action.

Until recently, Holocaust films did not attract the criticism of their Nazisploitation counterparts. Christoph Classen looks at the way *Schindler's List* and films like it have been adopted into both popular culture and the historical memory of the Holocaust. Classen traces the truth within these films, and how cultural memory has popularized many motifs from the Holocaust, including the actual locations where those events took place. He is careful in his criticism of this development, and instead focuses on the acceptance of such films. He observes that it is 'striking how cautious expert historians are when they criticize the movie. Now and again one can find a general skepticism about the filmic representation of history as such, which expresses especially the historians' concern about losing to popular film and television productions their privileged position to interpret history' (Classen 2009: 79). Tim Cole and Mark Dery are two writers who are unafraid to critique Hollywood's response to the Holocaust. In his essay 'Shoah Business', Dery draws on Cole's critique of the 'branding and blockbustering of the unspeakable' where the unspeakable itself, the Holocaust, is being devoured by eager audiences (2012: 87). Dery is extraordinarily critical of the consumer culture that cropped up around these films in the 1990s. He suggests that 'the Holocaust is being trivialized, merchandized, and through feel-good Hollywood confections and theme-parked museums, Americanized all around us', a trivialization that includes the purchase of 'Holocaust-related toys, lit lite, postcards, and games' (Dery 2012: 87). This consumerist habit around the Holocaust is trivializing – as is fascination for the image of the Nazi – yet mainstream Hollywood films made prior to 9/11 have in some ways become sacrosanct. While their attitude to the Holocaust is still in debate, it is clear that these films take the character of the Nazi seriously, and attempt not to exploit it. As critics note, while these films may exploit the Holocaust, the one thing they do not exploit is the fashionable Nazi.

The Fascist aesthetics of contemporary Nazi films

Since September 2001, the figure of the Nazi has had an increased presence in popular culture, in films, and in Nazi-inspired themes and imagery. The current renaissance of 'Nazisploitation' differs from its earlier incarnation, and its 'narrative conceits have permeated big budget studio productions and mainstream popular culture' (Magilow 2012: 6). Hollywood has released films that abandon the desaturated documentary-style aesthetics that dominate the WWII or Holocaust narrative. It instead enters a territory where the Nazi is stylized, fashionable, sexualized, and in many cases, human enough to engage the viewer's sympathy. At the same time, totalitarian themes have cropped up in unexpected films, which also borrow stylistic elements from the Third Reich. Black, red, and white return as the colour scheme for stylized super-villains who fight for absolute control in futuristic, fantasy, and even adolescent cinema. It seems today's Hollywood Nazi narrative borrows from the themes illustrated in Marvel's post-9/11 *Captain America* comics. The protagonists are heroic, and patriotic, and the antagonists are fashionable Nazis who have an identity and leave a lasting visual impression.

Valkyrie is a beautifully shot action and suspense film, which traces the actions of Colonel Claus von Stauffenberg, who attempted to lead a political coup that would begin by assassinating Hitler. Film critic Emanuel Levy noted that costumes were a key component to the design of *Valkyrie*, and the film's director, Bryan Singer, 'wanted to be authentic as possible while still being richly cinematic' (Levy 2008). Singer's portrayal of Hitler is not cartoon-like, recognizing that the action of the film takes place during Hitler's decline. At the same time, Singer and his costume designer, Joanna Johnston, recognize the force, power and tragedy of the German uniform. The narrative also departs from traditional WWII and Holocaust films in that the Nazis themselves are the protagonists, and Colonel Stauffenberg is a sympathetic character who cares for his wife, his children and his soldiers. He cares so much for Germany that he wishes to overthrow Hitler and the hateful Third Reich. In the end, Hitler's men stop Stauffenberg and execute him, along with his collaborators. The depiction of Nazis in *Valkyrie*, while not exactly exploitative, is sensationalist, and reflects a narrative popular among dystopian post-9/11 cinema. Like the protagonists in *Inglourious Basterds, V for Vendetta,* and the *Harry Potter* series, Stauffenberg recognizes the oppression of the evil regime in which he lives, and attempts to vanquish it.

Inglourious Basterds boasts a controversial history-twisting plot with all the rich decor that one can expect from Quentin Tarantino. The film's costume designer Anna Sheppard suggests that the costumes in Tarantino's film are not styled in relation to clothing actually worn in Nazi-occupied France. Instead, she suggests, they are as flamboyant as the aristocracy that wears them, and notes that 'many previous films on WWII have brought down the costumes rather than make them elegant or expensive-looking' (Laverty 2009). Sheppard explains that she could dress everyone extravagantly since the film's narrative featured two film stars and the Nazi elite who prepare to attend a film premiere. While Sheppard did not elect to exploit the Nazi image per se, the narrative itself allowed for a high degree of glamour.

The film *Iron Sky* enjoys all the freedom of a science fiction satire, in which Nazis, living on the dark side of the moon, return to Earth in the near future when a Sarah Palin caricature is US president. Humour is clearly a central anchor in such an absurd plot, but reviewers failed to find it. *Hollywood Reporter's* David Rooney states, 'the plot doesn't quite hang together toward the end, but the real problem is that the jokes are just not there' (2012). *Variety's* Leslie Felperin notes that 'the high concept behind sci-fi comedy *Iron Sky* is an immediate winner, and the trailer has already built an instant following via a viral marketing campaign, but sadly, the final product is much more amusing in theory than in execution' (2012).

The film *Iron Sky* is unique not only as a Nazi narrative, but as an action narrative. Interestingly enough, it is the women who drive the plot; they have the power to rule and affect the course of action. *Iron Sky* exploits Nazi imagery and costuming within a work of fiction, and its design borrows heavily from the dieselpunk aesthetic (Gauzot 2011). This aesthetic is a subcategory of the cyberpunk movement and merges pop-culture styles from the 1920s to the 1950s with those of today. One of the often quoted references on the Internet states that the 'diesel era' was a time defined by warfare, Art Deco, pulp heroes, swing music, and noir gumshoes … [Dieselpunk's] goal is to create something unexpected by merging the Zeitgeist of the past with the technology and attitude of the future' (Gauzot 2011). Using the dieselpunk aesthetic, *Iron Sky* then reinvents the Nazi uniform and the Nazi 'world'. This world belongs to the past; computers are still the size of rooms, and buildings, machinery, and furniture borrow motifs from art deco. Despite its old-fashioned look, the technology is clearly advanced enough for the Nazis to have created structures, ventilation systems, mining techniques and gravity sufficient for human beings on the Nazi moon bases. The uniform is as pristine and sharp as the uniforms in *Salon Kitty* and *Valkyrie,* and both civilians and military personnel in this world wear some variation of a uniform. Yet the uniform plays another role in the second act when the president's campaign manager, Vivian Wagner, designs gothic-industrial Nazi-inspired uniforms for the president's 'campaign troops'. These uniforms, complete with sleek leather accessories, corsetry, industrial fashion boots, and red-and-white armbands offer a modern and fashion-forward rendition of the Nazi uniform. Wagner does not stop with uniforms, but instead redesigns the president's entire campaign with Nazi-inspired propaganda, speech writing, and body language. The film does not make clear if Wagner understands the history or visual context of these designs, however, it is a campaign that she, the president and the voters all take quite seriously.

All of these films are unapologetic in their proliferation of the Nazi image. They are obsessed with Nazi or fascist design in a way that seems perverse, over the top, and unashamed: uniforms are exceptionally well presented and worn by beautiful people; sets feature vast architecture, scattered with swastikas and red, white and black colour motifs, sometimes without purpose. The film *Valkyrie* in particular includes stunning architectural sets, and the swastika even appears at the bottom of a beautiful swimming pool, as a pin-up boy straight out of Heroic realist propaganda expertly swims across it. The extravagance and redundancy of the imagery in these films, in which the Nazis inevitably meet their demise, trivializes these figures just as concentration camp imagery does the Holocaust. In addition, however, these Nazis are sexualized, not unlike those of the Nazisploitation films of the 1960s.

Unique and responsible post-9/11 Nazi narratives

With the exception of *Iron Sky*, the unabashed Nazisploitation films emerge primarily from Hollywood. European films portraying Nazis seem focused principally on historical narratives about protagonists trapped in Nazi occupation, and less interested in objectifying the Nazi as fashionable and sexy. Other films, with a more European sensibility, such as *Downfall* (Hirschbiegel 2004) and *The Counterfeiters* (Ruzowitzky 2007) seem to borrow from narratives and aesthetics much closer to the Holocaust films that predate 9/11. There is reason to suggest that this new wave of Nazisploitation is primarily a product of Hollywood, and, therefore, the United States (US). *Downfall*, a European production based on a true story, engendered some controversy. It tells the story of Hitler's final days in his Berlin bunker and at times portrays him as someone to pity. Glamour in the film is ridiculed or non-existent and the Nazis are slightly unkempt in their uniforms; those who maintain a polished look in order to appease Hitler in the final hours appear – like Eva Braun in her attempts to stage luxurious parties – to have lost their grip on reality. Hitler himself teeters between depression and verbose anger. Yet, Nazi or not, he is merely human, as are the lives of the Berliners around him. *Downfall* neither exploits the Nazi allure, nor paints them as sympathetic characters. The pity it induces in its audience is in relation to Hitler's hubris as he wastes his life building a hateful regime, and one that will not endure.

The Counterfeiters begins with a man gambling in Monte Carlo. He then remembers a time when he belonged to a group of artists who were arrested and forced to forge British pounds for the Nazis, as part of Operation Bernhard: the Nazi goal was to inflate the British market with fake currency, and thus weaken its economy. Having complied in the forgery of the British currency the men devise plans to delay reproduction of the US dollar. As the war ends, the Nazis threaten to shut the printing operation down, but instead must flee Russia's advance. The counterfeiters are then discovered by other prisoners, who perceive them as SS officers and threaten to kill them. This 2008 film, unlike American releases of the same period, did not glamorize the Nazi characters. Its colour palette is muted and the focus of the story is the counterfeiters, with the Nazis there to enforce their labour or punish them when disappointed. *The Counterfeiters* concentrates on the issue of responsibility, both individual and collective, acknowledging the actions of the forgers in their attempt to weaken the Nazi regime.

Downfall and *The Counterfeiters* are distinctive productions within the Holocaust and war narratives of the post-9/11 era. They make an effort to explore the idea that human beings must do what they can to stand up to tyranny. These films therefore put responsibility for such atrocities not only on the governing powers, but on the civilians who live under their rule.

Nazis Nazis everywhere!

While Hollywood churns out Nazi films, popular culture has become enamoured with Nazi-styled fashion, Internet memes, and media which either seeks to beautify fascist aesthetics, or poke fun at Nazis in trivial ways. For example, the fashion industry seems hooked on military style and aesthetics, which draw on the subtle, utilitarian, and functional uniform of the 20th century. Daniel Dykes confesses to tracking military trends in fashion since 2008 (2010). Josh Patner's article traces the 2010 trend of military fashion, primarily as it relates to men. Patner asks, 'is chic-ing around in quasi-military gear weird when there's a real fight going on?' (2010). Patner suggests not – because fashion escapes the 'quotidian reality':

> … today's military style escapes the realm of the real, doing without fatigues and camouflage. The best of the new clothes make no reference to the battlefield. These are hero's clothes in the glossy, *Top Gun* sense, with romanticized military flair – hard-edge details rather than a show of brute force (2010, n.p.n.).

He continues to point out that counterculture in the 1960s made military fashion popular as hippies and rock stars began wearing army surplus clothing to protest against the Vietnam War.

Dykes also observes how military-inspired fashion continues to reject baggy surplus outerwear and 18th- and 19th-century Georgian and excessive Victorian ornamentation, and instead opts for the simple, edgy and understated details inspired by uniforms of the 20th century (2010): 'yesterday's sloppy surplus and wearable dissent is a thing of the past. Fall's classic military looks are sharp and tight, offering a fashionable salute to the precision and function of uniforms. The only statement the wearers are making is that they want to look sharp' (Dykes 2010).

While most fashion bloggers will not go so far as to say that 'Fashion has gone Nazi', their fashion editorials visually betray the Nazi inspiration. The blog, Trendhunter displayed a spread on Military-Inspired Trench Coats, which showcased Victoria Beckham in peak caps and light grey double breasted trenches and tunics next to a *Valkyrie* screen shot of Tom Cruise sporting a light grey Nazi tunic and peak cap. (Trendhunter 2009). This 'posh military aesthetic' manifests in the Nazi uniforms of the 2008–2009 Nazi films, and seeps into other action, fantasy and science-fiction genres of the post-9/11 era.

In his introduction, Daniel Magilow points out that Hitler and the Nazis have not only found a new place in cinema, but they have penetrated the media arts in everything from video games to Internet memes (2012). Parodies of Hitler's famous rant in *Downfall* continue to decorate YouTube despite the company's decision to avoid copyright lawsuits from Constantin Film AG and remove such viral videos as of April 2010 (Magilow 2012). These parodies feature a defeated Hitler taking his anger out on his top men as Berlin crumbles in the face of Russian forces. The English subtitles in these parodies, however, have been changed to depict a Hitler who is angry about being banned from Xbox, Sarah Palin's resignation, or the fact that so many people are making parodies of *Downfall*.

A famous satirical cartoon, *Der Bonker*, also became an Internet phenomenon in 2006. Created by Walter Moers, this short depicts Hitler sitting on the potty, whinging about Germany's defeat, Churchill's success, and his loneliness, to a bebop reggae beat. The *Guardian* journalist Katy Duke outlined the controversy in an article published in September 2006. Duke notes that prominent German Jews have complained about portraying the 'Father of the Holocaust' in such a way, and that the Jamba ringtone company faces a commercial and economic backlash because it has the video and its tune available for mobile phone download. Walter Moers claims that Hitler should be parodied, though Lea Rosh, co-founder of the Berlin Holocaust Memorial, said she does not believe this topic is one that should be joked about (Duke 2006). Jewish publicist Henryk M. Broder noted the cartoon is a 'refreshing way of looking at an old topic.' Duke quotes Broder saying 'that Hitler was a murderer – we know that, it doesn't have to be the topic of every thesis. But Moers shows wonderfully what kind of a wretched, useless gasbag the Germans fell for. And that's groovy' (Duke 2006, n.p.n.).

In the midst of these debates and controversies, Hitler and the Nazis have taken the Internet by storm. In addition to *Downfall Parodies* and *Der Bonker, Epic Rap Battles of History* features a two-part music video where Hitler and Darth Vader battle through rap and rhyme, only to be vanquished by Stephen Hawking in the final video. *Grammar Nazis* is a parody of the opening scene of *Inglourious Basterds* where Colonel Hans Lander interrogates Perrier LaPadite regarding the missing Jews in his village. Lander corrects LaPadite's grammar because the Nazi Party takes grammar seriously. So seriously, in fact, that Lander kills himself after using a dangling participle. The web-comic *Hipster Hitler* depicts Hitler as his attempts to be an ironic, 'uncool' hipster often get in the way of his ambitions, or at least partially explain some of his flaws as a character. Some cartoons depict Hitler doing strikingly 'unhipster' things such as striking out against feminism because it is 'cool in England,' riding a bike on a battlefield to 'save gas,' or hiring a famous fashion label to design uniforms because its window display features understated, eye-catching, subtle and so very *avant-garde* uniforms.

Iron Sky as a demonstration of 'Nazi popularity'

The film *Iron Sky* was the result of collaboration amongst different talents around the world. Funded largely through crowdsourcing, *Iron Sky* was able to engage its audience in advance of production, an audience who then participated in the culture the film created (Rooney 2012). These fans supported the film by donating money, buying 'war bonds,' mock propaganda posters, and related *Iron Sky* merchandise. Despite the crowdsourced energy behind the film, critics gave *Iron Sky* a mixed reception. The film and its distribution suffered due to its limited budget; it could not afford the technological, advertising and distribution advantages of contemporary mainstream films. However, the film's alternative methods of funding, quirky narrative and crowdsourced fan base meant it received some critical acclaim from alternative and less well-known critics. *Iron Sky*, which premiered at the 62nd Berlin International Film Festival as a part of its Panorama programme, did not get long theatrical runs from the mainstream distributors, and well-known commentators were critical of the film (Rooney 2012). The distributor Revolver Entertainment attempted to release *Iron Sky* for one day only in UK cinemas, which led to accusations from the film-makers that they had been misled: Revolver was obliged to revise its decision when online fans demanded a longer release. In many ways, it was this crowdsourcing, the cult-like popularity of the idea of Space Nazis, that prompted the film's wider distribution throughout mainstream cinema in large cities.

It is difficult to determine whether *Iron Sky* struggled to find a wider release because it featured Nazisploitation, or because its narrative serves as a commentary and satire on the US political machine, and the global greed for the last energy sources on the planet. The plot could be described as insensitive, comical or innovative, depending on the viewer. The action takes place in 2018 and weaves classic Nazisploitation villainy with a post-9/11 political subtext that mocks the patriotism and propaganda style of US politics. Also, *Iron Sky* portrays the US as a totalitarian regime in the making. It has everything in place for such a regime, including patriotic propaganda, absolutist xenophobic slogans, military pomp, and a desire to dominate the universal supply of natural resources. Further, the fictitious president approves of taking campaign advice from the two Nazis who find their way to the moon.

Iron Sky also features action/adventure elements common in other post-9/11 sci-fi or fantasy films set against the backdrop of totalitarianism. When the Nazis attack, they lay waste to New York City, which serves as a reminder of the destruction that met New York on 9/11. The imagery of dramatic explosions and crumbling buildings toppling over panicked pedestrians match the clips that news stations aired to tell the story of the September 11 attacks. These images can also be found in other films released post-9/11, including *Cloverfield* (Reeves 2008) and *Harry Potter and the Half Blood Prince* (Yates 2009).

Conclusion

In an era where the enemy has become a faceless terrorist, and the Nazi can appear heroic, it seems that today's unabashed Nazisploitation, in film, digital media, the Internet and other platforms of pop culture, engages a willing audience. Are Nazi-themed weddings and blogs dedicated to glamorizing Hitler demonstrating a nostalgic fondness for the figure of the Nazi – or are Nazi devotees a sign that society has lost its sensitivity on the subject of the Holocaust? The cinematic examples assessed here suggest that a newfound era of indefinite warfare – enhanced by heightened security, patriotic propaganda, xenophobic slogans, and more restrictive civil liberties, has encouraged narratives that glorify warfare and patriotism. Yet the films also offer a critique of those same restrictions, and show the fear, and the threat to freedom, of totalitarianism. Likewise, Internet phenomena like *Hipster Hitler* or the *Downfall* parodies illustrate how warning signs of fascist uprisings form a background of commentary on today's geopolitical landscape.

Iron Sky, within the terms set out here, seems to parody the post-9/11 film, and it does so responsibly by showing how a world can fall apart under tyranny. As an action film set against the backdrop of a totalitarian regime, *Iron Sky* has features found within other films of this post-9/11 genre; the Nazi characters, too, reflect the aesthetic opulence that has defined Nazis in post-9/11 cinema. The critique of the American political system is a central theme, exposing as it does the anxieties of the post-9/11 world. In other words, *Iron Sky* can be categorized alongside action films that manifest a post-9/11 rhetoric; the film, however, simultaneously enacts a critique of that same rhetoric. This critical stance is currently problematic (if not taboo) because it questions the military and political actions of the US since the events of September 11. What appears least taboo about these films are the parading figures of the very glamorous Nazis.

References

Birkenstein, J., Froula, A., & Randell, K. (eds) (2010). *Reframing 9/11: Film, Popular Culture and the 'War on Terror'*. New York: Continuum.

Bleiker, R. (2009). *Aesthetics and world politics*. Basingstoke: Palgrave Macmillan.

Cann, N. M. (2009). 'Nazi // Occult // High Fashion' from the Penumbra Report, http://nathanmaxwellcann.info/2009/12/22/nazi-occult-high-fashion/. Accessed 9 September 2012.

Classen, C. (2009). 'Balanced Truth: Steven Spielberg's *Schindler's List* among History, Memory, and Popular Culture', *History and Theory*, 47, pp. 77–102.

Dery, M. (2012). *I Must Not Think Bad Thoughts: Drive-By Essays on American Dread, American Dreams*. Minneapolis: University of Minnesota Press.

Duke, K. (18 June 2006). 'Hitler internet cartoon causes storm in Germany', *The Guardian: MediaGuardian*. London: UK.

Dykes, D. P. (2010). 'Military Fashion: Women's Military Clothing Trend', http://www.fashionrising.com. Accessed 16 June 2012.

Felperin, L. (2012). 'Iron Sky', *Variety Film Reviews*. http://www.variety.com/review/VE1117947071/. Accessed 1 September 2012.

Ferrera, A. N. (2010). 'Fashion's Forgotten Fascists', http://www.vice.com/read/fashions-forgotten-fascists. Accessed 14 September 2012.

Gauzot, M. D. (2011). 'What is Dieselpunk?', http://www.thesteampunkempire. Accessed 13 August 2012.

Goddard, S. (2005). 'Siouxsie Sioux: The Life & Loves of a She-Devil', http://www.untiedundone.com/020105b.html. Accessed 13 August 2012.

Guenther, I. (2004). *Nazi chic? Fashioning women in the Third Reich*. Oxford: Berg.

Heller, D. A. (2005). *The Selling of 9/11: How a National Tragedy Became a Commodity* (1st ed.). New York: Palgrave Macmillan.

Kellner, D. M. (2009). *Cinema Wars: Hollywood Film and Politics in the Bush-Cheney Era*. West Sussex: John Wiley & Sons.

Laverty, C. (2009). 'Inglourious Basterds: Costume Lowdown', http://clothesonfilm.com/inglourious-basterds-costume-lowdown-by-anna-sheppard/5602/. Accessed 13 August 2012.

Levy, E. (2008). 'Valkyrie: How Joanna Johnston Dressed the Third Reich', http://www.emanuellevy.com/comment/valkyrie-how-joanna-johnston-dressed-the-third-reich-7/. Accessed 13 August 2012.

Lupano, M. & Vaccari, A. (eds) (2009). *Fashion at the time of fascism: Italian modernist lifestyle, 1922–1943*. Bologna: Damiani.

Magilow, D. H. (2012). 'Introduction: Nazisploitation! The Nazi Image in Low-Brow Cinema and Culture', in D. H. Magilow, E. Bridges & K. T. Vander Lugt (eds), *Nazisploitation! The Nazi Image in Low-Brow Cinema and Culture*, pp. 1–21. London: Continuum International Publishing Group.

Patner, J. (1 September 2010). 'Military Chic During Wartime? Yes, Sir!: All Dressed Up With No War to Go', *The Wall Street Journal* [online edition], http://online.wsj.com/article/SB1000142 405274870408210457551632064646464294.html. Accessed 12 June 2012.

Rooney, D. (2 December 2012). 'Iron Sky: Berlin Film Review', http://www.hollywoodreporter.com/review/iron-sky-berlin-film-review-289733, Accessed 14 June 2012.

Sanchez-Escalonilla, A. (2010). 'Hollywood and the Rhetoric of Panic: The Popular Genres of Action and Fantasy in the Wake of the 9/11 Attacks', *Journal of Popular Film & Television*, 38: 1, pp. 10–20.

Sontag, S. ([1975] 2002). 'Fascinating Fascism' from *The New York Review of Books*, Vol. XXII(1) Feb. 6, 1975, reprinted in *Under the sign of Saturn: Essays*, pp. 73–108. New York: Picador.

Thies, J. (2012). *Hitler's Plans for Global Domination: Nazi Architecture and Ultimate War Aims*. Oxford: Berghahn.

This, C. (2012). 'Captain America Lives Again and So Do the Nazis: Nazisploitation in Comics after 9/11', in D. H. Magilow, E. Bridges & K. T. Vander Lugt (eds), *Nazisploitation! The Nazi Image in Low-Brow Cinema and Culture*, pp. 219–37. London: The Continuum International Publishing Group.

Trendhunter (6 March 2009). 'Military-Inspired Trench Coats: Victoria Beckham Shows How to Rock Military Street Style', http://www.trendhunger.com/trends/military-style-the-posh-way. Accessed 14 August 2012.

Video and game credits

Alejandro (2010). Music video of Lady Gaga performing 'Alejandro'. US: Interscope Records (Universal Music Group).

Deus Ex (and series) (2000–2012). Video game. US: Ion Storm.

Dr. Horrible's Sing-Along Blog (n.d.). http://drhorrible.com. Accessed 12 November 2012.

Warhammer 40k (and series) (1987–2012). Tabletop miniature wargame. Nottingham, UK: Games Workshop.

Film credits

Amorim, V. (2008). *Good*. M. Segel. UK: Good Films.

Aramaki, S. (2012). *Starship Troopers: Invasion*. Joseph Chou, Edward Neumeier, Caspar Van Dien. US: Sony Pictures Home Entertainment.

Benigni, R. (1997). *Life is Beautiful*. Gianluigi Braschi, Elda Ferri. Italy: Cecchi Gori Group and Miramax Films.

Brass, T. (1976). *Salon Kitty*. Ermanno Donati, Guilo Sbarigia. Italy: Coralta Cinematografica, Cinema Seven Films, and Les Productions Fox Europa.

Cavani, L. (1974). *The Night Porter*. Esa De Simone, Robert Gordon Edwards. Italy: The Criterion Collection.

Curtiz, M. (1942). *Casablanca*. H. B. Wallis. US: Warner Brothers.

Daldry, S. (2008). *The Reader*. Donna Gigliotti, Redmond Morris. (Sydney Pollack, Anthony Minghella received credit posthumously). US: Mirage Enterprises, Neunte Babelsberg Film, GmbH and The Weinstein Company.

Dmytryk, E. (1958). *The Young Lions*. A. Lichtman. US: Twentieth Century-Fox Film Corporation.

Edmonds, D. (1975). *Ilsa: She-Wolf of the SS*. D. F. Friedman. US: Aetas Film Production.

Herman, M. (2008). *Boy in the Striped Pyjamas*. D. Heyman. UK, US: Miramax Films.

Hirschbiegel, O. (2004). *Downfall*. B. Eichinger. Germany: ConstantFilm.

Lang, F. (1941). *Man Hunt*. K. Macgowan. US: Twentieth Century-Fox Film Corporation.

Miller, F. (2008). *The Spirit*. Debra Del Prete, Michael Uslan, Gigi Pritzker, William Lischak. US: Lionsgate and Odd Lot Entertainment.

Polanski, R. (2002). *The Pianist*. Gene Gutowski, Robert Benmussa, Roman Polanski, Alain Sarde. France, Germany, Poland, UK: Focus Features, Universal Studios.

Reeves, M. (2008). *Cloverfield*. J.J. Abrams and Bryan Burk. Paramount Pictures.

Riefenstahl, L. (1935). *Triumph of the Will*. Leni Riefenstahl. Germany: Reichsparteitag-Film and Universum Film AG.

Ruzowitzky, S. (2007). *The Counterfeiters*. Josef Aichholzer, Nina Bohlman, Babette Schröder. Austria: Filmladen, Universum Film AG and Studio Babelsberg Motion Pictures.

Singer, B. (2008). *Valkyrie*. Chris Lee, Gilbert Adler, Christopher McQuarrie, Bryan Singer, Dan Snyder. US: Twentieth Century Fox.

Spielberg, S. (1981). *Indiana Jones and the Raiders of the Lost Ark*. George Lucas, Frank Marshall, Howard Kazanjian. US: Lucasfilm Ltd. and Paramount Pictures.

Spielberg, S. (1984). *Indiana Jones and the Temple of Doom*. R. Watts. US: Paramount Pictures.

Spielberg, S. (1993). *Schindler's List*. Gerald R. Molen, Steven Spielberg, Branko Lustig. US: Amblin Entertainment and Universal Pictures.

Stevenson, R. (1971). *Bedknobs and Broomsticks*. B. Walsh. UK, US: Buena Vista Distribution/ Walt Disney Studios.

Sturges, J. (1963). *The Great Escape*. J. Sturges. US: Mirisch Company and United Artists.

Tarantino, Q. (2009). *Inglourious Basterds*. L. Bender. Germany, US: The Weinstein Company, Universal Pictures.

Teigue, J. M. (2006). *V For Vendetta*. Film Index International. US: Warner Bros Entertainment.

Vuorensola, T. and S. Torssonen (2012). *Iron Sky*. Samuli Torssonen, Tero Kaukomaa, Michael Cowan, Oliver Damian, Cathy Overett, Mark Overett. Finland, Germany, Australia: Walt Disney Studios Motion Pictures Finland.

Wirkola, T. (2009). *Dead Snow*. Harold Zwart, Tomas Evjen. Norway: Euforia Film.

Yates, D. (2007). *Harry Potter and the Order of the Phoenix*. David Hayman, David Barron, Lionel Wigram. Film Index International. UK, US: Warner Brothers Entertainment Inc.

Yates, D. (2009). *Harry Potter and the Half-Blood Prince*. David Hayman, David Barron. UK, US: Warner Bros. Entertainment Inc.

Yates, D. (2010). *Harry Potter and the Deathly Hallows*, pt. 1. Kristan Giordano, Carla Hawkes. UK, US: Warner Bros. Entertainment Inc.

Yates, D. (2011). *Harry Potter and the Deathly Hallows,* pt. 2. David Hayman, David Barron, J. K. Rowling. UK, US: Warner Brothers Pictures.

Zwick, E. (2008). *Defiance*. Pieter Jan Brugge, Edward Zwick, Marshall Herskovitz. US: Paramount Vantage.

Notes

1   For one example, see http://izismile.com/2011/07/20/asian_nazi_wedding_15_pics.html.
2   See http://drhorrible.com/.
3   For one example, see http://izismile.com/2011/07/20/asian_nazi_wedding_15_pics.html.
4   For example, see http://DeviantArt.com.
5   This game is reviewed on http://boardgamegeek.com.
6   See Allison Nella Ferrera's 2010 interview with Mario Lupano and Alessandra Vaccari, http://www.vice.com/read/fashions-forgotten-fascists.
7   http://www.untiedundone.com/020105b.html.

Chapter 3

Branding the muscled male body as military costume

Heather Smith and Richard Gehrmann

Introduction

The military uniform covers the body of a soldier and constitutes the primary visual reference point. But the fashion of war incorporates more than just the physical covering of the body, and increasingly includes the very body of the soldier itself, a body that has changed noticeably during the 21st century. The military body has become more muscular and its shape has become part of the changing 'uniform' for male soldiers and, while possibly these changes also impact female soldiers, the focus here remains on the males. This new brand of the muscular and masculine soldier has been shaped by a body-obsessed popular culture and, in the Australian case, differs markedly from earlier representations of the Australian manly body. This chapter considers selected representations of the changing male military body throughout the 20th century, contrasting these with the heroic male body found in the contemporary conflict in Afghanistan and the male body represented in contemporary film and popular media.

When considering fashion and war in popular culture, some of the most eye-catching and immediate components of the visual image are those that clothe the soldier's body. The polished boots and sinister dark clothing of the Nazi soldier and the resplendent perfection of the tall, red-coated British guards outside Buckingham Palace represent antithetical varieties of the ceremonial variant of military fashion. In contrast, the disciplined khaki drill worn by soldiers of the First World War (WWI) and the Second World War (WWII), and the diffused lines of the modern combat camouflage uniform embody the less decorative but much more utilitarian efficiencies of the military costume worn in combat. Uniforms are the visible coverings of the soldier past and present, and constitute key aspects of both the soldiers' self-identity and also their representation to the wider world. To both self and others, the uniform evokes a range of distinct feelings and emotions. As Jennifer Craik notes, uniforms can have meanings that range from conformity and order to subversive eroticism (2003) and, clearly, these meanings can also be highly contested for soldiers. But the fashion of war, like other kinds of fashion, is a system of interconnected relationships joined to a dynamic whole (Carter 2003) and therefore incorporates more than just the physical covering of the body. This chapter suggests that this cover increasingly includes soldiers' bodies, and these body shapes have changed noticeably in the 21st century. Just as the medals and emblems attached to soldiers' uniforms represent a given society's historical acknowledgement of their experience, service or courage, the shape and bulk of their bodies and the inked tattoos of today's soldiers provide their own meaning.

This new branding of the male soldier's body emerges from the contemporary popular culture milieu that challenges how modern-day professional soldiers are perceived, understood and defined. Images of the sculpted physique, often tanned and stencilled, adorn the screen and page with increasing frequency, from 'The Commando', a trainer in the popular reality television show *The Biggest Loser*, to the hyper-masculine characters in Kathryn Bigelow's film *The Hurt Locker* (2008). Therefore it is timely to examine the evolving 'brand' of the male soldier along with the parallel appearance of equally bronzed, buffed and tattooed body-builder-types. Recently, popular culture has elevated this phenomenon, so it acts as an inter-modal terminal in the brand's life cycle (Holt 2004). The brand, as seen through the lens of popular culture, acts as designer, manufacturer, curator and exporter to millions of plugged-in viewers and page-turning consumers. Progressively, the time-honoured values and virtues of ideal soldiers are being superseded by the modern reality which chooses to venerate male soldiers and their engineered physicality. Recurring examples from contemporary popular culture appear to authenticate this trend of excessive emphasis on body shape, and compel the authors to explore the ramifications of the body-obsessed brand in contrast to the hearts and minds of today's serving military men and women.

The soldier as masculine

The military sphere is not solely the domain of men, and the wars of the 21st century illustrate this truth. For example, between 10 and 14 per cent of the United States (US) veterans of the wars in Iraq and Afghanistan are women, and they fight, are maimed, and die alongside their male counterparts (Hassija et al. 2012). Contemporary modern armies of the developed world increasingly acknowledge the role and importance of the growing numbers of female soldiers, but male identification with the 'brand soldier' remains deeply embedded. In earlier wars, where male soldiers constituted the overwhelming majority of combatants, the male body provided a valuable focal reference point for effective discussion and analysis, as Bourke has shown (1996). In the current wars in Afghanistan and Iraq, female soldiers have transitioned from their previous marginal position and challenged the masculine image. However, the soldier as masculine remains a dominant trope, and women's incorporation into the image has proved problematic in popular representation (Holland 2006; Höpfl 2003).

So, soldiers exemplify, and are traditionally viewed as, an embodiment of masculine virtues – courage, strength and determination – and such virtues form the core of the 'brand soldier'. Military actors generally represent specific and easily identifiable physical values that are closely linked to western concepts of masculinity. Greek and Roman civilizations promoted physical representations of strength and manly appearance through heroic statues and painted images, representations that have been deeply embedded in western history as components of the ideological construct of what makes a soldier, and that have shaped the iconography of the commemoration of war (Carden-Coyne 2009, see also Peoples 2014). In the ancient Greek Olympics, the image of the beautiful athlete was strongly linked with the image of the physically strong warrior, represented by the Spartans (Jenkins & Turner 2009). These associations of the soldier with manly beauty appear throughout the 20th century, when soldiers at Gallipoli were depicted as the equals of ancient Greek heroes such as Hector, Ajax and Achilles, and praised for their 'absolute beauty' (Mackenzie 1929: 65–66).

Representations of the Australian 'digger'

This representation of the physically handsome and therefore desirable soldier is also deeply embedded within the Australian historical experience, and is reinforced in popular culture with the iconic representations of Australians that constituted the national tradition known as the Anzac legend. The Australian national holiday of Anzac Day, celebrated on 25 April, is a commemoration of the landing of both Australian and New Zealand soldiers at Gallipoli (in modern Turkey) in 1915. In Australia, the place of Anzac Day in the popular psyche and the strong associations of those soldiers with national identity, heroism, militarism and maleness are highly contested notions (Damousi 2010; McKenna 2010). In chronicling the exploits of the Australian soldiers (or 'diggers') in WWI, writers helped to popularize the image of the lean yet strong Aussie diggers. Both their physiques and innate qualities could be admired and their sacrifices respected. They became inspirations for future generations, evoking the heroes of ancient Greece (Londey 2007). The WWI diggers are represented in paintings by war artists such as George Lambert, and also in the statuary of war memorials in Sydney, Melbourne and throughout Australia. Arguably, the Anzac soldiers reached their pinnacle of representation in the figures used to decorate the Hall of Remembrance at the Australian War Memorial in Canberra, completed in 1941. Large memorials to soldiers became the dominant model in Australian capital cities, but the stylized representation of the masculine soldier's body was also ever present in local communities (Inglis & Brazier 2008). The statue of the Australian soldier, often standing with head bowed and his rifle reversed before him, was a ubiquitous feature of Australian suburbs, provincial cities and country towns. It remains as a dominant signifier of Australian military masculinity. Yet while these figures are masculine, they are not overly muscled or exaggerated. These bodies could personify the Everyman rather than the Superman.

The images of muscular yet lean Aussie diggers were perpetuated a generation later in the imagery associated with WWII. Official war artist Ivor Hele, among others, created images to commemorate the sacrifices of those represented and to inspire a new generation. Hele's posthumous painting of the Victoria Cross recipient Thomas 'Diver' Derrick shows a ruggedly handsome muscular man whose physical image is that of strength, but whose body image does not go beyond the boundaries of a normal masculine body type. Derrick is not portrayed as airbrushed, buffed or polished, but as a more raw and unfinished image of a soldier. The portrait of another Victoria Cross hero, Jim Gordon, might have revealed a great soldier in the eyes of the Australian War Memorial director, Alan Treloar, but for its artist, William Dargie, the exhausted Gordon is clearly 'not a tireless soldier-hero' (Bevan 2004: 18–19). Perhaps one of the most recognized images of WWII's New Guinea campaign was George Silk's 1942 photograph of Papuan supplies carrier Raphael Oimbari helping the temporarily blinded Private George 'Dick' Whittington. This iconic war image – incredibly, it was taken with just one spontaneous shot – became *Life* magazine's Picture of the Month and continues to resonate today just as it did in WWII (McDonald and Brune 1998: 138–39). The photo shows Whittington as a barefoot, maimed and unarmed figure clad in ill-fitting and dirty clothing, walking with the aid of a stick and Oimbari's helping hand. He is undoubtedly a determined soldier but clearly not the buffed warrior. Ironically, the muscled body and traditional costume of his non-combatant helper are more superficially warrior-like than is Whittington himself.

Australian soldiers in Vietnam

It should be noted that following WWII, Australians often relaxed their views on the representation of the soldier as a manly and finely sculpted figure. In the Australian Vietnam War era film *The Odd Angry Shot* (Jeffrey 1979) the actors performing the roles of the supposedly elite soldiers of the Special Air Service (SAS) present a cast of interesting and diverse characters that challenge the audience's credulity. The unmilitary appearance of Graham Kennedy and Graeme Blundell do not match up with the more chiselled physique of Bryan Brown or John Jarrett. None of the actors match contemporary assumptions of what Special Forces soldiers should look like. Kennedy and Blundell may have had star status in the 1970s Australian thespian world but by present-day standards of the buffed masculine ideal they are clearly aberrant in posture, size and muscle definition (Bertrand 1988). Their physiques differ from contemporary expectations, as the imagery present in today's popular culture conditions the audience to imagine the muscled soldier as both normal and desirable. It is certainly true that the genre of Vietnam War films reflects an era of disillusionment far removed from the mythic heroism of WWII (Bjerre 2011: 223). One explanation is that the characters 'unmanly' demeanour, and, in some cases, their aged, balding and flabby bodies, might be no more than the sentimental miscasting of otherwise good actors. The storyline of this film addresses aspects of the war that leads McCarthy to see it as a blend of MASH-style tragi-comedy and mateship (2001). Even if a contemporary Afghanistan war film chose to replicate these themes, the casting choices of ageing or even flabby actors to represent soldiers would not be made today, especially for any film that hoped to achieve commercial success or to convince an audience now accustomed to the more muscular brand of soldier. A very different image of the SAS hero was to emerge in the era of the 'war on terror'.

Australian soldiers in recent history

From 2001, members of the Australian Defence Force have served in the Middle East alongside their US allies, and the representation of the military body of this new generation exhibits a marked difference. These are more image-conscious soldiers, Generation X products of a different era. In the downtime between patrols, soldiers in contemporary wars have ample opportunity to sculpt their bodies, and there is speculation that some take the risk of accessing illicit bodybuilding aids not openly available in Australia (Oakes 2010). In the American military, emphasis is placed on the cult of bodybuilding and the military is seen as 'a place where bodies are transformed' (Hinojosa 2010: 184). The need to present a massively muscled physique has infused Australian military consciousness and soldiers already enthusiastic about maintaining physical fitness have shown little hesitation in replicating the American bodybuilding obsession. While earlier cultural representations of the military might have emphasized soldierly traditions of smoking and heavy drinking, contemporary soldiers on operations drink little, smoke less, and train hard (Richard Gehrmann, personal observation).[1] Today, soldiers train to achieve power, strength and, where possible, perfect muscle definition, and are provided with few alternatives but to 'work or work out' (Moran 2013).

Such dedication will earn a select group of hopeful young soldiers admission to the challenging roles available in prestigious elite and highly paid units such as the Special Air Service Regiment or the Commandos. The punitive fitness regimes required to pass selection mean that such young soldiers are aware of the effects of alcohol and tobacco, and they carefully consider their decision to indulge in products that would provide only short-term pleasure but could impair their physical fitness and limit their military career options. While excess can take place at the end of the deployment, military service in a dangerous and highly regulated war zone is conducive to abstinence and, once alcohol and tobacco are moved to the margins, the gym becomes one of the few options of escape, especially for those not on patrol (McPhedran 2013).

This might be a formal structure with exercise cycles and weight machines, or an improvised open-air gym of home-made concrete weights and steel chin-up bars suspended from the tops of the ubiquitous HESCO rocket protection barriers (Richard Gehrmann, personal observation). Working out in the gym can fill spare time in a soldier's day, and regular attendance is validated by a military culture that perceives this as a highly worthy and desirable pastime for deployed soldiers ('Life at Patrol Base Wali', 2010). There are role models for those sculpting the new military body. One need only look at Victoria Cross recipient Corporal Ben Roberts-Smith to understand the physical and psychological allure that his figure may hold for many as a template of the perfect modern Australian soldier whose physical form matches the bronzed, buffed and tattooed masculine image (see Plate iii). Roberts-Smith was awarded the Victoria Cross for Australia as a result of acts of bravery during fighting in Afghanistan in 2010 (Pedersen 2012). While the media also recognized the bravery of the war's other two Victoria Cross recipients, Roberts-Smith attracted extra attention. His tattooed body carried representations that evoked the values of military masculinity and comradeship, including the phrase 'I will not fail my brothers', which unequivocally embodies long-standing Australian military values of mateship and commitment (Neighbour 2011: 8; Nicholson & O'Brien 2011). His decision to pose in the popular fitness magazine *Men's Health* further increased his profile as an attractive Australian military superhero who combined the rugged physicality of the battle-hardened soldier with the 21st-century masculine metrosexual family values of the devoted husband and parent. The imposing physique contained in his 202-centimetre frame shown half naked on the cover of the magazine is undeniably a statement about his military body, and the accompanying article detailed his punishing training regime that was specifically designed to prepare him for war (Cordingley 2012). This body is far more sculptured, toned and shaped than those of the soldiers of previous wars. Compared to earlier images of elite soldiery, such as Lambert's ascetic Light Horsemen of WWI or Dargie's more muscled Jim Gordon, not to mention the fictitious military bodies presented in the Vietnam-era movie *The Odd Angry Shot*, the body of Roberts-Smith is striking in its incongruity with previous wartime heroes.

The contemporary military body

The created representation of the physically perfect and muscled soldier is an idealized trope, but of course the health and average size of serving soldiers has been increasing for over a hundred years. Today's military bodies are the product of a wealthy society, and far removed from the poor state of public health in late 19th-century Britain that led to the rejection of two-fifths of applicants for military service in the Boer War (Hatton 2011: 952). The increasing affluence of the developed world has produced the startling differences. Of those who enlisted in WWI, there were contrasts between the physiques of the healthy and well-nourished middle classes, the less well-developed working classes, the more sturdy bodies of sportsmen or physically strong workers from the mines and the docks, and the 'ragged bodies of the poor' (Bourke 1996: 12). At the start of WWI the minimum requirement for Australian recruits was a 34-inch chest measurement (Carlyon 2001), a diminutive male body when compared to the muscled build represented by images of soldiers today.

Modern popular culture is body-centric, emphasizing muscles and proportional form and using tattoos to further decorate the body. The act of reshaping the human form to create bulk musculature leads to increased fitness and, with the release of endorphins during exercise, can be an enjoyable pastime. In one sense this is a harmless pastime (unless the soldier ingests dangerous anabolic steroids) but can the cultural predilection for muscle bulk possibly have deeper ramifications for the psyche of soldiers serving in today's military? Popular culture perpetuates this body image, and, while it may be assumed by both male and female soldiers as aspirational, muscle bulk has become the domain of the male soldier in particular. These trends present a challenge for male soldiers who might have achieved an excellent standard of physical fitness but whose body shape does not match the current 'brand soldier'. Not all soldiers can match this ideal, and, even for those that do, the inevitable impacts of increasing work demands, the effects of age, and a sedentary, office lifestyle make retention of the bronzed and buffed image an increasingly difficult challenge (McDonald 2010; Hinde 2009).

In 2007, the Australian Army adopted a model of nine core behaviours. These were:

every soldier an expert in close combat;
every soldier a leader;
every soldier physically tough;
every soldier mentally prepared;
every soldier committed to continuous learning and self development;
every soldier courageous;
every soldier takes the initiative; every soldier works for the team; and,
every soldier demonstrates compassion.

('I'm an Australian soldier' 2007)

Examination of the nine behaviours shows that, while physical strength is clearly important, a range of other attributes are also highly valued. Indeed, physical toughness or strength – much less that of the sculptured physique – is only one of the behaviours formally listed, and other more cerebral attributes such as teamwork, compassion and continuous learning are presented as equally important. One obvious conclusion is that even the Australian Army itself does not emphasize the ideal of the bronzed and buffed soldier, an ideal currently pursued by many of its own members. Is there a danger that this current focus on the buffed soldier might become privileged at the expense of other attributes of the 'brand soldier'?

To understand the evolving body of the soldier it is necessary to explore this paradigm of 'branding'. In today's hyper-visual world, the detritus of business and enterprise is ever present. From highway billboards and cinema screens to cereal boxes and kids' toys, one cannot escape the heady concoction of images, messages, trademarks and aspirations. At best they can be alluring and rousing, transporting the viewers to another place comprised of new thoughts, sensations and possibilities. At worse, these images can be gruesome or downright exasperating which, in some cases, makes them all the more distinctive (if not memorable). En masse, these stimuli generate a powerful vortex of agenda and strategy, designed to interest, attract, persuade and win over modern consumers. These continual streams of relentless and tantalizing images make up what consumers have come to know as 'branding'.

The soldier as 'brand'

The notion of 'brands' and 'branding' have become synonymous with many aspects of human endeavour. Sport, the arts, politics and even philanthropy are enfolded in 'brand-wrap' and often adorned with the elaborate bows and ribbon of substantial marketing and advertising campaigns (Smith 2013). Currently, the process of brand-wrap has become synonymous with how consumers view the world they live in, and branding is both anticipated and quickly assimilated. The idea of the personal brand was first presented by influential management guru Tom Peters, who believed that people needed to define themselves as brands and, in fact, create 'Brand You' (Peters 1997: 84).

So branding migrates outwards from the domain of corporate business, products and services. Increasingly, people and places are defining and redefining themselves as 'brands' and positioning their offer or image so that it occupies a distinct and valued place, relative to competing items, in the target audience's mind. According to Kim Harrison, 'a corporate brand needs to be an accurate reflection of what the organisation is, how it performs, how it is different or unique among its competitors and what image or identity is being projected' (2011: 628). Similarly, individuals engineer brands for themselves which highlight their perceived uniqueness and emphasize their desired identity in a manner that turns them into the product, 'in effect, engaging in self-commodification' (Lair, Sullivan & Cheney 2005: 319). Intentional or otherwise, these human brands can become formidable forces, especially in the case of high-profile leaders, celebrities and well-known personalities who may, over time, be outshone and surpassed by their public brand. In fact, Naomi Klein noted that the graphic designer Tibor Kalman suggests 'the original notion of the brand was quality, but now brand is a *stylistic badge of courage*' (emphasis added).[2]

The ever-growing presence of intentional branding coupled with the 24/7 distribution network of contemporary media means consumers are guaranteed to be immersed in constructed identities across their multiple work, home and social spheres. Unsurprisingly, these brands appear in, or emerge from, the popular culture where it is almost impossible to detect if they are factual or faux. Once established, perception is reality for these brands which mutate for larger market share while remaining steadfast to their creators' vision. 'The reason consumers lean towards a particular brand is because they trust it' (Harrison 2011: 628). Who is more trustworthy than a country's soldier? Here, the re-construction of soldiers' bodies, fuelled by popular culture, has become both compelling and influential.

In the popular reality television show *The Biggest Loser*, which is now broadcast in Australia, New Zealand, the UK and the US, buffed and beautiful personal fitness trainers are teamed with obese contestants desperate to 'battle the bulge' (Network Ten 2006–present). In the Australian series, each of the three trainers have adopted and honed their unique brand, none more so than ex-military man Steve Willis. With his signature dark glasses, black T-shirt and combat fatigues, Steve is a picture of hard muscle, brawn and model looks. If his professional military experience is not enough, the army-style trousers make it clear, as does his alias, 'The Commando.' The sleeve of tattoos on his well-developed right upper arm adds to the branding of 'Commando': his physical and psychological prowess are encased within the identity of a soldier. Since his screen debut, Commando's popularity has soared amongst Australian audiences. On his profile on the show's website it states, 'To kids, he's an action man come to life and they love him.'[3]

Other trainers on *The Biggest Loser* are identified by their names, but Steve Willis is the only character identified on the basis of his former occupation as a Special Forces soldier. But the military associations with attaining fitness on *The Biggest Loser* are not confined to the character of The Commando. The programme itself drives contestants to compete to lose weight using what appears to be military-style training fused with imagery of endurance and inspiring feats of strength (Hadley 2012). The programme clearly represents the fat, the unfit and the uncommitted as failures, and deifies the slim, the healthy and those who try hard and subsequently push themselves beyond their limits of endurance. While The Commando's body represents years of his own hard work, dedication and physical training, and presents a physical image that no contestant can possibly achieve in several weeks, it does provide inspiration for contestants and is attractive to many (Johnston 2013). Thus the values embodied in The Commando and the values embodied in *The Biggest Loser* are inextricably linked.

From real-life action men to miniature plastic varieties, characterizations of the soldier are not difficult to find. Action figures are an enduring bestseller and firm favourites in the highly competitive children's toy market, and are often linked to military-style movies or games. The enduringly popular G.I. Joe figure from Hasbro has been available since 1964, but a visit to department stores or toyshops will unearth a dizzying selection of these toys, including Halo Battlescape, Transformers, Combat Creatures, and True Heroes. Weapons, armed vehicles, play soldiers and even camouflage clothing can be purchased with the enticing marketing superlatives of 'fight', 'destroy', 'action' and 'adventure'. Not surprisingly, these toys are overtly masculine in design and function which further perpetuates the stereotype that soldiers are male. These toys contribute to cultural assumptions about what soldiers should look like and perpetuate the myth that soldiering is focused on muscle, along with the attitudes of search and destroy.

The film industry is also a hotbed of soldier constructs that emphasize and idealize the physical. These constructs appear in a range of war films that chronicle the imagined experience of soldiers in Afghanistan and Iraq over the past decade. Such soldiers are universally represented by actors whose physical form matches that of the idealized version being discussed, and it is obvious that such representations in popular media will only further enhance the desire of today's soldiers to meet this often unreal expectation.

Conclusion

In Kathryn Bigelow's Oscar-winning film *The Hurt Locker* Jeremy Renner portrays a hyper-masculine hero who presents the complete package – big, strong, muscular – a package that, throughout the movie, is tied tenaciously to other qualities such as courage and sacrifice.

These masculine attributes are combined with his masculine physiognomy, an image of physical bigness only further enhanced by the padded and protective bomb disposal protection he often wears. The hero is a big strong man, who epitomizes masculine values through both his heroism and his altruism; he is an easy soldier to like because he saves rather than kills and, in Tim Blackmore's words, is 'an invulnerable, unbeatable charismatic' (2012: 323). In other television representations of the soldier, such as *Generation Kill*, the physically strong stereotypical masculine shape is also prized. Yet it is important to remember that *The Hurt Locker* is a fictional account based on Mark Boal's interviews and his experiences as an embedded journalist and screenwriter (Johnston 2009). This representation, however, is foregrounded to such an extent that it is afforded a documentary realness. Certainly, such images match the shape that is marketed as the image of today's soldier.

Through the media, popular culture delivers many more examples which venerate the body and make it stridently clear that big is best – and better still with an excessive tan and 'killer' tattoos. As shown here, the muscled body acts as a costume that has become synonymous with 'brand soldier' for men in the 21st-century military, and it seems improbable that this will change soon. The effects of popular culture's infatuation with the muscled body on societal attitudes and behaviours demands further investigation. What is clear is that perceptions of the ideal soldier are unlikely to include the lean and laid-back body portrayed in the Vietnam era, or the emaciated figures of soldiers who survived the terrors of building the Burma Railroad (Lomax 1996). Clearly, further study is needed to determine the ramifications of the body-obsessed 'brand soldier' on the hearts, minds and, especially, bodies of today's real servicemen and women.

References

Anon. (2013). 'About the show – The Commando', *The Biggest Loser*, http://thebiggestloser.com. au/the-commando.html. Accessed 13 June 2013.

Anon. (3 March 2010). 'Life at Patrol Base Wali', *Australian Department of Defence*, http://www. defence.gov.au/op/afghanistan/gallery/2010/20100303a/index.htm. Accessed 31 July 2013.

Bertrand, I. (1988). 'From silence to reconciliation: the representation of the Vietnam War in Australian film and television', *Historical Journal of Film, Radio and Television*, 8: 1, pp. 75–89.

Bevan, S. (2004). *Battle Lines: Australian Artists at War*. Sydney: Random House.

Blackmore, T. (2012). 'Eyeless in America, the Sequel: Hollywood and Indiewood's Iraq War on Film', *Bulletin of Science, Technology and Society*, 34: 4, pp. 317–30.

Bourke, J. (1996). *Dismembering the male: Men's bodies, Britain and the Great War*. London: Reaktion Books.

Carden-Coyne, A. (2009). *Reconstructing the body: Classicism, modernism, and the First World War*. Oxford: Oxford University Press.

Carlyon, L. (2001). *Gallipoli*. Sydney: Pan Macmillan.

Carter, M. (2003). *Fashion classics from Carlyle to Barthes*. Oxford: Berg.

Cordingley, G. (7 April 2012). 'A body prepared for any battle', *The Sunday Times*, http://www.perthnow.com.au/news/western-australia/a-body-prepared-for-any-battle/story-e6frg13u-1226321016581. Accessed 10 July 2013.

Craik, J. (2003). 'The Cultural Politics of the Uniform', *Fashion Theory: The Journal of Dress, Body and Culture*, 7: 2, pp. 127–47.

Damousi, J. (2010). 'Why do we get so emotional about Anzac?', in M. Lake and H. Reynolds (eds), *What's Wrong with Anzac? The Militarisation of Australian History*, pp. 94–109. Sydney: NewSouth Publishing.

Hadley, B. J. (2012). 'Self-making as public spectacle: Bodies, bodily training and reality TV', *Scope: An Online Journal of Film Studies*, 24.

Harrison, K. (2011). *Strategic Public Relations: A Practical Guide to Success*. South Yarra: Palgrave Macmillan.

Hassija, C. M., Jakupcak, M., Maguen, S., & Shipherd, J. C. (2012). 'The influence of combat and interpersonal trauma on PTSD, depression, and alcohol misuse in US Gulf War and OEF/OIF women veterans', *Journal of Traumatic Stress*, 25: 2, pp. 216–19.

Hatton, T. J. (2011). 'Infant mortality and the health of survivors: Britain, 1910–50', *The Economic History Review*, 64: 3, pp. 951–72.

Hinde, S. (21 February 2009). 'Army fronts up to battle against obesity', *Sunday Mail*, http://www.couriermail.com.au/news/national/our-troops-in-battle-of-bulge/story-e6freooo-1111118925468. Accessed 31 July 2013.

Hinojosa, R. (2010). 'Doing hegemony: Military, men, and constructing a hegemonic masculinity', *The Journal of Men's Studies*, 18: 2, pp. 179–94.

Holland, S. (2006). 'The dangers of playing dress-up: Popular representations of Jessica Lynch and the controversy regarding women in combat', *Quarterly Journal of Speech*, 92: 1, pp. 27–50.

Holt, D. (2004). *How brands become icons: The principles of cultural branding*. Boston, MA: Harvard Business School Press.

Höpfl, H. J. (2003). 'Becoming a (virile) member: Women and the military body', *Body & Society*, 9: 4, pp. 13–30.

Inglis, K. S., & Brazier, J. (2008). *Sacred Places: War Memorials in the Australian Landscape*. Melbourne: Melbourne University Press.

Jenkins, I. & Turner, V. (2009). *The Greek Body*. London: British Museum Press.

Johnston, M. (19 July 2013). 'Biggest Loser star, Commando Steve, hits town', *The Northern Star*, http://www.northernstar.com.au/news/commando-hits-town/1950908/. Accessed 2 August 2013.

Johnston, S. (25 August 2009). '*The Hurt Locker*: Interview with Mark Boal', *The Telegraph*, http://www.telegraph.co.uk/culture/film/starsandstories/6055329The-Hurt-Locker-interview-with-Mark-Boal.html. Accessed 15 May 2013.

Lair, D. J., Sullivan, K., & Cheney, G. (2005). 'Marketization and the Recasting of the Professional Self: The Rhetoric and Ethics of Personal Branding', *Management Communication Quarterly*, 18: 3, pp. 307–43.

Leahy, Peter (3 May 2007). Message from CA Lt-Gen Peter Leahy, 'I'm an Australian soldier', *Army: The Soldier's Newspaper*, http://www.defence.gov.au/news/armynews/editions/1165/features/feature01.htm. Accessed 12 July 2013.

Lomax, Eric (1996). *The Railway Man: A POW's Searing Account of War, Brutality and Forgiveness.* New York: Random House.

Londey, P. (2007). 'A possession forever: Charles Bean, the Ancient Greeks, and military commemoration in Australia', *Australian Journal of Politics and History*, 53: 3, pp. 344–59.

Mackenzie, C. (1929). *Gallipoli Memories.* London: Cassell and Co.

McCarthy, G. (2001). 'Caught between Empires: Ambivalence in Australian films', *Critical Arts*, 15: 1–2, pp. 154–73.

McDonald, A. (December 2010). 'Fat of the Land', *The Monthly,* http://www.themonthly.com.au/issue/2010/december/1357604782/alyssa-mcdonald/fat-land. Accessed 31 July 2013.

McDonald, N. and Brune, P. (1998). *200 shots: Damian Parer, George Silk and the Australians at war in New Guinea.* Sydney: Allen and Unwin.

McKenna, M. (2010). 'Anzac Day: How did it become Australia's national day?', in M. Lake and H. Reynolds (eds), *What's Wrong with Anzac? The Militarisation of Australian History*, pp. 110–34. Sydney: NewSouth Publishing.

McPhedran, I. (6 May 2013). 'Bored diggers pump iron at gym after being confined to main base in Tarin Kowt', *news.com.au*, http://www.news.com.au/national-news/bored-diggers-pump-iron-at-gym-after-being-confined-to-main-base-in-tarin-kowt/story-fncynjr2-1226635608107. Accessed 2 August 2013.

Moran, J. (31 March 2013). 'It's a long way to Tarin Kowt if you wanna rock 'n' roll', *The Sunday Telegraph*, http://www.dailytelegraph.com.au/news/opinion/its-a-long-way-to-tarin-kowt-if-you-wanna-rock-n-roll/story-e6frezz0-1226609575527. Accessed 31 July 2013.

Neighbour, S. (April 2011). 'Comment: The ANZAC Spirit', *The Monthly*, p. 8.

Nicholson, B. and O'Brien, A. (24 January 2011). 'Pledge to "brothers" inspired VC bravery of corporal Ben Roberts-Smith', *The Australian*, http://www.theaustralian.com.au/news/nation/pledge-to-brothers-inspired-vc-bravery-of-corporal-ben-roberts-smith/story-e6frg6nf-1225993318791. Accessed 10 July 2013.

Oakes, D. (16 November 2010). 'Drug abuse soldiers ordered out of Afghanistan', *The Age*, http://www.theage.com.au/national/drugabuse-soldiers-ordered-out-of-afghanistan-20101115-17ug7.html?skin=text-only. Accessed 15 May 2013.

Pedersen, P. (2012). 'The falling leaves of Tizak', *Wartime Magazine*, 57, January. https://www.awm.gov.au/wartime/57/falling-leaves/. Accessed 10 July 2013.

Peoples, S. (2014). 'Embodying the military: Uniforms', *Critical Studies in Men's Fashion* 1:1, pp. 7–21.

Peters, T. (31 August 1997). 'The brand called you', *FastCompany*, 10, pp. 83–87.

Smith, H. (2013). 'Brand-wrap', http://www.wishbone.com.au/announcements/brand-wrap. Accessed 31 July 2013.

Film and television credits

Bigelow, K. (2008). *The Hurt Locker*. Kathryn Bigelow, Mark Boal, Nicolas Chartier, and Greg Shapiro. US: Summit Entertainment, Universal Studios. Australia: Roadshow Film Distribution.

Jeffrey, T. (1979). *The Odd Angry Shot*. Tom Jeffrey, Sue Milliken. Australia: Samson Productions, the Australian Film Commission, the New South Wales Film Corp, Roadshow Entertainment.

Network Ten [Australia] (2006–present). *The Biggest Loser*. US: National Broadcasting Company. Australia: Crackerjack Productions (2006), Freemantle Media (2006–2010), Shine Productions (2011–).

Notes

1   Richard Gehrmann's personal observations were made during two tours including: first tour in Iraq from August 2006 to February 2007, and during that deployment he went to Afghanistan in November 2006, second tour in Afghanistan from October 2008 to June 2009.

2   See Kalman, T. (1998, 13 December). 'Variations: A cover story', *New York Times Magazine*, p. 124, quoted in Klein, N. (2001). *No Logo*. London: Flamingo, p. 26.

3   See Commando's profile on http://thebiggestloser.com.au/the-commando.html.

Section II

Fashion and the military

Chapter 4

In the service of clothes: Elsa Schiaparelli and the war experience

Annita Boyd

Introduction

Elsa Schiaparelli is renowned as 'the' imaginative couturier who wowed fashionable Parisian café society with her provocative and individualistic apparel during the inter-war years. Shortened to 'Schiap', her name became synonymous with Surrealism, and her creative and daring designs shocked the fashion world and challenged preconceived ideas of dressing. Schiap pioneered padded and broadened shoulders, re-emphasized the waist, and raised hemlines (and eyebrows). Coco Chanel, her contemporary and rival, referred to her as, 'that artist who makes dresses.' Schiaparelli was greatly influenced by art movements of the period and collaborated with artists so that her designs revelled in colour and fantasy. Yves Saint Laurent described her invention of the now famous colour 'Shocking Pink' as an 'aggressive, brawling and warrior pink' (White 1995: 13). Utilizing the sharp lines of Cubism and dreamlike images of Salvador Dali, Schiap used the body as architecture on which to shape her clothes. Much of her work is severely structured, even at times employing Victorian features such as a bustle which drew on the much-adored clothes of her grandmother's era. Although the severe silhouette was her staple, some of her 1930s evening wear demonstrates expertise in soft draping, and her later collections employed drastically sloping shoulders, contrary to her famed severe frame. Today, Schiap is considered a master of versatility, creating not only variety across her playfully themed collections, but also within a single garment.

To date, very little has been written about how Schiaparelli spent her life after the closing of her Place Vendôme shop in 1954. Even less has been published on her post-war fashion, with the exception of the perfumes and accessories to which she licensed her name. The general consensus is that she was out of step with post-war sensibility, which led to the eventual failure of her career as a couturier. Broadly, this gap in commentary falls into two periods: 1945–1954 (coinciding with the Paris shop's closing, her filing for bankruptcy and the publication of her autobiography, *Shocking Life*); and 1955–1973 (the time of her death). This discussion will cover the extent to which war and the military influenced both Schiaparelli's designs and how they were marketed. A closer inspection of her work reveals how Schiap's wartime experiences filtered into her garments and accompanying promotional campaigns. Schiaparelli did appropriate some military design elements throughout her fashion career and these can be located in earlier work as well her post-war designs, but these elements were dispersed amongst the many other influences incorporated into her ground-breaking collections.

Elsa Schiaparelli survived both the First and Second World Wars (WWI and WWII), living in Europe and New York. The outbreak of WWI began shortly after her disastrous marriage to philosophy lecturer Count Wilhelm Wendt de Kerlor in London. Soon after, the couple travelled to Nice, where they remained until the war was over. In 1919 they travelled to the United States, and settled in New York City. However, de Kerlor's philandering ways worsened and he left the family not long after the birth of their daughter, Yvonne (Gogo). The family was left destitute, so Schiaparelli's survival depended on her ability to utilize the friendships made during the voyage to America. These friendships provided introductions to the artistic circles of Greenwich Village, and renowned artists such as Marcel Duchamp and Man Ray would later have a significant creative impact on her work. In their portrayal of women, the Surrealists often used mannequins or other objects, a dehumanizing tendency seen, for example, in Man Ray's image of a woman's back as a violin. However, as O'Mahoney states, women artists and designers chose to participate in the Surrealist movement, since:

> Surrealism's ultimate emphasis on the examination of the inner being sanctioned a close analysis of their own individualities, allowing their works to reveal many of the complexities and problems inherent within gender-designated roles in society (O'Mahoney, in Martin 1999: 14).

Schiaparelli's work would later reflect the playfulness of Surrealism in her infamous 'shoe hat' as well as designing clothing that re-considered women's attire during the world wars, as discussed below.

While in New York, Schiap's daughter Gogo was diagnosed with a walking disability. Blanche Hayes, a rich divorcee who had befriended Schiap, convinced them to return to Paris to seek medical treatment, and provided a free domicile (Baxter-Wright 2012). Later, Schiap would rent a small flat of her own, and meet the world's most celebrated fashion designer of the time, Paul Poiret, who showered her with beautiful clothes. In this atmosphere, Schiap made her fashion debut with her distinctive black-and-white *trompe l'oeil* sweater with the knitted bow. An initial order of forty sweaters and skirts from a New York buyer prompted Schiaparelli to rent a garret at Rue de la Paix, wherein she located her workshop. This precipitated the start of her new sportswear business, dressing celebrity actresses and women in high society. As the premises became too restricting, Schiap relocated to the now famous 21 Place Vendôme atelier, where she would flourish and fulfil her destiny as haute couturier. Later, the boutique at No. 21 would become a tourist destination, alongside the other iconic French landmarks (Schiaparelli 2007: 65, 66). Elsa Schiaparelli, the Italian, now fully established in her credentials as a proud Parisian designer, became a French citizen.

'Hard chic'

The sharp, 'hard chic', and rather masculine fitted look of padded shoulders, nipped-in waist and narrow hips that Schiaparelli perfected would suit high-profile customers such as Katherine Hepburn, Greta Garbo and Joan Crawford. The look complemented their body shape and their lean, angular facial features. As Bolton and Koda note, the moniker '"Hard Chic" comprises designs that reference menswear, military and service uniforms, and industrial materials and fastenings applied with deliberate severity' (2012: 22). It was a style designed in keeping with the new athleticism associated with the so-called New Woman who would now compete in the masculine public domain, for example, at the revived Olympic games. Schiap emphatically rejected the Victorian ethos of concealing the body, especially any physical 'flaws' associated with women's figures. In contrast, the 'Schiaparelli look' defended a new role for the female body – as highly active. Embellishments she added to 'hard chic' included padding, quilting, detailed Lesage embroidery, highly decorated boleros and turbans – all elements that could metaphorically protect the female body from assault. This 'hard chic' look was extended to incorporate a more military appearance, with the addition of metal buttons and clamp fastenings, epaulettes and accessories such as capes. Schiap's provocative release of the 'Wooden Soldier Silhouette' earned her the title 'carpenter of clothes' (Watt 2012). These distinctive angular lines provided strength but retained elegance. This silhouette was adopted later by Hollywood designers such as Adrian, exemplified in the 1939 film *The Women* (White 1995). Schiaparelli also played with other military elements, appropriating the Maginot Line blue and Foreign Legion reds (Ewing 2001: 118), Cossack coats, and plumed headwear. Despite the fact that Schiap's design collections ceased throughout WWII, this signature military look continued to be very popular with women throughout this period. Military dress was reflected in the action-ready clothing of famous movie stars, and was also symbolically linked to a strong female population – women who supported the wartime industries at home, in hospitals and ambulance services, and in the countryside in increasing numbers.

Wartime tensions in America and Europe

The pared-down, even masculine Schiaparelli 'look' was copied widely across the US by local designers. Schiap was ambivalent about this practice at first, but in her later writings she reflects on it as flattery, feeling complimented that her designs had been so successful. 'The moment that people stop copying you,' she held, 'it means that you are no longer any good and that you have ceased to be news' (Schiaparelli, in White 1995: 87). French purveyors of haute couture, however, would confront her with this popularity at the close of WWII. In 1945 Schiap was compelled to attend a meeting with representatives from the Chambre Syndicale de la Couture in New York, who used this information against her. They suggested that American fashion had thrived at the expense of French couture, and that she had been instrumental in this event (White 1995). It was ironic that Schiap, who had done everything possible to promote the French clothing industry, and to continuously uphold the good name of France, even from abroad, found herself ostracized from the very group she sought to promote.

Politics again intruded during her stay in New York. Elsa Schiaparelli had been regarded with suspicion throughout WWII by the Germans, encouraged by the fact that the majority of her shareholders were Jewish (Watt 2012: 149). Others believed she was against the French Resistance; then it was rumoured that she was anti-British. Finally, accusations of fascism were hurled after she (unknowingly) wore a hat made by a German milliner working in France, which prompted a visit by the US Federal Bureau of Investigation (Schiaparelli 2007: 150; Watt 2012: 149). It is significant that the mere wearing of a hat could have such connotations. The Germans did not place any ration restrictions on buying hats; they were 'points free', meaning 'they could be purchased without any vouchers or clothing cards, and so would become the major fashion item of the war years' (Guenther 2004: 217). This resulted in the hat's elevation to the pinnacle of fashion innovation. In 1940, the German women's magazine, *Die Dame,* would claim, '*Alles ist Hut*' – the hat is everything (Guenther 2004: plates 25 & 26). Beyond Schiap's control was the fact that the French couturiers chose to furnish uniforms for the German soldiers, acquiring concessions for the high fashion industry for dwindling raw materials. As Guenther explains:

> Every yard of fabric wasted was a yard less of fabric that could be sent to Germany. Every flamboyant hat worn by a French woman, the designer Schiaparelli asserted, was a "symbol of the free and creative spirit of Paris," a "slap in the face for the Nazis" (2004: 211).

But in fact this extravagance could, instead, be read as Nazi collaboration. Irene Guenther teases out this question: was a French woman wearing a lavish hat a mark of resistance, and in particular would that same hat be read as 'bad fashion' if worn by a German woman? Guenther questions this notion of fashion as 'resistance'. Did the headgear signify a personal response to the restrictions of war, or a broader political statement about the war itself? So Schiap, an Italian-born French woman, wears a German-made hat in America – this challenged the Allied authorities. Hats had been very important for Schiap during WWII, as exemplified in the anecdote that she sewed several thousand dollars into the fur trim of one hat, funds that were entrusted to her by American friends, to deliver to others who had been left destitute in France. Schiap relates that she lost the hat during a rush to board a train, but miraculously it was returned to her, its secret contents intact (Schiaparelli 2007).

On the other hand, the practical operations of Schiap's business attracted attention. Her rival, Chanel, ceased to do business during WWII, but the salon at Place Vendôme No. 21 continued to operate at a reduced level with fewer staff, and later came under German administration. Even so, nearly sixty percent of French haute couture houses remained open and at their own premises at the insistence of Lucien Lelong, head of the Chambre Syndicale, despite Nazi attempts to relocate them to Berlin or Vienna (Guenther 2004).

It is easy to see how Schiap, Italian by birthright, and distinctively Italian in name, was vulnerable to rumours about her disloyalty to the Allies. But Schiaparelli hated Mussolini and was horrified at the fate of her country of birth. The notion that she may have been complicit with the military, either overtly or covertly, is difficult to countenance. In 1940, Schiap delivered an ambitious lecture tour of the US (42 towns in eight weeks) to strengthen the French economy, urging Americans to buy French high fashion. Other industries in France were under German control, but fashion still retained some independence. Schiap was welcomed in the US and acquired almost celebrity status, drawing audiences in the thousands. Despite the ship transporting the small collection for display being sunk en route, she managed to get the dresses remade at the last minute, and bravely carried on, to the acclaim of mass audiences.

Following the tour, Schiap returned to France, but, under threat and fearing for her safety, she was smuggled by influential friends out of Europe and back to the US. During her US residence, all of her efforts previously directed to fashion she channelled into the war effort, working chiefly for the Red Cross in New York City, as did her daughter Gogo. They both engaged in fundraising activities for various charity groups, including the Quakers, who were known for their activism for peace. She would not return to France until after WWII, when she would be greatly disappointed at the kind of clothes produced during the Nazi Occupation of France.

Post-war realities

During the war, and in the early years afterwards, there had been severe rationing and restrictions, and many fabrics and other dressmaking items were difficult or impossible to obtain (Guenther 2004). On her first return to Paris, after her lecture tour, Schiaparelli came armed with pins, as steel was a scare resource. Throughout Europe, but especially in Britain, strict rules determined the type of garments that could be made: how much fabric and in what styles. Not since the French Revolution, and before that the Middle Ages, had sartorial codes been in place where the relevant decrees were implemented through sumptuary law (Ewing 2001: 139). Schiap, not fazed by these shortages and restrictions, found other ways to continue her creative dressmaking practice. When faced with a problem, Schiap improvised. Dog chains were used for fasteners, and day dresses became evening gowns with the pull of a drawstring and the removal of a detachable collar. This was a solution to both material shortages and to the strict budgets of the buyers. The period between September 1939 and spring 1940 was a strange one in French history. Known as the *drôle de guerre* (phoney war), it appeared as though the realities of war had not yet hit France (White 1995). In a fight against unemployment and to heighten morale, the Chambre Syndicale de la Couture Parisienne marshalled their designers to show the world the very best of French couture (White 1995). Their efforts were rewarded after Americans crossed the Atlantic en masse to attend, despite the dangers of travel. Schiaparelli's collection was extremely well-received, and featured many convertible garments – these offered a new 'look' on a single garment in order to make the best use of scarce fabric supplies – wrap-around dresses, elasticized waists, and other garments with big pockets that could be filled with supplies in times of emergency.

Elsa Schiaparelli, although *the* most beloved queen of French couture, especially in New York, struggled to keep this moniker post-war. She herself confessed that she was not in touch with the moment. She drew on her established reputation for clever design features that had worked for her in the past, but her reliance on the pre-war elegance of slender lines seemed out of step with the times (Schiaparelli, in Watt 2012: 160; White 1995: 208). As with the Surrealist movement itself, Schiap's provocative Surrealist creations during the 1930s had outlived their moment (O'Mahony 1999: 15). The 'outrageous' did not seem relevant after the war years of military combat accompanied by civilian austerity, and the severe cut of her masculine suits became too reminiscent of military garb, as shown in Figure 1 (Baxter-Wright 2012). Schiap then made radical attempts to change her designs, softening the line of her dresses with sloping shoulders, offering large trench coats, but these designs did not find favour with the buying public (Watt 1995; Baxter-Wright 2012). Elsewhere, Coco Chanel, was able to relaunch her house, seizing the moment to bring back a modified version of her now famous suit. Buying customers wanted a new femininity and Chanel, along with a newcomer, Christian Dior, were destined to rebuild the French reputation for innovative fashion. In 1947, even though fabrics had remained scarce, Dior showcased a silhouette that met this desire: the New Look. Dior's New Look recalled an earlier version of womanhood, with lengthened skirts, full petticoats and a softer bodice (Watt 2012; White 1995). In response, Schiap claimed, mistakenly, that the New Look would not last (Schiaparelli 2007: 168): in fact it remained in vogue around the world throughout the 1950s and into the 1960s.

In February of 1947, in contrast to the extreme femininity of the 'indulgent' Dior look, Schiaparelli displayed her wares in an advertisement for a 'Petite Parisienne' suit in *American Vogue* (1947: 122). The model in the illustration appears to have just stepped off the set of *Casablanca* (see Figure 1). She sports a high-plumed fez, with double-capped-shoulders on a side-buttoning jacket with one large external side pocket, and a knee-length, narrow panelled skirt, and gloves. She also wears what are probably signature Schiaparelli rhinestones. Her strong brows evoke Joan Crawford, and the whole look is very Rosalind Russell. The overall severity is the antithesis of Dior's New Look, every element being different. The outfit covers and protects the body, in classic 'hard chic' style, and the bulky sharp shoulders that taper to a slim hip retain the triangular masculine look perfected by Schiap in the late 1930s. This suit was available at Saks Fifth Avenue in New York City, advertised as 'Designed for the younger figure'. But in post-war America, Schiap's designs of the war years no longer suited the aspirations of young women. They turned away from the 'hard chic' profile after they viewed Dior's deeply feminine dresses and voluminous skirts in the pages of *Vogue* three months later. As Watt reports, 'in its May 1947 issue, *Vogue* led with Christine Dior: "Dior – Christian Dior – is the new name in Paris"' (2012: 150).

There was also a new kind of clientele: 'the newly rich wives of grocers, butchers and provision merchants' who wanted to see a 'casual American sensibility' (Watt 2012: 150).

Figure 1: 'Petite Parisienne', *American Vogue* (1947) February 15.[1]

It is curious that Schiap, after spending the last four years residing and working in the US, did not understand the Zeitgeist. However, her New York years offered a respite from the fashion industry, even to the extent of retreating to a Long Island cottage to restore her sense of self. This self-imposed exile from dressmaking took its toll on her awareness of contemporary fashion sensibility (Schiaparelli 2007: 128–129, 158; White 1995: 199).

There was a set of factors that led to Schiap's downfall as a designer. First, the use of master fashion illustrators, central to the Schiaparelli image, began to fall out of vogue, to be replaced by high-profile photographers (Watt 2012). This was partly due to the rise of the photographic industry during WWII and to the post-war availability of former wartime photographers. Next, the introduction of entrance fees for buyers at fashion shows increased costs, while the ban on the release of press photographs until a month after a collection delayed access to the public. Further, the prohibitive cost of a couture dress as a result of post-war inflation seriously affected Schiap's efforts to regain her foothold as a French fashion house. Her attempts to counter these restrictions caused Schiaparelli to license her name to other manufacturers, but it was not enough to save her atelier. In 1954 she showed her final collection, and in the same year filed for bankruptcy (Watt 2012: 151).

Schiaparelli markets wartime sensibilities: Memories and realities

In the first example, in 1949, the magazine *The New Yorker* printed an advertisement for ties, from Bachrach Menswear, Madison Avenue, New York (see Plate iv). The accompanying text reads as follows:

> voila Papa! Schiaparelli does ties for men
> If your daddy has a recurrent nostalgia for the Ritz Bar, the Place Pigalle and the shops around the Place Vendôme, you will make him so-o-o happy with these. They are just what you'd expect from the rich imagination and gifted hands of Schiaparelli ... witty, Parisian, and wholly original in design and color treatment.

The black-and-white hand-drawn illustration features a rotund, bearded gentleman, reclining in a comfortable chair, surrounded by a woman, presumably his wife, two small children dressed in Victorian clothes, and a 'French' poodle. He is suited and smoking a cigar. On the wall behind him is a portrait of Napoleon Bonaparte. The happy domestic setting appears rather old-fashioned, and one might assume that he is either the children's father or grandfather, a veteran of WWI. Beneath them are four men's ties featuring bright patterns. The sketch and copy clearly signal nostalgia for his time spent as a soldier, on leave in Paris, especially at the Place Vendôme, which lies in the shadow of the Vendôme Column, originally erected by Napoleon to celebrate the victory of Austerlitz (Schiaparelli 2007: 64). The overall tone of this advertisement is reminiscent of a day that Schiap relates in her autobiography, when she encountered WWII American soldiers queued up outside her shop at the Place Vendôme to purchase some little remnant of Paris to take back home to their sweethearts or mothers, a scarf, a fragrance or a hat:

> ... but what puzzled me was the very long line of G.I.s quietly waiting to enter the shop ... I asked a girl I did not know what was happening, and she answered:

"The G.I.s? They are queuing up to buy presents to take home. Most of them buy perfume" (Schiaparelli 2007: 155–56).

In the advertisement, the 'Papa' figure depicts a nostalgic mood, driven by remembering good times he spent in Paris as a young man, perhaps including any romantic encounters with French women. The first location mentioned in the advertisement is the famous Ritz, a very upmarket bar in the exclusive hotel: as The Ritz was occupied by the Germans in WWII, it must indicate that the man is nostalgic for Paris during WWI.

It should be noted that the word 'nostalgia' was coined in the 17th century when it was used to describe the symptoms of soldiers diagnosed as suffering from homesickness. The term, which then migrated into the vernacular, is used somewhat differently here, however, as the soldiers addressed by the advertisement are assumed to be missing Paris rather than their own homes. Even before Schiap opened her salon there in 1934, Place Vendôme had a reputation as a luxury shopping district, just as Place Pigalle was known as the risqué cabaret area. American soldiers, returning from a different war, had pined for the various delights of the city before, as can be found in the lyrics of this popular 1918 song by Lewis and Donaldson:

How ya gonna keep 'em down on the farm
After they've seen Paree'
How ya gonna keep 'em away from Broadway
Jazzin' around, and paintin' the town …
Mother Reuben, I'm not fakin
Tho you may think it strange
But wine and women play the mischief
With a boy who's loose with change.

Clearly, Schiaparelli chose nostalgia as a selling point for her men's ties in 1949. The advertisement capitalizes on the recent return of soldiers from France after WWII, assuming this would spark memories in an older generation of men who served in the Great War (WWI). These 'old soldiers', even though thousands of their comrades lost their lives, could be reminiscing about their own tours of duty. Schiaparelli remembers this of the time immediately after WWII: 'Paris was full of G.I.s who were rich in cigarettes, nylons, and black market goodies. They hid in the Bois de Boulogne, necking and strutting down the Champs-Élysées' (2007: 161). In the advertisement, Bachrach is offering the romance of Paris in the form of a Schiaparelli tie, the finest France can offer a gentleman without having to travel abroad. Note that the ad is saturated with Frenchness. The juxtaposition of 'daddy', with the children's exclamation 'Papa' is characteristic of America's ongoing Francophilia. The address seems somewhat ambiguous, but 'daddy' can refer to the man depicted in the advertisement, as well as the father of the woman reading the magazine, also a potential consumer. It is the women, possibly shopping for a Father's Day gift, who will be well aware of the Schiaparelli name as synonymous with fashion (Plate iv).

In the second example, other types of wartime realities exert their influence on Schiaparelli's designs. Those influences began with her New York years in the American Red Cross. Nevertheless, these designs connect in their sympathies and through the direct outcome they had on uniforms for women in service, whether paid or voluntary.

> When I was with the Place Vendôme I did some work with the Salvation Army, visiting their wonderful canteens and rest houses near the front in the company of General Barret … The Salvation Army commissioner asked me to design a uniform for the women workers on modern lines, much like the dress I wore during this trip. The uniform which was made and accepted was blue with a red collar and blue apron, but we did not have time to put it into production. I have just learned that they used it later, after all (Schiaparelli 2007: 106–07, 107).

By 1962, Schiaparelli was able to capitalize on her reputation for utilitarian women's garments with her designs for nurses' uniforms for Preen (see Plate v). Even though her high fashion business folded in 1954, eight years later the New York Preen catalogues (actually called the *Preen Uniform Fashion Guide*) bear the name of her salon – 21 Place Vendôme, Paris, France – on the cover. It is evident that the institution of nursing has its organizational origins in military practices, drawing heavily on its discipline. Schiaparelli, having served as a nurse's aide, understood the necessary practicalities of a working outfit, while still maintaining stylish femininity (Schiaparelli 2007: 136; White 1995: 198). Decades before, she had designed practicality into her innovative tennis culottes, allowing for freedom of movement while retaining modesty, something that became a subject of controversy on the court (Baxter-Wright 2013: 23). But these nurses' uniforms must have a direct link with Schiap's personal wartime experience. Here, she observes herself as a figure of irony, as she notes that she is a French couturier who now, after the war wears such odd attire, a moment in her biography that is profoundly affecting:

> The sight of Schiap, so-called Queen of Fashion, walking through the streets of New York at 6 a.m. in flat, white canvas shoes, white cotton stockings, and a blue cotton apron, had its funny side … As a nurse's aid she had of course to do the humbler jobs, generally given to the charwoman, but that was not really hard because it filled her with passionate interest and gave her a feeling of self respect … all this gave her a feeling of humanity again … and it saved her soul (Schiaparelli 2007: 136–37).

Doubtless, while Schiap designed these uniforms, she would have graphically recalled her time in the American Red Cross, when she first encountered dead bodies and tended the suffering first-hand. The strength she gained during that period would sustain her for decades to come, and these Preen uniforms are, in some way, a nod to those years of humanitarian service and her own passionate dedication (see Plate v).

Preen is proud to serve the woman who works in white … nurses, doctors' assistants, beauticians, dieticians, and waitresses who perform the many vital and important tasks, which help keep this nation healthy and happy.

We match your sense of dedication with our own. All the skill at our command goes into creating the uniform styles you want. And thanks to the genius of Mme Elsa Schiaparelli, and other top flight designers … in a Preen uniform, you'll always be fashionable on the job …

The tailoring and detailing of each Preen uniform must meet our rigid standards of quality and meticulous workmanship (Preen 1962: 2).

Note the emphasis on 'serving.' The Preen company targets the women in service industries, whether medical, health, cosmetics or hospitality, and returns the favour with its own dedication to service and perfection. As varied as these professions are, their commonality is acknowledged as providing service to the nation's health and well-being. As a uniform provider, Preen recognizes no hierarchical distinction within these services, and promotes Schiaparelli as the talented French designer who fully appreciates this sense of equality. In her French atelier she appreciated egalitarianism, by insisting that the sewers, or 'girls', who worked there should enter through the front door.

Finally, note the use of such phrases as 'the skill at our command' and 'rigid standards.' This militaristic language had always been associated with the command structure of the nursing profession but subsequently became ubiquitous in the vocabulary of advertising and modern management, representing standardized and efficient mass manufacturing.

The Preen guides not only feature '… the latest in uniforms, [but also include] dresses, shoes, jewellery, lingerie, and other accessories' (Preen, Fall 1962: cover). Rather than haute couture, Schiap designed affordable garments aimed at the working woman, most of it selling for less than ten dollars. Further, Schiaparelli had always been a pioneer in utilizing new fabrics manufactured from synthetic fibres (Baxter-Wright 2013: 41; Watt 2013: 66). As post-war industries boomed, so did payment plans, and Preen encouraged its customers to use credit, with Preen's Easy Pay Plan, suggesting 'your wardrobe can always be up-to-the-minute with on-the-job and off-the job fashions that you can wear while you pay' (Preen 1962: 2). The 'wear while you pay' would have been a major shift in sensibility for the independent Schiap, who ruled in her autobiography that a woman 'should pay her bills' (Schiaparelli 2007: 211). The Preen company's emphasis on fashion was underscored by their use of a brunette model who strikingly resembled the First Lady, Jackie Kennedy, complete with bouffant hairdo (see Plate v). This conforms to the fashion trends of the time, as 1962 was the height of the Kennedy era in politics, and Jackie was a fashion icon for women worldwide. Even store mannequins bore likenesses to her (Cassini 1995: 66).

Under the model's photograph, the copy boasts, 'You'll be sure to catch plenty of Oh's and Ah's wearing this professional beauty' (Preen 1962: 7). This offers a more alluring image than one normally associates with the nursing profession. Another uniform 'fashioned for flattery' offers a coat-style uniform with an off-centre opening, and 'fashionable French cuffs' (Preen 1962: 15). Yet another, which looks more like a day dress, is titled the 'Double Duty Classic.' This classic Schiaparelli form features a detachable jacket: 'Here is comfortable adaptability in a uniform that's really two outfits for the price of one' (Preen 1962: 7). As we've seen, Schiap was an innovator of convertible outfits, stressing the need for versatility, particularly in the years approaching war. Her Cash and Carry collection of 1939, in particular, afforded several functions per garment (White 1995: 181).

These two examples – the nostalgic tie advertisement and the Preen uniform catalogues – demonstrate that the post-war Schiaparelli, although no longer engaged with her Paris salon, continued to have creative and active business interests in American clothing companies, and continued to trade on the solid reputation of her Parisian brand, whether licensed or not. They all draw on the practicality, the images, and the emotions associated with the war experience, and, what's more, are steeped in the idea of Frenchness. Schiaparelli herself may or may not have had direct input into the marketing of her designs for these companies, but she did engage in personal appearances worldwide to promote her perfumes and accessories (White 1995: 216). Nevertheless, the association of these military tropes with the Schiaparelli name was well entrenched in the public imagination.

Concluding remarks: The Elsa Schiaparelli revival

In 2012, several new books were published on Elsa Schiaparelli (Baxter-Wright; Parkins; Watt). In 2011, the Victoria & Albert (V&A) publication of her autobiography *Shocking Life*, written in 1954, was reprinted, after being out of print for decades. In 2012, the Metropolitan Museum of Art held the exhibition, *Prada and Schiaparelli: Impossible Conversations*, and published their catalogue as a beautiful work of art in itself (Bolton & Koda 2012). The well-known film director Baz Luhrmann was engaged to produce a film starring Judy Davis (as Schiaparelli) and Miuccia Prada, which screened as part of the exhibition. The year 2012 also marked an extraordinary event: the relaunching of the Schiaparelli name and shop at the exact location of the original at No. 21 Place Vendôme (note that this had been attempted in previous years but with limited success). The website accompanying the launch introduces viewers to the brand's history, and current goals, using typically French-styled animations.[2] This renaissance of Schiaparelli intends not just to recapture but to rework the dreamlike Surrealist style for which she was famous. But it is unknown if these so-called 'neo-Schiaps' will attempt the sharp military look that became her signature. The issue remains: to what extent, if any, will current wartime experiences impact upon contemporary fashion? The current climate can be viewed as that of a perpetual state of war – where combat is highly technological, remote from the developed world, albeit ubiquitous in the media. It is possible that body shapes and inclinations do not point contemporary fashion towards the 'protective body armour' that was employed during WWII. The padded shoulders of power dressing had made a

Plate i: Movie poster from *Iron Sky* (Vuorensola, T. and S. Torssonen (2012)). © The Picture Desk, Kobal Collection.

Plate ii: Movie poster from *Salon Kitty* (Brass, T. (1976)). © The Picture Desk, Kobal Collection.

Plate iii: Victoria Cross recipient Corporal Ben Roberts-Smith.

Plate iv: 'voila Papa! Schiaparelli does ties for men', *The New Yorker* (1949: 5).

GEM DACRON*

"DOUBLE DUTY CLASSIC"

Here is complete adaptability in a uniform that's really two outfits for the price of one. See the way the beautifully shaped skirt bells away from the deftly cropped jacket with its pearlized buttons and a beguiling two-buttoned half belt in back. Remove it and you're trimly proficient in a sleeveless and collarless charmer, with a zippered back and two inserted skirt pockets with pearlized buttons for that extra pretty touch.

Sizes: 7 to 15 — 8 to 18.

100% DUPONT* DACRON GEM $12.98
Style S21864 — Short Sleeves

DACRON* & COTTON $9.98
Style S21764 — Short Sleeves

*—DuPont polyester fiber

You'll have the prettiest back in town wearing this unique coat style with its fascinating back splendor of pleats and buttons. The laundri-proof snap fastener closure on the ultra-feminine pleated flare skirt with inserted pockets assures you of sheer, heavenly comfort. You'll be sure to catch plenty of Oh's and Ah's wearing this professional beauty.

Sizes: 9 to 15, 12 to 20.

DACRON* & COTTON LINETTE $11.98
Style S2732 — ¾ Sleeves
Style S21732 — Short Sleeves

PREENMOUNT POPLIN $7.98
Style S2232 — ¾ Sleeves
Style S21232 — Short Sleeves

7

Plate v: Nurses' uniforms (Preen spring and summer uniform fashion guide (1962: 7)).

Plate vi: 'Royally Screwed', Kate Sylvester (2008).

Plate vii: David Cameron Visits Community Enterprise Project in Manchester. Photographer: Christopher Furlong. © Getty Images News.

Plate viii: Woman selling Dutch wax fabric in the Open Market, Kumasi, Ghana. 1997. Photo by Denise N. Rall.

Plate ix: *Nelson's Ship in a Bottle,* Yinka Shonibare, MBE (2010). Photographer: Dan Kitwood. © Getty Images News.

comeback in the 1980s, when women started to climb the corporate ladder, and battled with men in the public sphere, just as the New Woman had done in the 1930s. The year 2011 also marked the tenth anniversary of the terrorist attack on the World Trade Center, in which Elsa Schiaparelli's granddaughter (Gogo's daughter), photographer Berynthia (Berry) Perkins (née Berenson), was killed. She was a passenger on the American Airlines jet that hit the North Tower (Baxter-Wright 2012). Perhaps, the return of Schiap to the public's consciousness is timely.

Globally, contemporary fashion is built on difficult terrain, and, as Elsa Schiaparelli said in her most quotable statement, 'In difficult times, fashion is always outrageous.'

References

American Vogue (15 February 1947). 'Petite Parisienne' [advertisement], p. 122.

Baudot, F. (1997). *Elsa Schiaparelli: Fashion memoir*. London: Thames & Hudson.

Baxter-Wright, E. (2012). *The little book of Schiaparelli*. London: Carlton.

Bolton, A. & Koda, H. (2012). *Schiaparelli and Prada: Impossible conversations,* preface to catalogue. New York: Metropolitan Museum of Art.

Ewing, E. (2001). *History of twentieth-century fashion*. London: B.T. Batsford.

Guenther, I. (2004). *Nazi chic?: Fashioning women in the Third Reich*. Oxford: Berg.

O'Mahony, M. (2000). 'Introduction', in T. Martin, *Essential Surrealists*. Bath, UK: Parragon.

Parkins, I. (2012). *Poiret, Dior and Schiaparelli: Fashion, femininity and modernity*. London: Berg.

Preen spring and summer uniform fashion guide (1962). New York, Paris.

Preen uniform fashion guide (Fall 1962). New York, Paris.

Schiaparelli, E. (2007). *Shocking life: The autobiography of Elsa Schiaparelli*. London: V&A Publications.

Schiaparelli Paris official website, schiaparelli.com/en/. Accessed 20 October 2012.

Watt, J. (2012). *Vogue on Elsa Schiaparelli*. London: Quadrille Publishing Ltd.

White, Palmer (1995). *Elsa Schiaparelli: Empress of Paris fashion*. London: Aurum Press.

Notes

1   For the advertisements reproduced in this chapter (Figure 1, Plates iv and v) copyright is undetermined after a diligent search. Should you own the copyright to these advertisements please notify the book publishers.

2   See schiaparelli.com/en.

Chapter 5

The discipline of appearance: Military style and Australian flight hostess uniforms 1930-1964

Prudence Black

Introduction

This chapter describes how military uniforms influenced the style of the civilian uniforms of Australian flight hostesses from the 1930s through to the early 1960s.[1] Both aircraft and uniforms evolved from the two major world wars. Uniforms, historically, articulated the human body in relation to the machine of war. Flight hostesses are linked, via their uniforms, to the aeroplane-machine in precisely the same way.[2] As a technology, uniforms shape and code the body so they become a unit that belongs to a collective whole. The flight hostess uniform, worn since the 1930s, is a technology that articulates a line of command and disciplines the body both physically and aesthetically. Uniforms, as the visible signifiers of the line of command, also represent subjection to regulated behaviour, so that the flight hostesses' appearance also articulates a code of behaviour. In the early days of aviation, flight hostesses were instructed, amongst other things, not to 'eat ice-cream while in uniform' (McRobbie [1986] 1992: 13). It is in these ways that 'the discipline of the uniform imposes an external power on the body' (Purdy 2004: 88). But if the uniform was born of the necessities of war, it is also gathered up by another, more cultural, formation. The uniform is also an aesthetic statement.

While uniforms necessarily represent uniformity as standardization, they also have the capacity to be fashionable. Elizabeth Wilson opens up that question thus:

> The uniform might seem the opposite of fashion, meant to submerge the personality rather than enhance it – with the exception of military uniforms, which have traditionally been thought to enhance machismo and glamour (Wilson [1985] 2003: 36).

The uniformity of the flight hostess uniform has been subject to the vagaries of fashion, and Wilson makes the same point using the example of the uniform of the WAVES (the women's section of the American navy), which was designed fashionably in order to attract recruits during the Second World War (WWII) (Wilson [1985] 2003: 36).

The discipline of appearance

The uniform, like any other form of dress, makes the body culturally visible in particular ways. What uniforms do most explicitly is communicate belonging through dress. The flight hostess uniform was (and still is) designed to identify which airline they worked for through the colour and the design of the uniform as well as through other insignia like buttons, badges and other highly regulated aesthetic details (Greco 2000: 147). Uniforms also indicate rank, a precise position in a hierarchical order. Professional specializations and roles must be clearly indicated, for example in the different uniforms of the captain and the flight hostess, and finer distinctions are made through finer detail, such as through colour or insignia. These are the ways in which uniforms must be semiotically explicit: the meaning of each detail must be precise. Everything is codified and nothing should, in theory, be left to personal initiative. In the same way that a military uniform allows a soldier to be easily recognized on a battle field, or a school uniform helps identify the student having the quick cigarette at the bus stop, a flight hostess's uniform must enable her to be easily recognized as working for a specific airline, and in cases of emergency. This 'hyper-grammar' of uniforms is where everything about a particular role is regulated, including the body and the gestures of the subject inhabiting it. The uniformed body is a complex set of relations between dress, appearance, movement and manners.

We can have uniformity in dress but that is not the same as a uniform. A uniform is the agent of an institution. Occupational dress, for example the overall, lab-coat or apron with its protective function, is not a uniform unless it is further equipped with some signification of an institution. A uniform is more than just a mode of dress; it must have more than the sameness of, for example, a group of men in suits. The uniform must take away the individual control that persons have over how they dress. And the uniform thus creates a fundamental and all-important distinction between self and non-self.

Nathan Joseph, in *Uniforms and Nonuniforms*, sees the uniform as a 'certificate of legitimacy': 'a symbolic declaration that an individual will adhere to group norms and standardised roles and has mastered the relevant skills' (Joseph 1986: 66–67). In this way, the uniform is only part of the equation. It 'is not only an emblem but also a reminder of the behaviour appropriate towards this emblem; it becomes a third factor in the interaction between wearer and other' (Joseph 1986: 66). We are reminded of this when someone wears a uniform in vain, and finds themselves in a court martial or a school detention. Scott Hughes Myerly, in *British Military Spectacle: From the Napoleonic Wars through the Crimea*, elaborates on the same point. 'Unlike civilian wear,' he argues, 'uniforms are designed and their use controlled not by those who wear them but by those who wield authority' (Myerley 1996: 34). Power always keeps its distance and for this reason 'power requires images and signs that maintain a level of caution while preserving the force and violence in the realm of imagery' (Bonami 2000: 128). The flight hostess too reflects a path to power, up through a permanent hierarchy where the ranks remain in place filled by anonymous individuals. Her uniform means that if she can't give you orders, then someone else will, for example the pilot. The pilots during flight are generally 'invisible', although we can always imagine them in the same way (white shirt, epaulettes, dark trousers, winged badge), appearing only as a reassuring voice from the speakers – the voice of authority – to state a name and give a less than technical weather report (sunny day, clear skies ahead, estimated arrival time …). It is important to note that while the flight hostess uniform has undergone many changes, the standard pilots' uniform for airlines remains a dark suit, with gold stripes on the sleeve to indicate rank, white shirt with epaulettes, and tie. But the flight hostess is the visible presence of not only the pilots' but the airline's authority.

Military-style: The Australian flight hostess

Flight hostesses were first employed in Australia by Holymans Airways, a small regional airline flying out of Tasmania. In March 1936, Marguerite (Rita) Grueber and Blanche Due received letters informing them they had been selected and would undertake a 'fortnight's training before commencing on the service run'. Three other 'girls' who had applied at the same time were put on reserve until the company's services grew. Initially Grueber and Due flew on the de Havilland Express DH86 but on 2 May 1936 Grueber was rostered to fly on the newly acquired DC-2 flight carrying 14 passengers between Melbourne and Sydney. The all-metal Douglas DC-2 'Bungana' was a 'new generation' airliner and 2000 people were at Sydney Airport, Mascot, to see the plane arrive. Rita Grueber wore the uniform that she and Due had been told to design themselves, with the instructions that they should be 'conservative and practical' (Witcomb 1986: 5). The uniform they designed was a navy two-piece suit with white shirt and tie. The slim-fitting skirt was below knee-length and worn with 'serviceable' lace-up shoes. The suit jacket had brass buttons down the centre and on the breast pockets, and it was secured at the waist with a buckled belt. A small, embroidered insignia badge appeared on the left-hand chest pocket. They wore a forage cap adorned with a brass star, similar to that worn by the RAAF (Royal Australian Air Force) of the time. The hat was to be worn at all times, including during flight. The uniform was made by a tailor in Collins Street, Melbourne, and Grueber and Due paid 4 pounds and 10 shillings each for the uniforms (Black 2011: 30). Instructions were given that there was to be no jewellery worn other than a wristwatch and the hostesses were not allowed to smoke or drink in public when staying overnight in hotels, even when they were not in uniform (McRobbie [1986] 1992: 15). Later, a looser-fit summer uniform with a double-breasted cream jacket with navy epaulettes and a skirt with a centre pleat was worn with the white shirt and tie and forage cap.

The details here about the first flight hostess uniform in Australia are pertinant because these details are reiterated in the hostess uniforms of all other airlines across the world at this time. It seems that almost all flight hostess uniforms of the time had a quasi-military style. In 1930, Ellen Church had become the first flight hostess in the world when she started work with Boeing Air Transport (later United Airlines). Shortly after her appointment seven other young women, all nurses, were recruited and they came on board as 'sky girls', wearing green wool suits with a matching green and grey wool cape and green beret. The jacket of the suit was double-breasted with white double stripes running along the length of the sleeve, two inverted pockets at the waist, and a breast pocket on the left-hand side.

The suit was worn with a white shirt and tie. Along with the more traditional military navy, dark green was a colour used for military suiting. In Australia in 1917 the Officers in the Australian Flying Corps wore a dark olive-green uniform with a hip-length 'maternity' jacket fastened to one side with concealed buttons, epaulettes and a buttoned side cap, and the Women's Royal Australian Naval Service (WRANS) established in 1941 wore a bottle-green uniform of a below-knee-length skirt, belted jacket and white shirt and tie worn with a forage cap.

Across the Atlantic, BOAC (British Overseas Airways Corporation) bought surplus Women's Royal Naval Service (WRNS) uniforms after WWII and service tricorne hats were also worn. This military-style uniform stayed until well after the war, while some of the clothing restrictions from that time were still in place. In 1946, couturier Georgette Rénal designed a navy suit, white shirt and beret for Air France flight hostesses (Anon 2006: 42). In 1958 *Life* magazine had a nine-page photographic spread which included a photograph of the flight hostesses who represented the 53 airlines flying into the United States. Nearly all of the hostesses, one representing each airline, are photographed wearing a navy suit, worn with a white shirt (by then, ties had gone from the uniforms) but still wearing the forage cap. Figure 1 illustrates the Australian National Airways (ANA) version of the military look that had been adopted throughout the world's airline industries (Anon. 1958: 68–77).

In 1936 Holymans Airways became Australian National Airways (ANA, and later Ansett), and by then there were six flight hostesses. By 1939 there were 18 hostesses and Hazel 'Matron' Holyman was employed to take over the selection of flight hostesses and she became the Hostess Superintendent.[3] It was Hazel's husband Victor Holyman who had been a pilot in the Royal Naval Air Service who had set up the first Holyman's Airways service

Figure 1: Prime Minister Joseph Lyon and ANA hostesses, 1938. Courtesy Collection of Home Hill, National Trust of Australia (Tasmania).

in 1932, flying a three-passenger de Havilland 83 Fox Moth from Launceston to King Island. In 1934 he and ten others were lost over Bass Strait in the recently acquired DH86 Miss Hobart (Strahan 1996). Matron Holyman was to remain with the airline until 1955, a time when ANA had 200 hostesses on the books.

Trainees would wear civilian clothes for the first few weeks and would not be fitted for a uniform until it was established that they were suitable for the job. The flight hostesses continued to buy their own uniforms, which they would purchase from Myers department store in Melbourne. The winter uniform was £7.7s and the summer dress was £4.4s. The summer uniform was a shirt with two breast pockets buttoned to the neck, and in early versions with navy epaulettes (by 1946 these were removed but they came back again in the summer uniform which was worn from 1958 to 1964), elbow-length short sleeves and a below-knee-length skirt with cloth-covered belt. A half wing badge was sewn onto the shirt above the left-hand breast pocket. It was Matron Holyman who stopped the company policy of hostesses paying for their own uniforms and also ensured that hostesses were provided with in-flight meals (Witcomb 1986: 33). Up until 1943 it was expected that all ANA flight hostesses would be trained nurses but in 1943 this rule was waived, as nurses were needed for the war effort. The uniforms had to be practical as it was cold on board: planes during the war were often unlined and unheated, and one flight hostess remembers wrapping newspapers around the legs of the passengers to keep them warm (Witcomb 1986: 39).

Ansett Airways started in Melbourne in 1936, and while they employed ground hostesses who wore uniforms similar to the ANA hostesses but with a Glengarry cap, they did not employ flight hostesses until 1946 and the introduction of the DC3 aircraft. The Glengarry cap was a slightly raised boat-shaped cap with a deep lengthwise crease originally worn by the Scottish military. Eve Sexton, who had flown with ANA, became the first Ansett flight hostess.[4] Tailors were employed by the airlines to make uniforms designed by senior flight hostesses.

The challenges of flying and appearing professional in their uniforms included the prohibition on appearing with suntanned skin – a challenge if hostesses were flying and having stopovers in the north of Australia. Trixie (Lange) Henderson who flew on ANA remembers, 'we didn't wear stockings up North, but I can assure you we were always worried that someone might report us to Matron' (Witcomb 1986: 20). The Gulf Run was a favourite for many of the hostesses: the route comprised a huge triangle from Cairns up to Mitchell River Mission and down to Normanton and back to Cairns. The temperatures would soar and it was standard advice to wear 'no stockings and little make-up', as the seams of the stockings would wrap around the front of their legs, and perspiration would drip off their faces (Witcomb 1986: 72). One flight hostess recalled that Matron was looking at some photos of a Gulf Run in far north Queensland and noticed the flight hostess with her cap off. The flight hostess in question had taken her small forage cap off and replaced it with a wide-brimmed hat to protect her skin from the sun (Witcomb 1986: 21).

Uniforms should be practical but while the military saw merit in the duty of polishing brass buttons, these buttons were the bane of many flight hostesses' lives. Not only did they have to polish their own buttons before and during trips away, but pilots would ask them to polish the brass buttons on their uniforms too. Nancy (Grant) Dan remembers one pilot flying low over her home in Melbourne, her mother in the garden waving at her with a tea towel, in exchange for the task (Witcomb 1986: 30). The difficulties of keeping these buttons clean was eventually acknowledged, and, along with a shift from a military to a more fashionable uniform style, the brass buttons were eventually replaced with gilt ones. Also impractical, and more suited for military parade, were the white gloves worn by hostesses on all Australian airlines until the 1970s. The white gloves were usually worn with the summer uniform while darker gloves, often in leather, were worn with the winter uniforms.

For women in the armed forces during WWII it was decreed that hair had to be an inch above the collar, and this rule, which became part of the regulations for flight hostesses, would remain in place until the 1970s (Witcomb 1986: 272). Matron Holyman had insisted that short hair was more practical and looked neater with the uniform, so flight hostesses would be asked during their interview if they were prepared to have their hair cut. During the 1960s many prospective flight hostesses wore wigs to their interviews, and continued the practice when they flew. The unvarying appearance of flight hostesses in their graduation photos indicates that many of them were wearing wigs, all having bought the same short bobbed style.

The uniforms were not only used for identifying the hostess on the tarmac and in the air. Helen Sommerville, who began flying for ANA in 1940, remembers walking home from the tram stops and being greeted by a milkman and a policeman (Witcomb 1986: 34): the flight hostess in uniform was an unusual but welcoming sight at that time of day. In 1946, Sommerville went on to become Hostess Superintendent for Trans Australian Airways (TAA).[5] Government-owned TAA was, along with Ansett, one of the two major domestic airlines in Australia.[6] TAA participated in the Queen's Royal visit to Australia in 1954, with the hostesses greeting and serving the Queen on board wearing (along with a forage cap) the white below-the-knee-length short-sleeved dress with a button-through front and navy epaulettes, a dress which they had been wearing since 1946, and would continue to wear, with minor alterations, until 1964. The uniform had been designed by Sommerville and was based on the uniform worn by the Women's Royal Australian Navy (WRAF). It consisted of a navy blue suit with gold bars on the jacket sleeve and a half winged badge worn on the left-hand side, a white open-neck shirt, and a raised blue cap with badge. Sommerville replaced the lace-up shoe with the more fashionable court shoe. Initially, some of the newly recruited flight hostesses had crewed in civilian clothes because of wartime shortages. Peg McGill who joined TAA in September 1946 wore her Women's Auxiliary Australian Air Force (WAAAF) Officer's uniform for the first few weeks of flying until her uniform was ready (McRobbie [1986] 1992: 34).

Regional airlines in Australia also had a military-style uniform (see Figure 2). Pat Jordan flew for MacRobertson Miller Aviation (MMA), a Western Australian regional airline in the 1950s; she started flying on the unpressurized DC3 from her family home in Broome in the far north-west of the state. She remembers that the uniform at the time was a 'khaki drab-coloured skirt and shirt and a maroon tie, and over that you had a coat with about four pockets and brass buttons and epaulettes and lots of brass to polish, including those giant

Figure 2: Edna Payne Flight Hostess c.1951
MMA. Courtesy of the National Library of
Australia.

double wings which in flight, when you bent over to do something for a passenger, used to stab you in the boobs' (Bunbury 1993: 117).

Just over ten years after Grueber and Due started flying in 1936, Qantas employed flight hostesses for the first time, in December 1947. The young women would work alongside flight stewards who, since 1938, had been working on the Hythe Short C Class flying boats. On board the flying boats the flight stewards would wear white serving jackets reminiscent of clothing designed for service work on ships. Their 'off aircraft' uniform was a khaki military-style suit worn with brass buttons. The uniforms had to be practical as, amongst other duties, stewards would have to take passengers in small boats out to the flying boats moored in Sydney Harbour. When the flight hostesses came on board, the khaki was replaced with a dark-blue, navy 'square rig' suit which they wore until the early 1970s.

Lady Hudson Fysh, wife of Sir Hudson Fysh, the chairman of Qantas, had selected the uniform, as it was suggested that she had a liking for the navy uniform.

The first Qantas flight hostess uniform was almost identical in style to the uniform worn by the Holyman Airlines hostesses. It was made by the Sydney department store David Jones, who had made uniforms for the military during the war, and continued to do so for a number of years afterwards. The navy-blue suit was worn with wartime lisle stockings, made from spun cotton, which tended to sag when worn, so that many Qantas flight hostesses would purchase nylon stockings in Singapore. There was also a greatcoat, which was seen by many of the flight hostesses as too bulky and heavy to lug around the world, despite the warmth.[7] The uniform was worn with a navy bag, kid gloves and navy forage cap and black lace-up shoes. Two-tone navy and white shoes could be worn with the white 'tropical' uniform which had buttoned flap pockets and epaulettes, fabric belt, and gilt QEA buttons with shanks.

Llyris ('Short') McIntosh started flying with Qantas in 1952. While having lunch at the fashionable Romanos restaurant in Sydney she meet Eileen Weedon, a flight hostess for British Commonwealth Pacific Airlines (BCPA), an airline formed in 1946 by the governments of Australia, Britain and New Zealand to fly the trans-Pacific runs. She was

Figure 3: Llyris ('Short') McIntosh Queen of the Air Competition, Johannesburg 1955. Courtesy of Llyris McIntosh.

taken by the khaki-coloured uniform, which was a double-breasted suit with epaulettes, fastened with two buttons at the waist and worn with a white shirt, brown gloves and with a matching khaki Scottish-style beret.[8] As a result of the exchange she applied for a job with Qantas. After succeeding in her interview, Llyris went to David Jones to be fitted for her uniform with another new flight hostess, Joan Ente. They convinced the tailor to nip in the waist of their winter uniform, in an attempt to make it more fashionable. When Marjorie ('Marj') de Tracy, the Flight Hostess Supervisor, checked the uniforms they were sent back to the tailor to have the waist let out (McIntosh 2006: 2). In 1955 Llyris represented Qantas in the International Queen of the Air competition in Johannesburg.[9]

During the 1950s many of the airlines across the world began to soften the look of the uniforms by removing some of the military features. They did this by removing lapels on the jackets, replacing the wartime-issue fabrics with softer cloth, and allowing more fashionable court shoes to be worn instead of the dated lace-up wartime-issue shoes, but it would not be until the mid-1960s that the military forage cap was finally replaced.[10]

The force of the spectacle

Along with the reasons given above, the military-style uniforms suited the flight hostess profession in ways other than just the practical aspects of providing suitable dress. Michel Foucault in *Discipline and Punish: The Birth of the Prison* used the figure of a soldier to describe what he later called the 'technologies of the self' – where the self is mechanized through a variety of mental and physical procedures. The body is transformed into 'an inscribed surface of events' through bodily habits and training which the uniform makes specifically visible (Barthes [1957] 1980). It is these military-style uniformed flight hostess bodies combined together that become phalanx-like as they stroll through airport terminals. In Lewis Mumford's histories of technology and science, he coins the term 'megamachines' to describe large hierarchical organizations which use humans like components of a machine (Mumford 1967 in Myerley 1996: 12–13). He describes how the qualities of machines, with their regularity, order and repeatable physical effects, have played a role in the development of western civilization, and within this argument he points out that uniforms are 'an outward token of an inner unison' and that, while the 'drill made [soldiers] act as one, discipline made them respond as one, and the uniform made them look as one' (Mumford 1967 in Myerley 1996: 12–13). As the army is a spectacle of force in action, so is the flight attendant a visual demonstration of corporate power, usefully located on the vectors of the international stage. The constellation of elements that constitute a spectacular event are all part of the flight hostesses performance with its attendant significations: the imagery, the routines, the gestures, the uniform.

While Mumford is interested in the concept of the machine as a formation, Siegfried Kracauer in *The Mass Ornament* provides another account of the same processes with an inflection that is particularly relevant to the uniformity of flight attendants. Kracauer's discussion of the 'feminized mass ornament' uses the example of the Tiller Girls' performance to discuss the aesthetic, temporal and subjective impact of modernity (Kracauer 1995). Formed in the late 19th century, the Tiller Girls were a militarily trained calisthenics/dance group who, like the flight hostess, were selected to conform to a standard weight and height. The flight hostess, like Kracauer's 'feminized mass ornament', represents a mass-produced, functionalist object with which the modern subject is invited to identify. In uniform, they are the disciplined, streamlined, modernist body. But the flight hostess presents an interesting variation on these critical visions of modern mechanization because, once in battle (once on board), her mass machinic formation dissolves. She becomes a 'hostess', a space of personal interaction however much she is still ordered with the *appearance* of power.

Conclusion

The uniform is thus the clothing of the modern disciplinary society. Evolving from a military set of regimes, designed to transfer and maintain authority, control and discipline, the uniform developed within civil society into the corporate suit, initially for men. Yet this uniform took on new forms in the 'heightened', futuristic and largely peaceful cosmopolitan and post-national (or at least transnational) domain of air culture. International airlines were and are both nationalistic and globally corporate in their branding. The female cabin crew uniform signals the maintenance of safety, thereby retaining its military function, but it is also subject to the vagaries of fashionable change, and as such creates an association between fashion and femininity. This new manifestation of the uniform created tension between control and release, stillness and dynamism that contributed a great deal to the mid-20th-century perception of the flight hostess as an eroticized glamorous figure.

By the 1950s, larger, pressurized jet-engined aircraft, such as the Boeing 707, were widely deployed, and at the same time increased rigour in applying standardized commercial regulations also meant that there was little variation between airlines (even the number of flight hostesses was based on the management of passengers in case of an emergency). So airlines discovered that one way of suggesting difference was through the appearance of their flight hostesses. Flight hostesses who had initially been employed for their ability to nurse, ensuring safety and then comfort, were now for the first time employed for their looks: 'Besides having to be white, under twenty-five, and certifiably unmarried, they had to undergo cosmetic training, hairstyling and lessons in how to charm male passengers' (Visser 1994: 3).

Modernism created a 'brave new world', and if it has been the task of postmodernism to endlessly revisit that world it should not be forgotten that it was modernism that offered not only the 'delight in mobility' which characterizes air travel and its attendant images but also the opportunity to 'thrive on renewal' that grounds modern fashion (Berman [1982] 1968: 96). The flight hostess became the exemplar of this modern world of travel, and through her uniformed body she articulated a new subjectivity: that of a cosmopolitan woman. In her uniform she appeared in the more unusual and quite new spaces (dubbed 'non-places' by Augé) of the aircraft, the airport and the international hotel (Augé 1995).

Today, many flight attendant uniforms the world over still refer back to an earlier era of aviation, their styling borrowed from the military-inspired suit of the late 1940s. They historicize the present in a time when a nostalgia for the 'golden days' of flying dominates in today's world of budget airlines. The flight hostess uniform allowed women to come 'on board' flight in a professional capacity. The uniforms of nurses and the military bind the excess of the female body and flight hostesses presented as a 'new form', requiring a mode of dress that was form-fitting but within the governing modernist aesthetics of the time.[11] The flight hostess was also distanced by the uniform, which placed her within an institution thus making her eroticized as inaccessible. Regimented people are always inaccessible, but the flight hostess has an allure when she 'breaks ranks' to minister personally to each customer, an important dimension of her image and occupational performance.

References

Anon. 'Buttons', http://museumvictoria.com.au/collections/items/1584133/buttons-nurse-s-uniform-world-war-i-australia-1915-1920. Accessed 1 May 2013.

—— (25 August 1958). 'Glamor Girls of the Air', *Life Magazine*, pp. 68–77.

—— (June 2006). 'New in Briefs', *Air France Magazine,* 110, p. 42.

Auge, M. (1995). *Non-places: Introduction to an Anthropology of Supermodernity.* London & New York: Verso.

Barthes, R. ([1957] 1980). *Mythologies.* London: Granta.

—— ([1967] 1983). *The Fashion System*, (trans. Matthew Ward & Richard Howard). New York: Hill & Wang.

Berman, M. ([1982] 1988). *All that is Solid Melts into Air: The Experience of Modernity.* New York & London: Penguin Books.

Black, P. (2011). *The Flight Attendant's Shoe.* Sydney: NewSouth Publishing.

—— (2009). 'Fashion Takes Flight: Amy Johnson, Schiaparelli and Australian Modernism', *Hecate,* 35, pp. 57–76.

Bonami, F. (et al.), (2000). *Uniform: Order and Disorder.* Milan: Charta.

Bunbury, B. (1993). *Rags Sticks and Wire: Australians Taking to the Air.* Sydney: ABC Books, p. 117.

Ewing, E. (1975). *Women in Uniforms: Through the Centuries.* London & Sydney: B.T. Batsford.

Foucault, M. ([1977] 1979). *Discipline and Punish: The Birth of the Prison.* London: Penguin.

Greco, L. (2000). 'Social Identity, Military Identity', in Bonami (eds), *Uniform: Order and Disorder,* pp. 145–52. Milan: Charta,

Hughes Myerly, S. (1996). *British Military Spectacle: from Napoleonic Wars through the Crimean.* Cambridge, Mass.: Harvard University Press.

Joseph, N. (1986). *Uniforms and Nonuniforms.* New York: Greenwood.

Kracauer, W. (1995). *The Mass Ornament: Weimar Essays* (trans. Thomas Levin). Cambridge, Mass. & London: Harvard University Press.

McIntosh, L. (2006). *Footsteps in the Skies*. Canberra: self-published.

McRobbie, M. ([1986] 1992). *Walking the Skies: The First Fifty Years of Air Hostessing in Australia 1936–1986*. Melbourne: self-published.

Mumford, L. (1967). *The Myth of the Machine: Technics and Human Development*. New York: Harcourt Brace Jovanovich.

—— (1970). *The Myth of the Machine: the Pentagon of Power*, New York: Harcourt Brace Jovanovich.

Purdy, D. (ed.) (2004). *The Rise of Fashion: A Reader*. Minneapolis: University of Minnesota Press.

Strahan, Frank (1996). 'Victor Clive Holyman', http://adb.anu.edu.au/biography/holyman-victor-clive-10713. Accessed 1 May 2013.

Visser, M. (1994). 'Heavenly Hostess', in *The Way We Are*. London: Penguin.

Wilson, E. ([1985] 2003). *Adorned in Dreams: Fashion and Modernity*. London & New York: I.B. Tauris.

Witcomb, N. (1986). *Up Here and Down There*. Adelaide: self-published.

Notes

1   The first civilians put in uniforms were in the mid 18th century during the time of King Frederick William I of Prussia, who had a fixation on military uniforms replacing court state dress.

2   Throughout this chapter the term 'flight hostess' refers to the title used in Australia during the period 1936 to 1964 when they were wearing uniforms with military features. In 1984 all Australian flight hostesses were renamed flight attendants.

3   Hazel Holyman had never been a nurse. Witcomb says she was so named because there were so many Holymans in ANA at the time (Witcomb 1986: 15).

4   Eve Sexton worked with Ansett until 1952 when she joined BCPA as Hostess Superintendent. She later became Assistant Hostess Superintendent for Qantas (after BCPA and Qantas merged) (Witcomb 1986, 12).

5   TAA was established in 1946, renamed Australian Airlines in 1986, and in 1996 it was sold to Qantas.

6   Known as the 'Two Airline Policy' this duopoly from the Australian Federal Government restricted the number of airlines flying between the major routes in Australia from 1946 until the 1990s.

7   In the 1960s some of the Qantas hostesses replaced the standard-issue coat while they were away from home base with more fashionable kangaroo-skin coats.

8   The BCPA buttons were made by Stokes and Sons Melbourne, Victoria of oxidized brass. In WW1 Stokes and Sons had made buttons for nursing uniforms, and Australian military forces between 1914 and 1945. http://museumvictoria.com.au/collections/items/1584133/buttons-nurse-s-uniform-world-war-i-australia-1915–1920.

9   See 1955 'Queen of the Air' the same year as Lyris. http://www.britishpathe.com/video/air-news-ann-price-queen-of-the-air/query/stewardesses.
10 For example, in 1953 the Qantas uniform changed; as the lapel was removed from the jacket; the tie no longer had to be worn; and the skirt was made straighter.
11 It was not only flight hostesses who were presented as a 'new form' in flight, as early aviatrices had to find ways of dressing to suit their pioneering endeavours (Black 2009: 57–76).

Chapter 6

Models, medals, and the use of military emblems in fashion

Amanda Laugesen

Introduction

The previous two chapters have detailed significant moments in the 20th century that have marked the ongoing relationship between fashionable garments and civilian uniforms and their uptake of military conventions (Boyd, Chapter 4; and Black, Chapter 5 in this volume). It is fair to say that in the 21st century's 24/7 news media cycles, any such connections between fashion and the military uniform are quickly exposed – and sometimes evoke a public outcry. Vehement public response followed two recent events: the use of military medals and other uniform insignia, one in New Zealand (with repercussions in Australia), and the second, in the United States (US). These two examples formented dissent in a variety of ways, the public mostly communicated via the Internet, which was then followed up with media commentary. It is also significant that they differ as to the various cultural responses from region to region. However, with the 2013 Agua Bendita collection of swimwear, including a one-piece suit with both shoulders ornamented with medals, these discussions of fashion's use of military emblems are far from over (Mercedes-Benz Fashion Week, Miami, Florida).

Two controversies

In April 2008, New Zealand fashion designer Kate Sylvester staged a fashion show as part of the annual Sydney Fashion Week. The show was titled 'Royally Screwed'. Sylvester intended the show to be subversive of royalty and its associated regalia. But what ignited controversy across Australia and New Zealand was the fact that the fashion models wore 'mock-military' dress with numerous military medals prominently displayed (see Plate vi).

Medals (all facsimiles of real service medals) worn by Sylvester's models included the New Zealand Operational Services Medal, the Australian Vietnam Medal, the United Nations Service Medal for Korea, the Crimean War Medal and the Second World War (WWII) Allied Service Medal. Many of these medals were worn on the models' left-hand side, the traditional display side that indicates that the wearer has served in wartime, as shown in Plate vi ('Kate Sylvester sorry' 2008).

Representatives of the Australian Returned and Services League (RSL), the pre-dominant veterans' organization in Australia and a prominent voice in public affairs, quickly stated their objections as soon as photographs of the fashion show hit the newspapers. Derek

Robson, National RSL Secretary, described the show as 'appalling and sickening'. He argued that the show 'demeaned the whole purpose of the commemoration of Anzac Day' and was 'disgraceful'; further, he declared, 'I am appalled on behalf of those who have committed so much. To do something so flippant and dismissive is unfathomable' (quoted in 'Kate Sylvester sorry' 2008). Major General Bill Crews, RSL National President, similarly spoke out, condemning the event as debasing 'the whole value system we have in Australia' (quoted in Jensen 2008).

Kate Sylvester quickly responded. She defended her choices by calling attention to the theme of the show – which was intended as a commentary on royalty rather than the military – but issued an apology. Her official statement commented that 'There was no intention of showing disrespect for returned servicemen, for whom I have the deepest amount of respect. I sincerely apologize to anyone I may have unwittingly offended' (quoted in Jensen 2008). Simon Lock, Sydney Fashion Week's general manager, defended the show, arguing that no disrespect was intended. He pointed out that all the medals that had been worn by the models in the show were facsimiles, rather than authentic artefacts ('Fashion designer says sorry' 2008). Sylvester later reported that she had bought the medals from stores in Australia and New Zealand, and had told the salespeople that they would be used in a fashion show; she was never questioned when buying them ('Models' medals upset RSA' 2008: 5). Robson accepted Sylvester's apology, but also commented, 'An apology is fine but the issue here is that we need to learn something about values and respect' ('Fashion designer says sorry' 2008).

The New Zealand veterans' organization, the Royal New Zealand Returned and Services' Association (RSA), similarly condemned the use of the medals by Sylvester. Commenting on the show, RSA National President Robin Klitscher, said 'There would be many veterans who would take offence at what she's done'. He added: 'It's a great pity when that kind of symbolism is taken lightly, and I would have to say that a fashion show would be interpreted by most veterans as "taken lightly"' ('Models' medals upset RSA' 2008: 5).

One year before, in the US, another controversy involving fashion and military service took place. Choreographer and judge on the popular television dance competition, *So You Think You Can Dance*, Mia Michaels, wore a United States Marines dress blouse, with the Marine emblems displayed upside down. The incident created a flurry of outrage, mostly expressed on the Internet. Hundreds of messages were posted on Michaels' website within twenty-four hours of the airing of the programme, many of which chastised Michaels, and told her that she should be ashamed of herself. On the following episode of the television show, Michaels apologized, acknowledging that she had upset some people and agreeing that the emblems were 'sacred to the Marines' and should be respected (quoted in Trippany 2007). It should be noted that almost all images of Mia in this blouse have been removed from the Internet, excepting photos that show the non-offending sleeve.

The controversy did not end there, however. On the same episode in which Michaels apologized, fellow choreographer Wade Robson choreographed a series of dance solos. These solos were done to an anti-war theme, with dancers dressed in matching T-shirts with the peace symbol printed on them. Nigel Lythgoe, executive producer of the show and judge, was subsequently forced to respond to more unhappy Americans who objected to what they perceived as a blatant political message. Lythgoe apologized to anyone who might have been offended, but also commented, 'Art should be allowed to make statements' (quoted in Trippany 2007).

While there was no official condemnation of Michaels in the way Sylvester was taken to task by the RSL in Australia, the American blogosphere lit up with public commentary about the offensiveness of her actions. Blog commentator and political conservative Terry Trippany wrote: 'The dress blues themselves are sacred to the men and women who have earned the right to wear them. Military personnel follow strict guidelines pertaining to dress codes. Even more importantly, fallen Marines are often buried in their dress blues' (Trippany 2007). An online comment attributed to a Lieutenant Colonel Patrick (last name unknown), a serving Marine, in response to the show was:

> As for Michaels, I think she honestly just didn't know the significance of the uniform or even know that she was wearing a part of the Marine tradition and history. I heard her apology last night and think she just made a mistake and meant no offense to the Corps. But that doesn't excuse her or all the people who saw her wearing it and didn't step in and let her know about the mistake ('Stupidity is not an excuse' 2007).

Each of these incidents tells us something about the ways in which war, the military, popular culture, fashion and public debate intersect. While the two controversies are perhaps ephemeral, the issues and emotions that they engage in are not. This chapter will explore some of the broader themes and issues raised by these two controversies, and some of the questions that it will seek to address include: Why is the wearing of military emblems or medals, particularly if they are perceived to be authentic, so controversial and likely to stir up an emotional response? How do debates over the use of military emblems and medals in fashion intersect with political debates over the memory, meaning and status of, firstly, past conflicts and veterans, and, secondly, the military and contemporary military involvements? And do these controversies reveal a perceived popular dichotomy between art (and creativity) and war?

The meaning of medals

Medals and emblems of military service have enormous symbolic importance in American and Australian culture. The medal first emerged as a symbolic award for particular actions or demonstrations of virtue in Renaissance Italy. Frances Stonor Saunders notes that, given as gifts, these medals indicated that the recipient was themselves 'an object of virtue' (Stonor Saunders 2009: 18). From the 18th century, military medals have been awarded, both as decorations for particular acts of bravery in war (for example, the Victoria Cross; the United States Congressional Medal of Honor) and as awards for service in particular military campaigns (for example, the British War Medal 1914–20; the American Asiatic-Pacific Campaign Medal).

The wearing of medals has become heavily invested with importance in 20th- and 21st-century American and Australian society. On Memorial Day in the US and on Anzac Day in Australia, veterans march, often proudly displaying the medals that they have earned as part of their wartime service (which may or may not indicate combat experience, but often does). As mentioned previously, only the actual recipient of an award or decoration can wear that medal on the left breast. There are also strict rules set out by (in Australia) the RSL, as to how these medals should be worn: for example, they should be displayed in a horizontal line, the ribbon should not exceed one inch in length, the uppermost clasp should be one inch below the top of the ribbon, and so forth ('Medal Wearing Protocol' 2012). Similar rules of etiquette apply in the US.

Family members, who often inherit military medals on the death of the recipient, can also wear these medals, although they are instructed to always wear them on the right-hand side. According to the RSL, '[t]here is no limitation or formal policy on what occasions they should be worn. ... [But] [t]hey should not be worn lightly or where it would be inappropriate to do so' ('Medal Wearing Protocol' 2012). On Anzac Day in Australia, family members will often march wearing the medals of their family member; this is usually the only day in the year that the medals will be worn in public.

The important meanings invested in military awards and decorations can be discerned through a number of different issues that have arisen in recent decades. For example, there have been numerous controversies over the wearing of medals by people who have not earned them and who fraudulently claim to be war veterans. The fraudulent wearing of medals is in fact a federal offence in Australia, as well as in a number of other countries. In Australia an individual can be imprisoned under the Defence Act for up to six months for improper use of service decorations (Jensen 2009).

The fraudulent wearing of medals and military uniforms has a long history, as Laura Ugolini argues (2011: 126). At times, such activity may have been for the purposes of deception and fraud, including financial gain. In 2005 in Australia, for example, Joseph Brain was found guilty of pretending to be a Vietnam veteran and subsequently claiming over $90,000 worth of state entitlements over a ten-year period. He was also able to convince the Department of Defence to issue him with two service medals. In deciding the case, the judge declared that Brain's fraud was 'an insult to those who did serve for this country' (quoted in Bentley 2005: 4).

However, the desire to wear decorations and claim veteran status can equally be linked to a desire for recognition (for example, by those who undertook war service on the home front, but received no official recognition for such work) or even be considered a consumer choice (Ugolini 2011: 126). The wearing of medals or uniforms by those who have no wartime service history is therefore not always done with malicious intent. There can be a strong fantasy element involved, with the glamour and status attached to uniforms and medals – the embodiment of ideas of 'patriotic manliness' (Ugolini 2011: 135) – being highly attractive to many. In 2010, Australian Colin Sinclair was outed as an imposter. He claimed to have fought in Vietnam and once he first engaged in lies about his supposed wartime experiences they got out of control. Sinclair had no desire to defraud (and nor did he), but clearly enjoyed the status accorded him within his local community as a veteran. Interestingly, Sinclair noted that he drew the line at wearing medals – if people asked to see his service medals, he would tell them that he had thrown them into the river as a protest (Robinson 2010: 3).

Another issue that reflects the important symbolism of war medals is the way in which they acknowledge and symbolize an individual's contribution to a nation's involvement in military conflict. This is highlighted most acutely in relation to those groups that historically have *not* been appropriately acknowledged for their military service. In the US, this has included the lack of appropriate recognition for certain groups, symbolized by the failure to award service medals to African Americans and Asian Americans in past conflicts, notably following WWII.

Asian Americans and African Americans were not awarded some of the US' highest honours in (and after) WWII. African Americans who served in that war received no Congressional Medals of Honor (America's highest military award) until 1995, after a concerted campaign to have several noted veterans given the award. In 1997, President Bill Clinton presented seven Medals of Honor to African American veterans, six of whom were no longer alive to receive the honour (McNaughton, Edwards & Price 2002: 15). A similar campaign was undertaken to recommend some Asian American veterans (including Japanese-Americans and Filipino veterans) for Medals of Honor. A total of 22 awards were given, again by President Clinton, to Asian American veterans of WWII in 2000.

Such belated recognition through the individual award of honours is significant in that it shows how medals – and what they symbolize – are important to the conception of recognizing military service to the nation-state (and hence the relationship of certain groups to citizenship of the nation-state). As the group of historians who helped to secure the awards for the Asian American veterans have written, 'America's memory of World War II became more diverse. … [T]he Medal of Honor review once again brought before the public eye examples of Asian American heroism. New generations learned about the genuine heroes in their midst.' (McNaughton et al.: 33). Medals thus can be seen to be important repositories for memory and meaning – and they can also be a means by which memory and meaning can be redefined as certain individuals and groups are restored to the public memory of war.

For veterans, however, medals are not necessarily always embraced and displayed with pride. One journalist recounts how his grandfather hid his WWI medals in a box, too wounded by the scars of war to ever talk about his experiences with his family ('Diggers' stories' 2011: 20). Veterans have also used medals to make political statements: for example, John Kerry, the future US senator and presidential candidate, as a member of the political group Vietnam Veterans Against the War threw away his war medals in 1971 as a protest against the Vietnam War (McCoppin 2004). More recently, one Iraq War veteran, John DeBlasio, told a journalist how he has put his medals away, not yet ready to confront what they might mean about his own contributions to, and experiences of, war (McCoppin 2004). For veterans, medals are not only symbols of their contributions to the nation, but can be personal reminders of traumatic and shocking events. Nevertheless, the symbolic importance of medals is once again underscored even when they are rejected or hidden.

For families, too, medals are important as symbolic artefacts. They are often regarded as precious family heirlooms, and prized as material forms of memory, a linkage between the present generation and a dead relative or loved one. Mementoes of a broad variety, including clothing worn by servicemen, their written records (for example, letters and diaries) and evidence of their service (documents and medals) can all be valuable to family, both in representing their loved one and in signifying and facilitating the family's link to national historical narratives (Ziino 2010: 131; Harrison 2008: 777).

In all of this, we can trace the importance of medals as symbols in society's understanding of, and coming to terms with, war, as well as the various ways in which war is remembered. We will now turn to considering the ways in which uniforms are regarded and how they function in society and culture.

Uniforms and culture

In the Mia Michaels television incident, the primary controversy centred on the fact that she wore the US Marines emblems displayed upside down. The Marines dress uniform is a distinctive one, modelled on a design that dates back to the 19th century, and is reserved for use at formal and ceremonial occasions. There are strict regulations that apply to its wearing. Marine Regulations state that 'wearing the uniform should be a matter of personal pride to all Marines.' Strict regulations apply as to personal appearance and presentation, and include activities that cannot be engaged in while wearing the uniform, such as endorsing a commercial product (Permanent Marine Corps Uniform Board). Michaels wore only part of a Marines dress uniform (on a television dance show), and that part of it was worn incorrectly.

In most societies, uniforms and their accompanying accoutrements communicate significant messages about identity, belonging and power, as a number of scholars, notably Jennifer Craik, have demonstrated (Craik 2003: 2005). Clothing is a social artefact and therefore communicates certain messages (Joseph 1986: 1). Uniforms in particular convey a certain set of meanings, and represent a set of characteristics that the wearer of the uniform embodies but is also expected to adhere to in their everyday behaviour. Various characteristics attached to uniforms might include: orderliness, precision, efficiency, gallantry, and patriotism (Joseph 1986: 107).

The wearing of a uniform, such as the US Marines uniform, is a sign of status and belonging, as well as demonstrating the wearer's (ideal) characteristics. The US Marine Corps, perhaps of all the US military services, is held to particularly high standards of dress, behaviour and character. Craik notes that uniforms are key markers of group identity and membership, and group social status (Craik 2005: 22). She adds that uniforms can also symbolize history, pomp and tradition. These features can all be seen as true of American attitudes towards, and understandings of, US Marines' uniforms.

As with the controversies over the fraudulent wearing of medals, occasionally people have worn military uniforms as a means of claiming status and benefits to which they are not entitled. In a recent 2012 incident, a young man from Southern California was charged under the 2006 Stolen Valour Act for wearing a Marines uniform, with service decorations (Peterson 2012). Michaels' wearing of the uniform was obviously not fraudulent, but like the fashion models wearing medals that they had not earned (and wearing them in what was considered an inappropriate context and manner), she was not considered to have the *right* to wear any part of the uniform.

Uniforms can act as a type of control device, particularly in terms of marking boundaries of inclusion and exclusion (Joseph 1986: 69). They mark the wearer as the member of a particular group, and it is necessary to be initiated into that group (in whatever way) to be eligible to wear the uniform and/or display the appropriate markers. This question of who has the right to wear/display the emblems was evident in the debates surrounding both controversies: it was clear that neither the fashion models nor Mia Michaels were 'permitted' to wear the emblems that they did. Their actions were considered unacceptable not only because they were not members of the groups permitted to display the emblems, but also because of *who* they were: fashion models and dance choreographers – and women.

Evident in some of the criticism of the Sylvester incident was the fact that those wearing these medals were *female* models. One Internet commentator, a serving Royal Australian Air Force officer, wrote, 'To let these scrawny females wear medals that only soldiers should wear is a disgrace.' Another said, 'Isn't this typical of the Metrosexual culture that is plaguing todays [sic] society. Absolutely no respect for the men these medals were made for' (comments to 'A Different Kind' 2008). While these kind of comments are not necessarily representative of the majority view – the anonymity afforded to people who comment or blog allows for less socially acceptable views to be aired – it does point to the fact that there is a gendered dimension to the wearing of uniforms and medals, and the fact that a female fashion model should display them was considered especially transgressive.

The linking of uniforms and masculinity has already been touched upon, but perhaps needs reiterating. While the linking of medals, uniforms and masculinity is not absolute – especially in recent decades when women can serve in combat roles – there nevertheless exists a link between military service, what is considered appropriate behaviour or characteristics of one in (or formerly in) military service, and masculinity. Craik notes that 'uniforms have played a dominant role in defining modes of masculinity' (2003: 138).

Furthermore, uniforms and military emblems have often been fetishized and sexualized in popular culture, including in sadomasochism, gay cultures, cross-dressing and transvestism. (Craik 2003: 129.) Craik traces an eroticization of the uniform back to the Napoleonic period (133); the sexually subversive possibilities of the uniform were being commented on by the end of the 19th century (135). High fashion has also appropriated the uniform, playing on the transgressive and sexualized associations that uniforms have in popular understanding.

Both the linking of military uniforms and insignia with masculinity, and the transgressive and sexually subversive possibilities of the military uniform, perhaps help to explain in part the objections raised within the two controversies described above. Fashion has often transformed the military uniform into a sexualized, transgressive image. Yet, as Craik has noted, such transgression plays on our knowledge of the rules of uniforms (2005: 210): we know what uniforms mean, and therefore the transgression makes sense. However, when the designer or artist goes too far in their transgression – especially when they tread into sensitive political and popular emotions – controversy can be generated.

It is also worth considering the importance placed on the fact that the medals and uniform in each of the two cases were perceived to be authentic. Authenticity was a key factor in generating objections. More general use of military style in fashion – for example, cargo pants or camouflage colours – raise few, if any, objections; such militarized fashion is almost completely normalized and acceptable in modern fashion. However, it is still impossible to normalize authentic (or apparently authentic) military emblems or regalia because they are *too* laden with social, cultural and political meaning. They still belong only to those who are considered to have earned the right to wear them.

The politics of war

It is important to contextualize the two incidents in order to understand just why they were so controversial. More broadly, it is important to consider why it is that some people take offence to the use of medals and uniforms – particularly those that are authentic or are presented as such – in fashion, television or similar contexts. While it can be argued that, historically, certain attitudes have prevailed regarding the meaning of military medals and the wearing of military emblems and uniforms, it is telling that these two controversies blew up at the particular point when they did.

The Internet was a primary medium in which public debate could be generated about each of the controversies, reflecting the political and social context in which each of the events took place. As mentioned previously, the response to the Mia Michaels controversy was largely limited to the online world. But this online debate also provides insight into the contentious politics surrounding the issues of war and the military which many 'ordinary' Americans had opinions about. At a time when the US was involved in controversial military engagements abroad, including the second war in Iraq (2003–present), issues such as Michaels' (incorrect) wearing of Marine emblems could become caught up in broader political debates about the war and recognition of the armed services who were serving overseas.

As was pointed out above, the main objections to Michaels (and the subsequent Wade Robson dance routines) were expressed primarily on politically conservative and right-wing Internet sites and blogs. By 2008, American involvement in Iraq, which had begun as a war aimed at regime change (deposing Saddam Hussein), had shifted to managing political and social change on the ground. As Richard Eichenberg (2005) has argued, many Americans have, historically, not been in favour of involvement in another country's internal conflicts; they also, understandably, have questioned conflicts that have led to significant battle casualties. By 2008, then, questioning of America's ongoing involvement in Iraq had significantly increased.

It is also worth noting that, according to Val Burris (2008), the current war was highly partisan, with more Republican supporters favouring the war in comparison to Democrats. This goes some way to explain why the right-wing blogosphere took up the Michaels issue. Critic Cassy Fiano, writing on the website 'Right Wing News', complained that the show did nothing to show support for the troops, called the show's participants 'moonbat liberals', and commented that what they had done was to 'add a new insult to an old argument by disrespecting our Marines' ('So you think'). Rather than regarding Michaels' wearing of the shirt as a fashion or consumer choice, it was considered to be a political statement against the war and against the military, seemingly reinforced by Robson's subsequent anti-war dance routines. It was possible for viewers who were so inclined to read the incorrect display of Marines emblems as more than an aesthetic and stylistic choice. It is impossible to know if Michaels was so motivated, as she did not say that she had deliberately chosen to wear the shirt and the emblems in such a way, nor did she openly comment on her views on the war or service personnel overseas. But the fact that some viewers instantly read her outfit as a political statement reminds us once again how military emblems are loaded with political and social meanings.

A possible comparison can be made with the meanings invested in the American flag after the World Trade Center attacks on September 11 2001 (9/11). As Ronald Ostman and Harry Littell comment, after 9/11, the American flag appeared everywhere. The flag was (and is) of enormous symbolic importance for many Americans, but was also used as a commercial product, appearing on a variety of consumer items, including fashion items (Ostman and Littell 2007: 45–46). Flags were used to assert American patriotism, and, importantly, were also used to define public spaces (Obajtek-Kirkwood 2007: 70; 59). At the same time, multiple political and cultural meanings could be invested in the flag, including anti-war expressions. Thus flags, like the medals and uniforms discussed here, have no stable meaning. Nevertheless, they are all heavily loaded with meanings and often become strongly invested with emotion and sentiment. In the same way, the response to Michaels' 'misuse' of the Marines emblems reveals how certain things are considered to be more than just fashion items.

This emotional and sentimental investment in certain symbols is similarly evident in the Australian controversy. In Australia, the Sylvester affair blew up because of the deep feelings invested in the Australia New Zealand Alliance (Anzac) legacy, which finds expression in the reverence accorded service medals. The timing of the fashion show, due to Fashion Week's proximity to Anzac Day (25 April, a public holiday in Australia), was unfortunate.

In the controversy, the RSL in particular laid claim to their role in the ongoing protection of the Anzac legacy, something that was clear in the comments they made on this incident. As historian Martin Crotty (2007: 190) points out, the RSL has played a continuing role in 'reminding people of just what a debt Australia owe[s]' to veterans. Historically, the RSL have played a role in undertaking acts such as securing legislative protection for the name 'Anzac'. They have also sought to protect and secure privileges for Australians who have served in wars. Crotty has further illustrated how, in the wake of WWI, the RSL helped to create a cultural understanding of the returned serviceman that placed them at the top of the hierarchy of Australian citizenship (193).

In both the Michaels and the Sylvester controversies, veterans and servicemen staked a claim for their own groups in society, privileging their status as veterans and members of the armed forces. In Australia, the RSL explicitly linked the incident to a supposed violation of 'Australian values'. Michael Keren and Holger Herwig (2009: 1) have suggested that veterans possess a particular 'sense of mission to pass on virtues believed to have been gained in war such as heroism, sacrifice, bravery, comradeship, abolition of class barriers, devotion to a higher cause, and ingenuity'. These virtues are promoted as those that are fundamental to the nation state. The authors also argue that these virtues and the status of the veteran have been under siege at various times, and that veterans have felt periodically as if their message – and their virtues – are considered to have no relevance and are ignored. It was clear in both the US and Australia at the end of the first decade of the 21st century that veterans and the military were seeking to reassert their authority in the public sphere; but this was tied to, as noted above, conservative politics in the US. This was also true in Australia, although the political embrace of Anzac has traditionally remained bipartisan.

The Australian incident took place in 2008, not long after the end of the lengthy conservative Liberal prime ministership of John Howard (March 1996 to December 2007). While prime minister, Howard had intervened in the shaping and political uses of Australian history, decrying the so-called 'Black Armband' school of Australian history that sought to focus on wrongs done to Indigenous Australians, rather than on the heroic achievements of Australians in events such as wars. The previous Labor prime minister, Paul Keating, had similarly intervened in historical debates, using the alleged British failure to prevent the fall of Singapore in WWII as a means of asserting Australian nationalism and supporting Keating's 'turn' to Asia (Bonnell and Crotty 2008). The subsequent prime minister, Kevin Rudd, was no less keen to appropriate the Anzac legacy as representative of Australian character and values. During his political campaign in 2007, he walked the Kokoda Track, following in the footsteps of Australian soldiers fighting in New Guinea in WWII; the journey was chronicled on the popular breakfast television show, *Sunrise* (Seven Network, Australia). Politicians have thus sought to make Anzac a sacred part of political and civic discourse and elevate it beyond criticism (as well as using the Anzac legacy to reinforce their political legitimacy and popularity).

In 2010, a number of Australian historians spoke out about the 'militarization of Australian history'. They argued that from the 1990s, Anzac Day and the Anzac legend became increasingly important in the definition of Australian nationalism. The Anzac legend and the 'spirit of Anzac' became increasingly sacrosanct, with all Anzacs (defined as any Australian veteran, not just veterans of WWI) considered to be national heroes (McKenna 2010: 112; Donaldson and Lake 2010: 91). These historians also pointed to the ways in which sentimentality and nostalgia have become the prevailing modes by which most people relate to Anzac Day (Damousi 2010: 96), and, by extension, this sentimentality is extended to our regard for veterans – and, to a point, current serving troops as well.

Responses to the Sylvester controversy can be found in Internet forums, and echo some of the broader politics of Anzac discussed above. The Internet became a venue for ordinary people to add their voices to these debates, and hence reveal some of the attitudes that Australian society has towards Anzac and its appropriation in fashion, and perhaps echoing some of the issues outlined by these historians.

While the fashion show did not spark the intense vitriol that the dance show did in the US, a number of people agreed with the RSL that Sylvester's use of the medals was 'tasteless', a faux pas', and a 'mistake' (Vogue Fashion Forum 2008). A number of Internet posters to the Vogue Fashion Forum commented that it had been potentially offensive to people who had served, one commentator writing that they thought it made 'a mockery of the extreme challenges and conditions the veterans have gone through'. Posters to the *Sydney Morning Herald*'s news blog were less forgiving. Here, the show was condemned as an 'absolute disgrace', 'trashy and tacky', 'insensitive and very poor taste' and 'an insult to those that have served in both current conflicts and in the past' (comments on 'A Different Kind' 2008).

The wearing of medals by fashion models in a fashion show prompted a range of emotional responses, echoing the emotions that have been invested in Anzac in Australia. These responses are partly political – they demonstrate how Anzac and war are not regarded as areas open for political debate and intellectual engagement, but are rather considered to be sacred and off limits. However, this has perhaps led to a lack of critical engagement with current military involvements. In the US, the wearing of Marines emblems by Mia Michaels on a television dance show touched a raw nerve because of the divisive politics of recent wars, a state of affairs that continues in the country today. For some Americans, Michaels' fashion choice was, first and last, a political one.

Conclusion: Art, fashion and war

The above discussion details the significant divide between those in the military establishment and those who pursue their own agenda when exploring the interrelationships between art, fashion and war. And yet the three have historically been intertwined. Artists have depicted war both to glorify and condemn it, and to reveal its horrors. Art has been put to war service, not least in propaganda. Fashion has been influenced by military styles, and military dress has been influenced by fashion (Boyd, Chapter 4; Black, Chapter 5; and Rall, 'Afterword' in this volume).

In the Michaels controversy, Nigel Lythgoe, producer of the dance show, spoke out to defend artistic choice. One critic of the Michaels incident noted that she regarded the dance show as entertainment, which she tuned into 'as a way to unwind', and that bringing politics into it – and making anti-war statements such as Robson did – was objectionable (Davey 2007). In the Sylvester controversy, a similar sentiment was never clearly articulated. But some commentators on Internet forums did note the ways in which fashion might be about 'art and self-expression', as well as 'commercialism and selling a product' (Vogue Fashion Forum 2008). Some defended her show on the basis that 'fashion is out to provoke', and commended her talent as a designer ('A Different Kind' 2008). Others cynically commented on the fact that such controversy helped to get the designer's work more publicity (Vogue Fashion Forum 2008).

In both the American and Australian cases, there were questions raised as to the extent to which artists can engage in political statements, and the extremes to which artists can go to make statements, political or artistic. Should fashion and art draw a line on the kinds of items they incorporate into their work? Should military emblems be kept sacrosanct? Personal opinion will vary on this; however, it is essential to understand the history and politics that generate debates surrounding the use or incorporation of military emblems and symbols into fashion. By interrogating such use and trying to understand why it generates such public controversy, this opens up new perspectives on the way in which contemporary society regards war, the memory of war, and the meaning of military participation and service.

References

Agua Bendita swimwear collection, Mercedes-Benz Fashion Week, Miami, Florida (18–22 July 2013). http://miami.mbfashionweek.com. Accessed 11 August 2013.

Anon. (29 April 2008). 'A Different Kind of Fashion Disaster', *Sydney Morning Herald* News Blog. http://blogs.smh.com.au/newsblog/archives/your_say/018044.html?page=fullpage# comments. Accessed 2 November 2012.

———— (3 December 2011). '"Diggers" stories inspired by my brave Pop', *The West Australian*, p. 20. Accessed 8 November 2012.

———— (30 April 2008). 'Kate Sylvester "sorry" for offending servicemen at Fashion Week', *The Daily Telegraph*. http://www.news.com.au/kate-sylvester-sorry-for-offending -servicemen-at-fashion-week/story. Accessed 8 November 2012.

———— (2008). 'Models' medals upset RSA: Kiwi designer says she did not intend to insult war veterans', *The New Zealand Herald*, p. 5. Accessed 9 November 2012.

———— (31 July 2007). 'Stupidity is not an excuse … a symptom, maybe, but not an excuse', *Volunteer Opinion Journal*. http//volopinionjournal. wordpress.com/2007/07/31/stupidity-is-not-an-excuse-a-symptom-maybe-but-not-an-excuse. Accessed 9 November 2012.

Bentley, A. (5 October 2005). 'Phoney vet shamed dishonourably accepted $90,000 and two Vietnam medals', *The Gold Coast Bulletin*, p. 4.

Bonnell, A. and Crotty, M. (2008). 'Australia's History under Howard, 1996–2007', *Annals of the American Academy of Political and Social Science*, 617, pp. 149–165.

Burris, V. (2008). 'From Vietnam to Iraq: Continuity and Change in Between-Group Differences in Support for Military Action', *Social Problems*, 55: 4, pp. 443–79.

Craik, J. (2003). 'The Cultural Politics of the Uniform', *Fashion Theory: The Journal of Dress, Body and Culture*, 7: 2, pp. 127–47.

——— (2005). *Uniforms Exposed: From Conformity to Transgression*. Oxford: Berg.

Crotty, M. (2007). 'The Anzac Citizen: Towards a History of the RSL', *Australian Journal of Politics and History*, 33: 2, pp. 183–93.

Damousi, J. (2010). 'Why do we get so emotional about Anzac?', in M. Lake and H. Reynolds (eds), *What's Wrong with Anzac? The Militarisation of Australian History*, pp. 94–109. Sydney: NewSouth Publishing.

Davey, D. H. (27 July 2007). 'Popular Dance Show Incites War Controversy', http://voices.yahoo. com/popular-dance-show-incites-war-controversy-466740.html. Accessed 9 November 2012.

Donaldson, C. and Lake, M. (2010). 'Whatever happened to the anti-war movement?', in M. Lake and H. Reynolds (eds), *What's Wrong with Anzac? The Militarisation of Australian History*, pp. 71–93. Sydney: NewSouth Publishing.

Eichenberg, R. C. (2005). 'Victory has many friends: US Public Opinion and the Use of Military Force, 1981–2005', *International Security*, 30: 1, pp. 140–77.

Fiano, C. 'So You Think You Can Make a Statement?', *Right Wing News*. http://www. rightwingnews.com/uncategorized/so-you-think-you-can-make-a-statement. Accessed 10 November 2012.

Harrison, S. (2008). 'War Mementos and the Souls of Missing Soldiers: Returning Effects of the Battlefield Dead', *Journal of the Royal Anthropological Institute*, 14, pp. 774–90.

Jensen, E. (3 April 2009). 'When Fashion Ignites Passion … Military Cross and Designer Dressed Down', *The Age*. http://www.theage.com.au/action/printArticle?id=450892. Accessed 11 November 2012.

Joseph, N. (1986). *Uniforms and Nonuniforms: Communication through Meaning*. Westport, CT: Greenwood.

Keren, M. and Herwig, H. H. (2009). *War Memory and Popular Culture: Essays on Modes of Remembrance and Commemoration*. Jefferson, N.C.: McFarland and Company.

McCoppin, R. (21 September 2004). 'Do Medals Matter?', *Daily Herald* (Illinois).

McKenna, M. (2010). 'Anzac Day: How did it become Australia's national day?' in M. Lake and H. Reynolds (eds), *What's Wrong with Anzac? The Militarisation of Australian History*, pp. 110–34. Sydney: NewSouth Publishing.

McNaughton, J. C., Edwards, K. E. & Price, J. M. (2002). 'Incontestable proof will be exacted: Historians, Asian Americans and the Medal of Honor', *The Public Historian*, 24: 4, pp. 11–33.

Obajtek-Kirkwood, A. (2007). 'A Small World – and its Flags – in a Much Bigger One', in A. Obajtek-Kirkwood and E.A. Hakanen (eds), *Signs of War: From Patriotism to Dissent*. New York: Palgrave Macmillan.

Ostman, R. E. and Littell, H. (2007). 'The Stars and Stripes in the Year after 9/11: "Rally Round the Flag" or "The Flag is a Rag"', in A. Obajtek-Kirwood and E. A. Hakanen (eds), *Signs of War: From Patriotism to Dissent*. New York: Palgrave Macmillan.

Permanent Marine Corps Uniform Board (2012). Chapter One. http://www.marcorsyscom. usmc.mil/sites/mcub/pages/uniform%20regs%20chapters/chapter%201_files/chapter%201. asp. Accessed 12 November 2012.

Peterson, G. (30 June 2012). 'Vets seethe after Stolen Valor Act overturned', *Contra-Costa Times*.

Robinson, R. (22 April 2010). 'For 20 years at services he mourned his Vietnam mates, now he admits … I'm an Anzac fake', *Herald Sun*, p. 3.

RSL South Australia (2012).'Medal Wearing Protocol'. http://www.rsl.org.au. Accessed 16 November 2012.

Stonor Saunders, F. (27 June 2009). 'Badge of Shame', *The Guardian*, p. 18.

Trippany, T. (27 July 2007). '"So You Think You Can Dance" Issues Apology Over Upside Down Marine Emblem'. http://newsbusters.org. Accessed 18 November 2012.

Ugolini, L. (2011). 'The Illicit Consumption of Military Uniforms in Britain, 1914–1918', *Journal of Design History*, 24: 2, pp. 125–38.

Vogue Fashion Forum. (April 2008). http://forums.vogue. com.au/archive/index.php/t-292945. html. Accessed 18 November 2012.

Ziino, B. '"A Lasting Gift to his Descendants": Family Memory and the Great War in Australia', *History and Memory*, 22: 2, pp. 125–46.

Section III

Framing youth fashion, textile artworks and postcolonial costume in the context of conflict

Chapter 7

Battle dressed – clothing the criminal, or the horror
of the 'hoodie' in Britain

Joanne Turney

Introduction

According to fashion theory, and particularly that which is concerned with clothing and identity, sartorial codes predetermine what we wear in specific environments, and for certain events and occasions. This largely unwritten knowledge (such as not wearing white to a wedding unless you are the bride) adheres to socio-moral conventions of dress at a given time, and creates parameters of acceptability that individuals then consent to or reject. Culturally, in the developed world it is generally inadvisable to wear ripped jeans to an interview for an office job or to wear a suit and tie to a beach party. Such knowledge is both practical and coded; it would be too hot in a suit at the beach, but also would appear too uptight to participate in the revelry afforded by the term 'party'. This basic sartorial knowledge, engrained in everyday experience, appears as common sense, and enables us to either fit in or stand out from the crowd. Likewise, we make judgements about the ethics, world view, personality traits and interests of others based purely on what is being worn and how. Therefore the relationship between clothing codes and gesture or the performitivity of both wearer and clothing is inherent in determining first impressions.

While it's true that we have become increasingly good semioticians at reading the fashion(s) of others (a shallow skill to some, perhaps), the symbolic potential of clothing to demonstrate identity also enables clothing to mask who or what we really 'are'. In these circumstances clothing becomes a costume, merely garb that enables us to fulfil a role. Our wardrobes can be seen as extensive dressing-up boxes, containing the potential to be both virgin/whore, master/slave, hero/villain.

But what does one wear to commit crime? Do potential burglars look to the iconography of Hollywood's jailhouse garb (black-and-white horizontally striped jerseys) in order to make 'correct' clothing choices? Obviously, this is a facetious comment; but as crime is central to socio-political debate and an omnipresent facet of contemporary daily life, clothing associated with criminality has become a potential means of identification and potential prevention. Does clothing mediate behaviour and can merely putting specific garments on elicit equally specific responses from those around us?

The aim of this chapter is to assess what has become, in recent years, a media furore and, by association, a moral panic, all of it stemming from a seemingly innocuous piece of clothing: the hoodie. The hoodie is a leisurewear garment: a sweatshirt with a hood; a knitted piece of mass-manufactured clothing, just like a T-shirt. It is ordinary: most people have one in their wardrobes. Hoodies are practical garments, keeping the wearer warm, with the added benefit of warming the head as well as the body. The discussion here draws attention to the mundanity of this garment. It is inoffensive, democratic even, readily available to everyone regardless of income, age, class, gender or educational background.

Youth, clothing, and social anxiety

In 2005, the Bluewater Shopping Centre in Kent banned the wearing of hooded garments (specifically hoodies) on their premises. Why was this? Why were hoodies so much of an issue? Indeed, Bluewater continued to sell them, so what was it about such a simple piece of clothing that produced such a drastic response? It seemed that, once the sweatshirt was worn with the hood over the head it took on transformative properties, changing from casual wear to something much more problematic, and indeed threatening, to the status quo. In the wake of rioting in urban areas in the United Kingdom (UK) in 2011, and in conjunction with attention to the clothing worn by the participants, the sweatshirt with a hood became the symbol of social disobedience. For a piece of mass-manufactured clothing, the hoodie's availability and ordinariness is significant in respect of its transcendence from wardrobe staple to *the* sign of criminality and criminal intent. By merely raising the hood, the wearer transformed from comfy dresser to something far more socially disturbing and threatening: 'Hoodies have created controversy after bans in some shopping centres and pubs, due to fears the clothing can hide potential offenders' identities or are "threatening"' (BBC 2006); and, 'The hooded top – the must-have fashion accessory for teenage boys – is being banned from shopping centres in the latest police crackdown on juvenile crime. Hats, including baseball caps, are also being prohibited' (Goodchild 2003).

Indeed, the garment became synonymous with its wearers, so both wearer and object became merged into the contemporary folk devil – the hoodie. By 2007, the hoodie had become 'faceless' as a piece of clothing as well as a stereotype described by then-shadow home secretary David Davis as something that formed part of a 'hooligan's tool kit' (Davis 2007).

But who (other than everybody) wears hoodies and to whom was Davis's statement addressed? This discussion will emphasize social concerns and attitudes to behaviours and peoples that extend way beyond the clothing they choose to wear, highlighting the *unheimlich* relationship between normative social propriety and that which is considered 'different' or deviant. Clothing under these circumstances is metaphoric; it sublimates deeper social anxieties, particularly those adjunct to personal safety, even mortality.

One of the many elements of this political and media discourse has emphasized the rise in teen crime in the UK, and an increase in anti-social behaviour, in particular, something seen as the instigator of more 'serious' criminal activity. The construct of what was to become the 'out-of-control teen' was met politically with the development of the 1998 Anti-Social Behaviour Order (ASBO), punishable by law via the Crime and Disorder Act, and those convicted became representative of another construct: 'Broken Britain'. The emotional relevance of this phrase later became evident in the compelling photograph of Prime Minister David Cameron with an unknown teenager shadowing his footsteps (see Plate vii.). In terms of clothing, teenagers wore hoodies and hoodies hid the wearer, thus facilitating engagement in criminal activity without the consequence of identification.

Youth culture since its inception in the early 1950s has always been shrouded with an air of disbelief and misunderstanding – deliberately so – separating youth from everyone else. Clothing has been central to this form of separation; a visual indicator of difference, a sign of rebelliousness. The hoodie, perhaps, is just another garment in a long line which includes jeans, T-shirts and leather jackets.

> It is not made of chain-mail, of Batman's off-cuts, or of the very fabric of evil itself. Indeed, nowadays, you're lucky to get one that's 100% cotton. And yet, the hooded top can strike fear into the heart of even the most courageous among us. A lone figure behind us on the walk home – hood up, head down – and we quicken our steps. Someone solitary and hooded at the back of the bus, and we opt for a seat near the front. A group of hooded teenagers on the street, and we're tensing our shoulders, clenching our fists (round handbag strap or house-keys-cum-weapon), training our ears for verbal abuse in order to emphatically ignore it. Just as leather trench coats are associated with goths, Matrix fans and ageing lotharios, so the hoodie has become a signifier of disgruntled, malevolent youth, scowling and indolent. The hoodie is the uniform of the troublemaker: its wearer may as well be emblazoned with a scarlet letter (McLean 2005: n.p.n.).

The deliberate distancing of youth clothing from that of the mainstream is significant not merely in its style but its gestural potential and its performativity. The clothing one wears is significant, but the ways in which clothes are worn are more so. The hoodie itself is not a threatening garment, but when worn with an attitude of disaffected youth, when paraded with a languid but aggressive gait, and worn with jeans or sweatpants with the crotch at the knee, the hoodie becomes a sign of difference. The interrelationship between clothing, youth and gesture, is not new; all youth cultural clothing, particularly that which is associated with violent groups who potentially threaten the status quo, embodies a sense of threat, which is heightened and perpetuated through media portrayal and commentary. For example, a young man in a leather jacket is transformed into legendary screen rebels like James Dean and Marlon Brando when the collar is upturned and he adopts a nonchalant swagger. Add a cigarette and the look, posture and the 'don't give a damn' attitude is complete. Indeed, like the hoodie, leather jackets are innocuous items of workwear re-appropriated by young men in the immediate post-war years, and worn with the stance and mindset of the Romantic outsider. As a counterpart to the business suit (the sartorial sign of the establishment), the wearing of a hoodie, particularly one with a zip, when combined with loose fitting trousers (as in a tracksuit) offers an obvious opposition to conformity; it is both suit and leisurewear, and lacking the structure of tailoring it is both casual in appearance as well as in its approach to white-collar work and the society it represents. Unlike earlier incarnations connoting the 'rebel', such as the leather jacket, the hoodie acknowledges contemporary surveillance culture, offering the wearer access to socially coded clothing at a low cost which facilitates ease of movement and personal concealment. Similarly, the hoodie does not have the subcultural kudos of previous youth clothing, as it is available to, and is worn by, everyone. These qualities make the hoodie a more confusing emblem of youth disaffection than the appropriation of the leather jacket, for example, and make it problematic in terms of social propriety and morality, and in criminal identification.

Non-conformity in a surveillance society

The fashion historian Aileen Ribeiro notes that morality aims to establish and maintain a group understanding of what is right and wrong, and that clothing, as a social signifier, functions as a means of 'belonging or indeed, isolation or alienation from the group' (Riberio 1986: 12). Clothing therefore in itself is neither 'moral' nor 'immoral', but subject to social mediation which the art historian Quentin Bell (1947) describes as a 'sartorial consciousness' (Riberio 1986: 12), cultivated by social norms and responses to changing socio-cultural circumstances. The development of a sartorial consciousness highlights the social impact of clothing, and more notably fashion, as both an aspect of the avant-garde and of everyday life, emphasizing a contradictory praxis that potentially challenges the norm. This distinction between culture and society is immediately recognizable as an implication of the modernist avant-garde – the quest to challenge and overthrow existing boundaries of acceptability, or an understanding of the importance of conformity. In the case of the hoodie, there seems to be no real fashion-led impetus in wearing the garment; it is not avant-garde, and appears to be unchallenging, primarily because it's so ordinary. It could be suggested, therefore, that unlike clothes worn deliberately as a statement of the rejection of the dominant ideology, hoodies became, merely by association, a symbol of youth, specifically disaffected youth, with no regard for the law – a threat to the law-abiding majority. Of course, the media furore over the intimidating presence of such clothes gave them a new 'street credibility', popularizing them further with a section of society isolated, it seemed, for wearing them in the first place. Thus the hoodie and their wearers became part of a self-fulfilling prophecy. As India Knight suggests in an article in *The Sunday Times*:

> Everybody is scared of hoodies: other teenagers, men, women – and dogs probably. That's why hoodies sell. No teenager is so well adjusted that he can't do without a bit of anti-social backup from his clothing (Knight 2005: n.p.n.).

The hoodie therefore appears to represent a clear distinction between wearers and the moral majority. It is both a sign of 'attitude' and the social stereotypes surrounding the problems of youth, and, more importantly, a signifier of moral decline, ASBO (anti-social behaviour order) culture and a general social downward turn.

The hoodie is, of course, a concealing garment; by wearing a hood, one can hide oneself from the glare of CCTV cameras and therefore potentially commit more crime without the consequence of identification and thus capture. A report in the tabloid newspaper the *Daily Mirror* noted:

> Hooded tops and baseball caps have been adopted by cowardly yobs up and down the land to hide their faces from CCTV cameras while they commit crime or terrorise victims unable to identify them (Allen 2005: n.p.n.).

While acknowledging the concealing properties of the hoodie, Eric Pickles, the Communities Secretary, warned rioting looters in London:

> This is a city with a lot of surveillance cameras and it's all right putting your hoodie on now, but you are going to have to put your hoodie on for a long time to escape justice. That stuff you stole over the last few days is going to lead directly to your arrest (Pickles 2011: n.p.n.).

One might regard the increased usage of CCTV cameras in towns and cities itself as a problem: it could be interpreted as a means of social control that infringes civil liberties, rather than a method of maintaining public safety. This is certainly a concern of the left-wing media. Writing in the *Socialist Review*, Andrew Stone notes:

> The government sees hoodies and caps as an affront to its surveillance culture. We're all meant to be constantly available for monitoring on the ever-present CCTV cameras. To want privacy, anonymity, is inherently suspicious, perhaps criminal. Hence the need to "stop and search" anyone wearing such clothes which, handily for the fashion police, are often worn by young black men. To be stuck on a street corner is equally unacceptable. They should be out doing something 'useful', preferably consuming in a privatised space where they can be observed and regulated (Stone 2005: n.p.n.).

Political ping-pong aside, the point is that the hoodie – worn by everyone from gangs to grannies – is universal, and as a concealing garment enables the wearer to seemingly merge into the background, whether the intention is criminal or not. As Braddock states in a recent article in *The Guardian*:

> For sure, a hoodie is a useful tool to avoid identification for a range of gang-related rituals. Yet for teenagers under intense peer pressure to conform to a collective identity, acceptance means adopting a prescribed outfit. For some, there may be no choice but to wear one and shoulder its associations. … David Cameron, in a rare outbreak of

understanding, told the Centre for Social Justice in 2006 that hoodies were "a way to stay invisible in the street. In a dangerous environment the best thing to do is keep your head down, blend in, don't stand out" (Braddock 2011: n.p.n.).

So concealment can be seen as a form of identification, of fitting in and following one's peers or as a means of *avoiding* criminal acts on the self. By lifting the hood, one can disappear and avert the gaze not only of the ever-present CCTV cameras or the police, but of criminals looking for victims.

The hood and the mask – real or fantastic

The hood as a sign of mistrust and suspicion, even horror, is not a new one. All of the great fictitious and mythical figures associated with evil or fear wear hoods, from the Grim Reaper, to mysterious hooded figures in Victorian novels through to the Hooded Claw in the Penelope Pitstop cartoons: the covering of the face or head hides the wearer's true identity, personality and intent. This has been recognized by reports into the 'horror' of hoodies. Gareth McLean writes:

> The big daddy of them all, the Grim Reaper, comes cloaked and hooded, as do the Four Horsemen of the Apocalypse, various minions of Satan, and harbingers of evil from all creeds, religions, mythologies, science-fiction universes and fantastical worlds of dungeons and dragons. "Hooded figures" appear in crime reports, horror films, nightmares …. For thousands of years, we have been bombarded with images of menacing hooded figures. Crabby youths wrapped in cotton/polyester-mix tops are just the latest entry in the catalogue of devils; they can't hold a candle to the Ku Klux Klan (McLean 2005: n.p.n.).

So hoodies are merely part of a mythology of folk devils; they are nothing new. Yet the creation of what has become a moral panic surrounding the wearing of hooded tops has entered the political arena in an unprecedented way. Youth crime, while significant to the argument, is not the central issue here: the political focus is on traditionally working-class, and unemployed, youth. It is the socio-economic associations of hoodies, its class, or the class of its wearers, that is central to the garment's outlaw status. Both urban and urbane, the top and its wearer are representative of a British underclass and a lifestyle alien to the moral majority. And it is these class associations, combined with an inability to recognize and identify wearers amidst a crowd, that creates and fuels an everyday terror; the balance between *good* and *bad* is blurred. Greg Philo, professor of sociology at Glasgow University, describes hoodies as part of:

> a long-term excluded class, simply not needed, who often take control of their communities through aggression or running their alternative economy, based on things

like drug-dealing or protection rackets. If you go to these places, it's very grim, the culture of violence is real. But for the British media, it's simple – bad upbringing or just evil children. Their accounts of what happens are very partial and distorted, which pushes people towards much more rightwing positions. There's no proper social debate about what we can do about it. Obviously, not all young people in hoods are dangerous – most aren't – but the ones who are can be very dangerous, and writing about them sells papers because people are innately attracted to what's scary. That's how we survive as a species – our body and brain is attuned to focus on what is likely to kill us, because we're traditionally hunters and hunted (Graham 2009: n.p.n.).

Such fear of covered heads can be aligned with the hoodie's similarity to the ski mask – which since the 1970s has become the literal face of the contemporary terrorist, photographed and displayed in both print and televisual media. The ski mask covers the whole face, with cut out eyeholes, rendering the wearer seemingly invisible. Such a garment is emotively significant because it implies terror on actual and metaphorical levels. Firstly, the presence of such imagery in the media and its association with actual acts of terrorism places the ski mask firmly in the public consciousness as a sign of political dissidence and fear; and secondly, the masking of the terrorist contributes to a sense of unease, in which that which is 'invisible' and potentially horrific could be lurking anywhere. In contemporary society, where the threat of terrorism pervades the social climate, such forms of dress become potent symbols of a collective fear, not merely of terror itself, but of difference – of race, religion, politics and so on, as indicated in recent media reports surrounding the wearing of the hijab by Muslim women.

The mask has a long history and significance within dress and display. The mask is ambiguous; it conceals the wearer, yet it offers the exciting potential of revealing the secrets which lurk beneath. The mask then acts as a fracturing device; it hides like a shroud, it camouflages and conceals, rendering the wearer oblivious to the concerns of vanity, to social norms and behaviours, all of which is viewed suspiciously by non-mask wearers. One might assume that this form of dress as anonymity is mysterious to the extent that we are always awaiting the moment of 'reveal' – the removal of the mask – which will in some way restore harmony. As Alexandra Warwick and Dani Cavallaro acknowledge:

Masks and veils further complicate the indeterminate nature of dress, by appearing to secrete the body, yet concurrently holding figurative implications that allude to their illuminating and hence revealing powers. Related to the central uncertainty is the mask's ability to both separate and connect individual bodies, and thus to amplify the function of clothing in general as both a boundary and a margin. In the language of symbolism, the coexistence of concealment and exposure, insulation and meditation, is one of the principal features of all screening garments and is conveyed by their explicit incarnation of the imperative of secrecy and the attendant invitation to unmask the secret (Warwick & Cavallaro 1998: 128–29).

The ski mask, however, is worn as an item of deliberate concealment; there is no potential 'reveal', which heightens its potency as a garment of threat. The mask conceals the face, but not the body; the body is present, but the face disappears. And this is the site of terror; the physical presence is amongst us, but we don't know from whom we could be under attack.

The body and its boundaries

Hoodies, unlike ski masks, are not merely garments that cover the head making the wearer 'faceless'. They are also nortoriously baggy, concealing the body of the wearer to the extent that they become gender neutral. Essentially the garment conceals, but it also conceals to such an extent that it disembodies. The hoodie can be described as demonstrating a surface of the abject, a break free from the boundaries of the body into a state of amorphousness. The body becomes ambiguous: it is neither man nor beast, inside or outside, veiled in a shapeless mass like a monster emerging from the quagmire. This can be seen as a move from the symbolic world of form, language and meaning into a realm of confusion, distortion and shapelessness; a realm beyond comprehension.

Such an analysis is appropriate for the discussion of youth clothing. The psychological concept of 'the abject' represents a move from the awareness of the womb into a state of differentiation, which parallels the ambiguous and transitional stage between childhood and adulthood; the lack of form implies a stage of transition in which one will either emerge into the symbolic realm or return to the quagmire from which it originated. Similarly, a state of abjection can be marked as a foray into nothingness, a means of displaying no form of identity, while simultaneously creating a primal one-ness. Hoodie-wearers demonstrate their creation of an unstable unity of perceived disaffection, but when the hood is worn, it offers a form of comfort: it shields the wearer from the gaze, not necessarily from CCTV cameras, but from the world outside. The wearers literally distance themselves from their surroundings by covering the head, concealing their identity and prohibiting social engagement. Such behaviour becomes a form of hiding, of fading into the background, like an ostrich with its head in the sand, exhibited by persons unable or unwilling to form a solid identity; an act that is far more psychological than it is anti-social. Nonetheless, such a desire to disappear is disquieting, as Peter Schjeldahl notes in 'The Empty Body', 'fashion is, we suppose … "nothing in itself". It needs a body in it to tell us something and then is constrained only to signify about that body' (Townsend 2002: 78).

The hoodie allows the body to disappear. It allows the wearer to move away from form that is both natural and bodily, and repellent, while creating attraction in the same measure. In the *Powers of Horror*, Julia Kristeva acknowledges:

Unflaggingly, like an inescapable boomerang, a vortex of summons and repulsion places the one haunted by it literally beside himself (Oliver 2002: 229).

For Kristeva, the abject is the inability to objectify the object, but in the present discussion the concept has traction through this concurrent juxtaposition of attract/repel: hoodies hide the wearer, conceal and disembody the body, moving it from shape to shapelessness, while at the same time drawing attention to its alien mass.

One could say similar things about other 'outsider' knitwear. For example, the black polo neck has become a mainstay in the wardrobes of intellectuals and fine art lecturers who consider themselves on the margins of society. The history of black in fashion is one which coincides with the emergence of European Romanticism and the cult of the outsider. It is a colour which defies fashion and its rules and as such is seen to transcend the frivolities of a quest for the new. Consequently, black has been categorized as a 'classic' in fashion terms, perhaps best demonstrated by the perennial 'little black dress', itself initially a form of oppositional clothing as devised by Coco Chanel in the 1950s in reaction to Christian Dior's 'New Look' (Holland 2004: 74). In menswear however, black is the colour of the rebel, the non-conformist and the hero.

Assuming the black

Black was the colour of revolutionaries, emerging as a style choice for those with Romantic sensibilities in the second half of the 18th century. The adoption of black under these circumstances created not merely an air of aggression, but one of masculinity and oppositional belief. It was the colour of anti-conformism and the anti-establishment and by association became a sign of social distance, of marginal thought and deed. As the Romantic tradition developed throughout the 19th century, black became associated with intense emotional feeling, the cult of the individual and the outsider. Literature drew on such characters, centralizing them as fictional heroes; passionate and un-tameable loners consumed by inner turmoil. Such men had little compassion or social responsibility, preferring or guided by higher concerns such as experience and the meaning of existence (Wilson [1985] 2003). By the late 19th century, black had become the colour of mourning (in the West), associated with loss and the distance between life and death, furthering the signification of colour with transcendence, the outsider or the other, and of other-worldliness.

With such a cultural heritage, it is unsurprising that black became part of the iconography of existentialism and the uniform of post-war intellectuals. Indeed, by the 1950s black had become associated with 'black' humour and nihilistic philosophy exemplified by the writing of Jean Paul Sartre (Holland 2004: 74).

One garment that encapsulates this form of thinking more than any other is the black polo-neck jumper. The garment is significant because when worn (and unlike the hoodie, which disembodies, or the ski mask, which obscures the head), visually it *decapitates*, visually removing the head from the body. The body disappears, but the head remains, often giving the impression of floating freely, unaided and unsupported.

The polo-neck jumper enables the wearer to present their face, but not their body. In contrast to the use of white, particularly as a background in fashion photography, where it enables the clothing to stand out and shine, black does the opposite – it conceals, hides and obliterates. When an intellectual wears a black polo-neck jumper, the statement is one of defiance; it says that the wearer is more than a body, more than a physical shell, and that their mind and soul is of paramount importance. This is reflected in popular culture; think Velma in her roll-neck in the *Scooby Doo* cartoons. Without a body, there is no canvas for cultural inscription, no empty space to carry brand names and logos, no vehicle on which to express the language of fashion, or other signs of social and cultural conformity. There are no signs to be read, no clues to identity through sartorial choice. Yet, of course, the garment's obvious refusal to communicate enables it to do so; to express a clear message of anti-conformity, and of the self as an outsider with a sensibility that claims a higher purpose. This is a technique used in the portraiture of the Old Masters, particularly Rembrandt, as Juliet Ash notes:

> Later, in old age, clothes have almost disappeared in Rembrandt's self-portraits, and instead the focus is on the expression on his face, on the poignant (lonely) presence of himself and his feelings (Ash 1999: 129).

The role of clothing as a vehicle through which to express identity is thus negated by a desire to focus on inner turmoil, on the self rather than society and its wider concerns. By deploying clothing in such a way, the subject/wearer distances themselves from the world, transporting them into an inner realm, supposedly enabling the communication of the psyche and soul.

In this respect, the hoodie represents the negation of the significance of clothing as a means of expressing identity. Here, identity is obliterated on two levels: (1) the body and face is concealed by the garments; (2) the garment is so commonplace that the wearer fits in with, rather than stands out from, the crowd. The garment, a subcultural oxymoron, does not distinguish the wearers from the society they may be rebelling against, its very ubiquity adding to the potential for continual fear. Yet wearing a hoodie allows wearers to isolate themselves from society; it is an attempt, perhaps, to produce an inward focus on their psyche and soul. Ultimately, hoods create a private space within a very public sphere; they create intimacy in a world of surveillance and social propriety. Hoods, therefore, are the embodiment of a 'private space' for contemporary urban nomads.

One might argue that clothes embraced so widely by the majority lose some of their meaning; but such clothes still bear traces of the outsider and retain the whiff of dissidence and criminality. So while wearers of the high-street black hoodie may not be criminals, yobs, or disaffected youth they may nonetheless want to project themselves as rebellious, and the garment acts as a cultural symbol of such sympathies. Indeed, garments that are associated with outsider culture are so easily recognizable that to wear them might be interpreted as 'lazy' dressing – dressing that requires little or no thought or imagination – which counteracts the notion of 'rebellion', intellect and difference.

Conclusion

The media furore surrounding the wearing of hoodies is essentially nothing new, and emerges as a response to the re-appropriated meaning of the garment – as a sign of opposition. In the wake of such bad press, hooded garments really need a change of image, particularly as they are not solely the domain of the young or the criminally minded.

The shapelessness of the hoodie conceals an unformed identity and appears to exist outside of the realms of comprehension; like the wearer, identity has no form and appears alien; both hidden and visible, repellent and interesting, simultaneously. As Jennifer Craik acknowledges, 'The "life" of the body is played out through the technical arrangement of clothes, adornment and gesture' (Craik 1994: 1); and if the body seems to disappear the onlooker is confused and fascinated.

So potent is this image of 'social menace as hoodie-wearer' that its use within the horror genre has revitalized British Cinema:

> Who's afraid of the big bad hoodie? Enough of us, certainly, that the smart money in British cinema is going on those films that prey on our fear of urban youths and show that fear back to us. These days, the scariest Britflick villain isn't a flesh-eating zombie, or an East End Mr Big with a sawn-off shooter and a tattooed sidekick. It is a teenage boy with a penchant for flammable casualwear (Graham 2009: n.p.n.).

Clothing cannot be immoral or horrific, but it can, and frequently does, encapsulate a mood of the times. Scapegoating a piece of clothing and marking it as an indicator of the anti-social highlights the garment as 'edgy', imbuing it with an 'attitude' of youth and rebellion. And so to the recent UK riots, where the hoodie was the garment *du jour* for rioters and spectators alike; a garment already vilified and cloaked in fear transgressed, capitulated and became a self-fulfilling prophesy. But here the 'youth' uniform was adopted by all ages, social classes and races, and one can assume that it was its accessibility and ordinariness that appealed, not merely to the young, but to everyone. Reuters reported from Hackney, East London:

> At a nearby housing estate, heavily tattooed Jackie, 39, resented what she saw as the media's portrayal of the riots as mindless youth violence. "This was not kids. This was youths and adults coming together against the crap that's been going on since the coalition," she said, referring to Britain's conservative-led government, which has made deep austerity cuts since coming into power last year to tackle a big budget deficit. "They're saying it's all young hoodies. Look at me, now I'm a hoodie," she said, putting her hood up, and with her small slender build instantly looking like the lithe teenage rioters shown in television

footage. "I was out in the riots. My 16-year-old daughter was calling me asking where I was," she said, chuckling (Abbas 2011: n.p.n.).

The hoodie may be a universal garment, worn by everyone, but is also appropriated as a sign of disaffection and lawlessness. It has become the garment of 'Broken Britain' worn as a sign of affiliation to the hidden masses – and anyone who wants to go looting.

References

Abbas, M. (10 August 2011). 'London Rioters Resent Media Image of Hooded Teen Thug', *Reuters News*. http://uk.reuters.com/article/2011/08/10/uk-britain-riots-hackney-idUKTRE 77942520110810. Accessed 12 August 2013.

Allen, V. and Roberts, B. (13 May 2005). 'Reclaim our Streets: Hoodies and Baddies', *The Daily Mirror,* online edition, pp. 8–9.

Ash, J. (1999). 'The Aesthetic Absence: Clothes Without People in Paintings', in Amy de la Haye and Elizabeth Wilson (eds), *Defining Dress*. Manchester: Manchester University Press.

BBC News, 12 April 2006.

Bell, Q. (1947). *On Human Finery*. London: The Hogarth Press

Braddock, K. (9 August 2011). 'The Power of the Hoodie', *The Guardian*. http://www.theguardian.com/uk/2011/aug/09/power-of-the-hoodie. Accessed 12 August 2013.

Craik, J. (1994). *The Face of Fashion*. London: Routledge.

Goodchild, S. & Lyon, D. (25 May 2003). 'Police Ban Hooded Tops from High Street', *The Independent on Sunday,* online edition, p. 13.

Graham, J. (5 November 2009). 'Hoodies Strike Fear into British Cinema', *The Guardian*. http://www.theguardian.com/film/2009/nov/05/british-hoodie-films. Accessed 12 August 2013.

Holland, S. (2004). *Alternative Femininities: Body, Age and Identity*. Oxford: Berg.

Knight, I. (15 May 2005). 'Let Them Wear Hoodies', *The Sunday Times*. http://www.thesundaytimes.co.uk/sto/news/article133978.ece. Accessed 12 August 2013.

McLean, G. (13 May 2005). 'In the Hood', *The Guardian*. http://www.theguardian.com/politics/2005/may/13/fashion.fashionandstyle. Accessed 12 August 2013.

Oliver, K. (ed.) (2002). *The Portable Kristeva*. New York: Columbia University Press.

Pickles, E. (9 August 2011). 'London Riots', *The Telegraph,* online edition. Accessed 11 August 2011.

Ribero, A. (1986). *Dress and Morality*. London: B.T. Batsford.

Schjeldahl, P. (2002). 'The Empty Body Part 2: Skin has no edges. Clothes do', in Chris Townsend, *Rapture: Art's Seduction by Fashion*. London: Thames & Hudson.

Stone, A. (2005). 'Boys in the Hoodies', *Socialist Review*, June. http://www.socialistreview.org.uk/article.php?articlenumber=9458. Accessed 12 August 2013.

Warwick, A. and Cavallaro, D. (1998). *Fashioning the Frame: Boundaries, Dress and the Body*. Oxford: Berg.

Wilson, E. ([1985] 2003). *Adorned in Dreams: Fashion & Modernity*. London: Virago.

Chapter 8

Dutch wax and display: London and the art of Yinka Shonibare

Davinia Gregory

Introduction

I recall watching Yinka Shonibare M.B.E. R.A. become an honorary Fellow of the Royal College of Art in the 2010 convocation ceremony. Seated behind him with the other graduands, observing him receive his umpteenth award as I was to receive one of my first, I felt an almost fatalistic awareness of a sort of culmination. Exhibitions and installations of Shonibare's work had punctuated my career up to that point for reasons no more uncanny than my having been working in London, concerned with black British criticism and post-colonial critique. Shonibare's work had been weaving itself into that city's cultural fabric as I had discovered and developed my academic specialism in its universities, libraries, museums and galleries. This chapter is in part a historiography of writings on the work of Shonibare. It examines them in order to uncover what are widely acknowledged to be his reasons for using the iconic Dutch wax batik textile in his work, and also to consider the extent to which that work has played a part in the endless battle for seamless, frictionless multiculturalism and pluralism in London. I refer to it as a battle and call it endless because, as is the same in any city, its contenders are constantly changing. Each new ethnic and social demographic, leading political party and cultural institution used as an arena brings with it a different history to be addressed, included or revisited. As a result cultural conflict waxes and wanes, and Shonibare's work is somewhere present at each juncture to encourage commentary and critique.

This chapter, therefore, positions the artist within a trajectory of contemporary artworks and postmodern commentary, but specifically as part of his tenure in London. His work can be examined in its context of the Young British Artists or compared to feminist and post-feminist artists, such as Helen Chadwick and Sarah Lucas (Hynes & Picton 2001). Such analyses have been covered, but in this case they illuminate the many layers of meaning held within his work. However, Shonibare must also be considered from the vantage point of cultural theorists who have written on race and class (Gilroy 2001; Hall & Jacques 1989), and also from the perspectives of researchers and curators such as Carol Tulloch, Peter Gorschlüter and Zoe Whitley (see also Oguibe 1999). These scholars have instigated and further developed the concept of Black British Cultural studies within British history as a whole. Therefore, Shonibare's striking work acts as catalyst not only for postcolonial enquiry but for a questioning that is specifically about Britishness, with a focus on the material world. As the curators above have noted, this artwork begins with objects that already exist, in Shonibare's case it is the 'language' of those historic objects which he borrows and adeptly applies to his own.

Finally, this chapter must necessarily acknowledge that Shonibare's work, while often depicting violent scenes, often does so with humour, as his portrayals of domination within cultural warfare offer a gentler touch. Thus, the chapter deals with the anti-militancy of his promotion of cultural pluralism as well as his stronger statements about his own 'otherness' (Shonibare 2012). Recently, the notion of 'class' has re-emerged as an omnipresent issue in the United Kingdom (UK), as a result of the global financial crisis and many unpopular decisions made by the government of the day. The viewer is reminded of this, as Shonibare's work ties questions of class inextricably to the current discourse(s) on colonialism. As such, this discussion explores over five years of artistic and critical commentary (between 2005 – 2010) on over five hundred years of London's history through the lens of Shonibare's artworks. It focuses on the subtle and more openly combative ways in which Shonibare's iconic batik sculptures were displayed in London during this time, and asks the question: does a cultural militancy have a place in Yinka Shonibare's work?

Yinka Shonibare and 'Africanness'

Shonibare's own identity has been described in a number of ways. He was born in the UK and raised in Nigeria, returning to the UK for university, and currently practises in London. Recently, curator Rachel Kent introduced him as a 'British-born Nigerian Artist' at the Museum of Contemporary Arts in Sydney (Kent, Hobbs, & Downey 2008). In the Museum's exhibition catalogue Robert Hobbs introduces him as a London-based, Nigerian expatriate (Kent et al. 2008).

The following extract from a speech at London's School of Oriental and African Studies is one of the most widely quoted statements from Shonibare (see Hynes & Picton 2001). Recalling his reaction when asked by a university tutor why he was making distinctly modernist work about world events that seemed unrelated to his African roots, he said, 'What does that mean? I'm a citizen of the world and I read the news, so I make work about these things.'

This consideration – that all world events relate to all people because they are all citizens of the world – can be identified as the artist's focal point from the very beginning of his career. When his tutor had asked why he was not creating things about Africa, with the justification that this would affect him more personally, Shonibare became interested in the tutor's assumptions that work about Africa would be more personal to him than work about Europe. What struck him most about this encounter was the fact that the stereotype surrounding him because of his visibility was so strong that the intricacies of his identity were forgotten. This moment is widely accepted among journalists and scholars who have told Shonibare's story as being the reason behind his persistent plays on stereotype. Instead of creating work that simply evoked 'Africanness', which would have presented his identity as one-dimensional, he set about trying to deconstruct preconceptions – 'question[ing] identity rather than celebrating it' (Hynes & Picton 2001). Shonibare still encourages his audiences to deconstruct stereotypes by making them explicit. He pushes them to their limits and repeats until they become visually jarring. Even though this fervour, which can be perceived as militancy, was born from a reaction to a limiting stereotype in his student days, it did have the effect desired by his tutor; his work became more impassioned and deeply personal. He sees identity as something that is partially imposed upon a person or thing; and he plays with the power of that imposition by applying the various identities existing within Dutch wax batik and other fabrics to various objects and shapes.

Dutch wax textiles and African identities

Almost every piece of writing about Yinka Shonibare's work has detailed in some way the origins, meanings and significance of Dutch wax batik cotton. It is the most instantly visually striking element of a large series he produced and the most consistent, having featured in almost every installation since his practice became fully established. Its bold prints form the front page of both his website and the book written about him, entitled *Yinka Shonibare MBE*. Some scholars have called it African print fabric but most have highlighted and focused on its transnational nature (Relph & Irwin 2010). In many of Shonibare's pieces it is the textile that causes audience members to pause, and then to reflect on the meanings inherent in the composition. For Manthia Diawara, the prolific writer on Shonibare's work, these textiles call to mind the sounds, smells and colours of the markets of his childhood on the African continent (see Plate viii). Moreover Diawara identifies what the artist found useful in the fabric; the language and agency that it offered market women in West Africa:

> Our identities get richer by multiplying themselves, and not through a return to purity and binary oppositions. As I look at Shonibare's work today I tell myself that African market women have always understood what still eludes many African artists. They know, as did my mother, that they can invent identities with the wax fabric (Diawara 2004).

Shonibare professionalized, stretched and re-contextualized this invention that African market women had been engaging in for generations, extending the role of art in the postcolonial discourse: to promote the new. By the time Shonibare was at art school, postcolonial theorists were busy locating the fixed identities imposed upon people and objects and breaking them down by exploring and endeavouring to understand them (Fanon 1967). However Shonibare's work has a function beyond this: while it has been informed by postcolonial critique, its visual nature enables it to 'pack a punch' in public places that goes beyond the written theories. It aims to be a visual intellectual irritant, and through humour and playfulness it offers a legitimate place for change that academic writing cannot. This is why it works so well as large-scale public art, and as a series of interruptions within pre-existing exhibitions and displays.

The origins of so-called Dutch wax cloth are still open to controversy, since the practice can be traced in a number of countries, and the earliest examples of the technique have been located in Egypt (Spée 1982). The technique of printing on fabric, with wax as a 'resist' to the dye, offers distinctive layers of complexity as the fabric can be repeatedly dipped into the dye with different colours emerging. However, new carbon-dating techniques have revealed that Indian textiles were carried to Java (Indonesia) to trade for Indonesian spices (Maxwell 2003: 56). This has pointed towards a very early exchange of textile patterns and techniques between Indonesian and the Indian subcontinent, including works dated to the mid-14th century, so the antecedents of these textiles may be more complicated than previously thought. Further, the journey of the patterned cloth from Indonesia, via Dutch traders to Europe gave the fabric its name: Dutch wax cloth (Relph & Irwin 2010). Further, following its introduction to the west, the fabric's reproduction met with significant European interventions – often mass-produced in Manchester and the Netherlands before being exported to West Africa – a different type of triangular trade (Relph & Irwin 2010).

For example, Shonibare's high-profile piece exhibited on the fourth plinth in London's Trafalgar Square, *Nelson's Ship in a Bottle* (see Plate ix), looks directly back to the British Empire and the great naval victories. It can even be seen to send a nod to the transatlantic slave trade but by inclusion of the Dutch wax cloth on the sails of the ship, it also brings to public attention the fact that Britain's naval history was not solely an outward-reaching exploration. It boldly acknowledges that influences and people from the empire were certainly brought back to Britian, whether willingly or not.

Shonibare's *Nelson's Ship in a Bottle* dramatically poses the question whether the Lady Britannia ruled the waves unscathed and unaltered, and his work boldly stood in Trafalgar Square for 18 months as an unabashed acceptance and celebration of the fact that She did not. That said, British trading practices permanently changed the way that Dutch wax patterned cloth entered Africa, and local production in countries like Nigeria have ceased (currently, most patterned cottons are produced in Asia). For Shonibare, authenticity and exoticism are pointedly *not* the issue here; it is the exposure and subsequent acceptance of the way things are that allow him to create a visual language that facilitates his own expression of such issues. As a young person, Shonibare saw the fabric in Nigeria, and first understood it just as Diawara did, as a system of political, religious and other codes inherent in the printed patterns, which signified and clearly stated the wearer's allegiances, thereby revealing parts of their identity. However he later became accustomed to seeing it in the markets of London's East End, and came to recognize in the fabric itself a melding of origin (Indonesia), manufacture (Europe), sale (Africa) and resale (African diasporic Europe) (Relph & Irwin 2010). Dutch wax challenges notions of Africanness by not being African in origin; but it clearly speaks *of* Africa. With his decision to use Dutch wax fabric, Shonibare comments powerfully on stereotypes and, furthermore, he asks questions about hybridity, impurity, belonging and origin. It is his playful deployment of the meanings that textile holds that enables him to say even more, provoking thought about fragmentation and the creation of new, individual identities from the rubble of obsolete ones.

Shonibare's critical use of visual language

Manthia Diawara continues his analysis:

> Shonibare's work challenges all of us to take transtextuality seriously. We're not black or white, Igbo or Nigerian, European or African. We are all of these at the same time and from time to time. Our identities get richer by multiplying themselves, and not through a return to purity and binary oppositions.

Diawara captures much of the core of Shonibare's work in his essay 'Independence Cha Cha: The Art of Yinka Shonibare', based on the exhibition at the Museum Boijmans Van Beuningen Rotterdam called *Yinka Shonibare: Double Dutch*. He emphasizes that it is multi-layered, with messages about the limitations of race as a construct and the subtleties of ethnicity, the violence of colonial endeavour, the remains of imperial and class constructs within Britishness, and humorous tongue-in-cheek references to the idiosyncrasies of British eccentricity, which Shonibare very much identifies as part of his own identity. It is interesting that Diawara uses the term 'transtextuality' rather than 'intertextuality' which would have immediately evoked semiotic theory, and the post-structuralist canon of writing from Kristeva to Barthes. The use of 'trans' not only clarifies that Diawara is referring to the postmodern extremes of infinite intertextuality in Shonibare's work, but also promotes an affinity with the theoretical 'beyond'. Yes, Shonibare isolates signifiers, using them intermittently and at will, but he does so in such a fluid fashion, easily pushing beyond boundaries that are already broken. In this manner he invokes Homi K. Bhabha in a way that is absolutely exemplary of a time of cultural hybridity that the theorist would claim is beyond postmodernity:

> The *beyond* is neither a new horizon, nor a leaving behind of the past … Beginnings and endings may be sustaining myths of the middle years, but in the *fin de siècle* we find ourselves in the moment of transit where space and time cross to produce complex figures of difference and identity … inclusion and exclusion (1994: 1–2).

The sense of disorientation and exploratory, restless movement that Bhabha goes on to describe are typical of Shonibare's work and this is why the prefix 'trans' is ultimately appropriate. In his early works on canvas he exemplified this quite simply and literally, referencing equally the black gold of Africa's resources that has flooded European economies during and since the centuries of colonization, and the abstract expressionist marks of Jackson Pollock (Bhabha 1994: 13). The paint excessively, sumptuously, violently and carelessly erupted from the multiple canvases and spilled onto the surrounding walls. Here, Pollock had broken free of his imaginings of himself as the future painter of a great modernist masterpiece and was experimenting with the freedom of artistic fragmentation. As Shonibare comments:

> There is no need for me to make one big heroic painting. I can actually take the language of this big, abstract painting and produce it in very small pieces, in fragments. I can actually break it down and reconstruct it (Hynes & Picton 2001).

Nancy Hynes and John Picton have written that when employing Dutch wax fabric in his work Shonibare 'teases out the signifiers and toys with them mockingly' (2001: 62). It is this mocking cynicism that portrays his resistance, or what some have termed his militancy (see the segment 'The headless colonials', Rall 2010). It can, in fact be argued that Shonibare's frustration reaches a peak in his photographic work, which becomes more personalized as he uses his own body as protagonist in place of the Dutch-wax-clad, headless mannequins. As opposed to decapitating or defacing protagonists within his reconstructions of well-known or easily read scenes, he replaces them with himself.

In these photographs, the complexities of the Dutch wax's subtle language of hybridity are abandoned; instead the viewer is presented with a short series of abrupt and direct messages about race and difference. In this way, Shonibare confronts his blackness head on and forces the audience to face the awkwardness of seeing it presented in a historically and culturally white-coded scene. These photographs add something unique to the body of Shonibare's work; they force the acknowledgement of the inescapable fact of his blackness. Although a cultural hybrid, he is still strikingly visible because of colonialism's effect on public consciousness and collective memory. Here, he displays the persistence of racism and hints at progress still to be made. He also subtly continues to expose the origins of racism in the gaps that have been made in history and culture, which, when correctly filled, make the story look very different. The Museum of Contemporary Art in Sydney's 2008 exhibition catalogue summarizes this perfectly by describing 'the way in which he insinuates himself into the centre of the work … [it] is a powerful assertion of the right of the "other" to take centre stage' (Kent et al. 2008).

Black militancy and cultural vigilantism

The presence of the typically African Dutch wax cotton adds complexity to this. With his focus on the work's transtextuality, Diawara therefore acknowledges not only post-structuralism, semiotics and Shonibare's use of the Dutch wax as one word in the complex language of each piece, but also cultural hybridity as outlined by Homi Bhabha in *The Location of Culture* (1994). By using the Dutch wax cloth, Shonibare sharpens a focus on plurality, on movement, on individual ownership and agency in the creation of national and ethnic identities. He promotes the idea that movement within and across the interstices of identity is to be desired and is forward-looking. He has described Dutch wax batik as 'a metaphor for interdependence', from the interdependence of nations on one another within the global economy, indeed the interdependence that they have always had because of trading relationships, right down to the interdependence of individual people, if only to define themselves against one another. This began very early on in his career. Hynes has acknowledged Shonibare's view of Africa and Europe as having 'invented each other' (Hynes & Picton 2001). Like the fabric and like the artist himself, everything and every person is presented as a cultural hybrid in his work. Furthermore this rhetoric of interdependence does not only stand in opposition to stereotypes surrounding ethnicity; it also applies to class, gender and sexuality.

So far, Shonibare has been presented as both militant and peacemaker: let him also serve as a cultural vigilante. This time the vigilantism is perhaps accidental and not immediately noticeable as it comes from a very specific and perhaps outdated meaning within the cloth. In the United States (US) and also for a time in the UK, batik cloth was adopted by black solidarity groups and imbued with a more militant meaning. Hynes and Picton take the Dutch wax into its diasporic context briefly, acknowledging its part in various movements across the Black Atlantic (Gilroy 2002). Consideration of its use in Europe and the US calls to mind the Black Power era of the 1960s and 1970s and the Black Arts Movement that accompanied it. Headwraps and items of clothing made from various types of batik cloth (in a visually indiscriminate fashion) were included in a series of signifiers that made a person appear radical no matter how passive their actions may have been. It restored a political edge to the Afro hairstyle, which by the late 1970s had become less of a political statement than a purely aesthetic fashion choice for many. When worn together with batik items and other pieces of clothing that denoted military dress, the Afro became a signifier of pan-Africanism and black solidarity as had been extolled by Jamaican Marcus Garvey and was being promoted by many of the Black Panthers and other politically active supporters of the American civil rights movement. This meaning still resonates for activists and others who see the political resistance in this cloth and Shonibare has teased it out and made subtle use of it within his work.

Along with the echoes of 1970s militancy, there is an intentional assertion in the way that the artist has employed the fabric on many occasions. Over the years, Shonibare has used this textile not only to accompany objects and figures but to dress them. In his early work he stretched the fabric over frames instead of canvas and painted on top of it in a minimal, modernist style. Later, when he had discovered his unique aesthetic, he stretched it again, but this time the fabric took centre stage, dressing the wall. He later dressed and renamed many other things, with varying success. The objects viewed as most successful were things that carried very strong signifiers of their own. He learned that giving a headless mannequin a name and stance already imbued with cultural significance achieved the best result: figures were given names from literature such as Charles Dickens, Jane Austen and the Brontë sisters. This is how 'by dressing a character like Dickens, for example, as an "African" Shonibare shows both a political and reverse side of identity.' (Diawara 2004). Furthermore, in the segment of her presentation entitled 'the headless colonials', Rall identifies the cheekily militant nature of the dummies dressed in Dutch wax cotton (2010: n.p.n.). In particular, Shonibare's large installation piece *Gallantry and Criminal Conversation*, which portrays a whole orgy of headless dummies, satirizes Victorian piety on the whole. Rall recognizes the headlessness as a violent 'postcolonial revenge'; a decapitation, and a representation of the colonizers as having no sense, being led not by their heads but by greed for gain (2010: n.p.n.).

The transtextuality touched upon above becomes increasingly intrinsic and complex as Shonibare begins to play not only with costume and dress history in this embrace of the 18th and 19th centuries and their signifiers of respectability and class, but also with the theory of 'The Other' as explicated by Edward Said, particularly as elaborated upon in *Culture and Imperialism*. Said associates the construct of culture with identity, explaining that it often simply serves to pit one country against another. He sees it as an arena, stage or battleground upon which ideological causes engage one another, vying for supremacy. He also identifies that it is often used as the opposite, a 'protective enclosure: check your politics at the door before you enter it' (1993: xiv). Shonibare challenges both of these functions by removing the power: he does this by removing the heads of the characters and, in the case of *Jane Austen and the Brontë Sisters*, he reduces them in size. In this way, he diminishes these figures from their position as foremost cultural symbols of English literature and injects the politics of colonialism as well by dressing them in the distinctly African Dutch wax cloth (Said 1993: 1). Here, Shonibare removes his gloves and wholeheartedly dives into the fray, encouraging the viewer to jump with him; but often his fight is against cultural conflict itself. Edward Said explains the need for this fight perfectly:

In time, culture comes to be associated, often aggressively, with the nation or state; this differentiates "us" from "them", almost always with some degree of xenophobia. Culture in this sense is a source of identity, and a rather combative one at that, as we see in recent "returns" to culture and tradition. These "returns" accompany rigorous codes of intellectual and moral behaviour that are opposed to the permissiveness associated with such relatively liberal philosophies as multiculturalism and hybridity (1993: xiii).

Yinka Shonibare on display, London 2005–2010

The year 2000 is repeatedly acknowledged as a golden year or turning point for Shonibare (Hynes & Picton 2001). His work was shown in a solo exhibition at the Camden Arts Centre (Fisher 2000); he contributed an installation piece in *Intelligence: New British Art* at Tate Britain, and displayed new digital work in the new Wellcome Wing of the Science Museum. His artwork's international scope was acknowledged as well: in 2000, he offered exhibitions in New York, Johannesburg and Rome and was selected to represent the UK in the following year's Venice Biennale. However London is the focal point for Shonibare, probably because it is the city upon which his work comments, and the city where he resides and creates. Shonibare has made public his allegiance to London on several occasions, but two questions need to be posed here: (1) why has London found Shonibare's art and its intellectual content so relevant? (2) why in this millennium so much more wholeheartedly than in the last? In other words, how far can the embrace be identified as the result of political waves or changes in London's cultural fabric, and how far the result of developments in Shonibare's work and ethos? An exploration of these questions will enable us to go some way towards establishing an answer to the 'militancy question'; analysing the changes in Shonibare's work in the context of a changing London and its institutions may help establish an understanding of his perceived mellowing in more recent years.[1]

In 1998, Shonibare won the Helen Hamlyn Foundation award of £30,000 which enabled him to focus on his creative work and, importantly, gain a far deeper understanding of the poststructuralist theories of semiotics, deconstruction and intertextuality. A self-professed student of Derrida, the next three years saw him producing a body of work that was increasingly complex in its play on meanings and in the conveyance of multiple, simultaneous messages. The exhibition *Diary of a Victorian Dandy* marks the beginning of this growth period and the exhibition *Dorian Gray* its culmination. After the success of 2000, Shonibare had some questions of his own to pose. *Dorian Gray*, a photographic series, explores his fear that becoming subsumed by the art world may be tantamount to being consumed by pride. Once again he placed himself in the frame, embracing the directness that the technique affords. During this period he began to adeptly fight the intellectual and social constructs of culture, class and race with easily readable intellectual constructs of his own. This can explain why Shonibare's work increased in prominence at this time, but was it the only reason?

At the beginning of this chapter it was noted that Yinka Shonibare's work is often described as excessive, a term even used by the artist himself. The bright vibrancy of the cloth acts as a signifier of Africanness, but the ornateness of the costuming is very much imbued with the excessiveness of western conspicuous consumption. Shonibare's interpretation offers up this consumption, but covers it with a semiotic layer of Africanicity which he has extracted and placed on the surface. This interaction between the two cultures has struck a chord with the 21st-century contemporary art world (Oguibe 1999).

Shonibare's early work uses this visual language to reinsert Africanness into the history of modernity. However after 2000, once the art world had fully embraced him, he no longer needed to continue reinserting Africa within his work. The work *was* the missing piece, not simply Africanness but hybridity itself, and thanks to the prominence of Shonibare's work and those who formulated the necessary postcolonial critique, museum curators were now ready to do the reinsertion. Shonibare, in collaboration with the curators, could begin to make a different type of statement. Before examining this, however, it is necessary to see what had happened to curators and their institutions, and how those changes were manifested in the early part of the last decade.

The year 2005 saw the academic and cultural mood in London experience one of its sporadic waves of high profile engagement with themes inspired by black criticism and postcolonial critique. This particular wave occurred in the wake of the Victoria & Albert Museum's major exhibition *Black British Style* (curated by Carol Tulloch in 2004) and the accompanying book, *Black Style* (Tulloch 2004) which would embolden the writings and inspire the academic explorations of undergraduate fashion and textiles students for years to come. A number of retrospective exhibitions at other galleries followed, all aiming to reappraise the collective memory of blackness and empire, particularly aiming to distinguish British and Caribbean histories from African American history while considering the relationships and similarities between the three. Two of the most prominent of these exhibitions were the Whitechapel Gallery's *Back to Black: Art, Cinema and the Racial Imaginary* (curated by Richard Powell, David A. Bailey and Petrine Archer-Straw) and the Michael McMillan exhibition *The West Indian Front Room* which caused a stir at the Geffrye Museum.

The Whitechapel's exhibition was the first of the decade to explicitly use Paul Gilroy's text *The Black Atlantic: Modernity and Double Consciousness* to bind the diaspora together as a unified theory and present it as a whole with many elements of shared history, while also identifying many areas where differences in national histories develop divergent ideologies and artworks (Gilroy 2002). McMillan can be compared with Shonibare as his installation also dealt directly with colonialism, imperialism and Britishness. This allowed Shonibare to reinsert cultural diversity into – and deconstruct established stories of – empire and 'home', rather than perpetuating them, as many have criticized McMillan for doing. The strength and uniqueness of Shonibare's use of Dutch wax became a primary vehicle for exploration, especially when examined in relation to the overtly plush but generically 'western' textiles used in the *Front Room* installation.

The year 2005 was important for London: it was also important for Shonibare. Just as the city was in the midst of embracing black criticism and multiculturalism, the artist who most championed these things was awarded an MBE. His acceptance of this award has been questioned repeatedly since then and he has been criticized for making a concession. Indeed, Shonibare's acceptance stands against his perceived militancy as it begs the question: after the postcolonial depictions of the headless colonials, after the questions raised in *Dorian Gray*, why would he accept the MBE and align himself with the power structure's colonial control?

Rachel Kent and her co-authors offer a reason for this in *Yinka Shonibare MBE* (2008). She suggests that it is his way of 'sticking two fingers up at the establishment', and this is a plausible, if unproven scenario. If there is one thing that is certain from all writings and interviews it is that Shonibare has no problem with labels. He uses them; they are the tools of his trade. What he despises is the rigidly categorizing effect they have when applied singly and without the choice of the recipient. Significantly, the label 'Member of the British Empire' was not thrust upon him: it was offered and he chose to accept it. He retained the agency in its application and it is agency that he cares about. This transferred the power back to him – by his standards, he has exercised as much power over his own identity by accepting as he would have by rejecting the award.

Furthermore the MBE completes Yinka Shonibare as his own work of art. He places importance on *dressing* his works, and on *naming* them. Similarly, in every photograph of himself, he is dressed exquisitely, often in brightly coloured suits like a postmodern dandy; a paragon of English eccentricity mixed effortlessly with dreadlocks, signifiers of an almost religious affiliation with Africa. Now he has named himself in the same way. His African name has been accompanied by the most British of honours and the task is complete. This is more than a joke, this is cultural hybridity completed and as such it becomes another weapon against cultural conflict in Shonibare's new type of militancy.

The bicentenury of British abolition

The year 2007, was important for London's culture and heritage institutions as it marked the 200th anniversary of the abolition of the British transatlantic slave trade. In this bicentenary year, Shonibare was thrust to the forefront of the London galleries' campaign to counteract the British government's established take on the abolition of the slave trade; one that failed to distinguish, for the most part, between the abolition of the *trade* in people from West Africa and the abolition of slavery as a practice across the British Empire, which did not cease until 1833 (Davidson 1961). More significantly, government-endorsed efforts at commemoration attributed the bulk of the glory to William Wilberforce, telling a familiar white, male and upper-middle-class history. This received and accepted story reached a mass audience by way of film: the blockbuster *Amazing Grace,* partially funded by the military and endorsed by Tony Blair's government, was marketed relentlessly and very widely viewed. The tactics employed by the galleries were exemplary. They did not put on separate blockbuster exhibitions, which would have paled into insignificance in comparison with the film, losing their message completely in the glare of bright lights. Instead they kept their permanent collections in place, acknowledging the fact that the received version of history will always exist – and they inserted trails within them. These trails depicted the people, stories, heroes and villains of slavery, empire and Britain that have been written out of history; that exist in the collections but remain held in archives, which schoolchildren never learn about, at least not as part of the national curriculum. In the National Portrait Gallery, Samuel Coleridge-Taylor was given his rightful place next to the other composers of his age, Olaudah Equiano was given pride of place as an abolitionist with William Wilberforce and Thomas Clarkson, Toussaint L'Ouverture and the Great Haitian slave revolt were credited for raising awareness of the horrors of slavery among people in Europe, and Queen Victoria's god-daughter Sara Forbes Bonetta was visually acknowledged on the Gallery's 19th-century floor. For the first time in the museum's history, a black ribbon ran through the Portrait Gallery, reinserted into the acknowledged annals of British history, if only for a limited time. This ribbon aimed at subtlety, but remained in stark visual contrast to the permanent collection, making it the most striking display point of the year. This poignancy is echoed in the same way as Shonibare's insertion of himself into the whitewashed historical scenes in *Diary of a*

Victorian Dandy. Here, he employed that familiar technique of 'powerful assertion of the right of the "other" to take centre stage'.

While the Portrait Gallery could make this stark visual intrusion by simply utilizing more of their permanent collection, the National Gallery and Victoria and Albert Museum (V&A) made the decision to push this idea of contrast and intrusion one step further by also including Shonibare's work in their *Scratch the Surface* and *Uncomfortable Truths* trails respectively. *Scratch the Surface* was a major feat of the National Gallery's interpretation department, not its curators.[2] It was a series of secondary wall text captions attached to two new acquisitions within the permanent collection, which aimed to 'contextualise the role of slavery in the lives of the two sitters'. The paintings were *Mrs Oswald* by Johann Zoffany (1763–64) and *Colonel Tarleton* by Sir Joshua Reynolds (1782). What made these so noticeable were the works created by Yinka Shonibare in response to the two paintings, *Colonel Tarleton and Mrs Oswald, Shooting*. By adding the shooting action, Shonibare also added violence and a tongue-in-cheek reference to the activities of the leisured classes, underlying their role in the countryside as types of predators.

The simultaneous exhibition *Uncomfortable Truths* at the V&A was, by comparison to the other two, an object-based exploration rather than one of portraiture. Its aim was to expose the slaving roots of the V&A's beautiful collection of 17th- to 19th-century tea cups, jewellery, cotton gowns, and other objects. It was accompanied by a conference entitled 'From Cane Field to Tea Cup' led and organized by the contemporary curator Zoe Whitley. The conference was inaugurated by Joanne Banham, who, significantly, had been a leader in the abolition-related events at the Portrait Gallery that year; a champion of the 'de-Wilberforcization' of the received history. The curator Whitley had just accepted the role of Head of Education at the V&A, and was delighted to be a part of *Uncomfortable Truths* – where the events, conference and exhibition demonstrated the importance of museum education within London's culture and heritage sector during this bicentenurial year of 2007. A trend to promote interruption and interpretation (whether verbal or visual) formed an important supplement to exhibitions and collections, and the exhibitions became integral to radicalization and/or reform of museum curatorial practice that continues to the present.

Therefore, it was no coincidence that Shonibare's work was chosen; it was supremely appropriate. What better work to illustrate a series of intrusions? Shonibare's effective visual invitations to the audience implored them to scratch beneath the surface of a whitewashed history, and in the process, become unafraid to face uncomfortable truths. The use of Dutch wax batik cloth and Shonibare's contemporaneity made the exhibits both striking and attractive to a wider audience. As stated earlier, the brightly coloured cloth forces the viewer to stop and question but importantly it does so with laughter, with excess and with beauty. Through this response to sensitive issues, London's galleries signalled that they were finally ready to laugh at themselves and their difficult social histories. Shonibare's work made fun not only of the class of people who had underwritten these galleries, but also of their excessive manner of living, in which the museums became complicit by transplanting and displaying the aristrocrats' luxurious living quarters. Shonibare's works, the *Victorian*

Philanthropist's Parlour (1996–97), and *Sir Foster Cunliffe, Playing* (2007) were placed in the V&A's Norfolk House Music Room. In signature Shonibare fashion, the name of the piece is significant. Sir Foster Cunliffe was the grandson of a Liverpool slave merchant. Positioning Cunliffe at play, posing with his rifle within the golden sumptuousness of the Music Room, not only intrudes on the audience's eye quite unapologetically but also makes evident that golden sumptuousness comes from violence. Placed in this way, Shonibare's work adeptly questions the material excess brought about by the slave trade as well as the social, political and cultural constructs designed to keep people across the empire locked in their respective social milieu, which inevitably leads to questions about class – a more universally inclusive category than race.

In 2010, the Tate establishment revisited and celebrated the work of Paul Gilroy through the major exhibition *Afro Modern: Journeys through the Black Atlantic* at Tate Liverpool, which was mirrored in London by a large-scale Chris Ofili retrospective at Tate Britain. In the same year Yinka Shonibare achieved his most prominent statement yet: *Nelson's Ship in a Bottle*, which remained on Trafalgar Square's fourth plinth until January 2012 (see Plate ix). In a poetic return, Carol Tulloch gave an address at the Afro Modern symposium in Liverpool. It is clear that Shonibare is also questioning primitivism, or the way in which the African continent is left out of the Eurocentric history of modernity and is persistently represented as both ritualistic and backward-looking.

Conclusion: A new type of militancy?

For a large part of his career Shonibare's work has not been considered as 'heavily militant' by most definitions. Nevertheless his work has, up to the present, remained heavily political. Primarily, his work engages with the politics of globalization and consumption. Perhaps it does not critique it directly, but it encourages the viewer to do so. Courtesy of the Dutch wax's busy brightness and Shonibare's endless layering, ruffling and mixing of the textiles, his work has been repeatedly described as excessive (Hynes & Picton 2001: 60). Here, it becomes a commentary on conspicuous consumption that has accompanied times of plenty throughout British and European history, although other parts of the globe have achieved their own levels of opulence (Smith 2002). With the British, it is Victorian emphasis on the decorative arts that comes to mind. Here, Shonibare's work remains importantly in tune with the public consciousness of London and the firm but subtle resistance that is most effective not merely against the establishment but against colonialism's most harmful legacies: binary oppositions, stereotypes, division and cultural conflict.

It has been said that Shonibare's early work was far more fervent and militant than his later work and indeed his acceptance of the MBE in 2005 can be read superficially as an admission of defeat: a hypocritical embrace of the establishment once that establishment had embraced him. However, such a conclusion suggests an ignorance of Shonibare's body of work. Starting with his use of the Dutch wax batik textile, loaded with its infinite lexicon of signifiers, and his thought-provoking subject matter, piece names and tableau composition and, finally, the way in which his artworks have been displayed in museums and galleries between 2005 and 2010, Shonibare's work rings true to his activism. Shonibare's work has mutated and become more complex since the year 1998, mutating his modes of protest. His work now stands and speaks for itself; its surroundings have become its message; he contravenes spaces that once evoked imperial might (such as the Music Room at the V&A, the National Gallery's atrium or Trafalgar Square's fourth plinth) into their opposites. This is a far more effective form of 'militancy'. Here, the very positioning of his work does the fighting; the role of the pieces themselves is to mock the establishment and convey the message.

This chapter has highlighted how Shonibare has dealt with the fact of blackness head on, not rejecting conflict, while also recognizing that participating in conflict, against the roles of essentializing stereotypes, fuels the struggle. Instead, Shonibare focuses on deconstructing the conflict itself. In accepting his MBE and combining it with, not juxtaposing it against, his African name and visibility as a dreadlocked, black British man and artist, he has also deconstructed its meaning.

If there is one conclusion reached by this chapter, it is that Shonibare has focused on pushing the boundaries of deconstruction and intertextuality in order to encourage independent critique in his audience. His work fragments and deconstructs, then probes the mind of the viewer. The cloth of Dutch wax is a tool for this, as are the historical references that make his tableaux readable and their titles pithy. He mocks sideways but he need not directly comment. In accepting the MBE he has, arguably, simply done this again very effectively – provoking his audience into dialogue. By being himself: a black Briton, a British Nigerian, a 21st-century Victorian Dandy and now an adamantly anti-colonial Member of the British Empire, he is only being what he always claimed to be – a cultural hybrid – and is embodying his subtle message of resistance against stereotype and enforced identity (Atha 1998; Halliburton 1999). This chapter has shown that the focus on subtlety and audience education through provocation of independent thought is arguably what makes Shonibare's work so relevant to the new, education and interpretation-focused method of presenting history in London's museums. As Shonibare concludes during an interview in 2010:

> Culture has a role to play. In a diverse society people have to find a way of being together, and that can only come from understanding other cultures. Otherwise, you're just fighting for space. But I'm from London, now. I've been here for 30 years. In Lagos, I would feel like a foreigner. The city has had such an impact on my work. If I'd lived somewhere else, I'm certain that my career would have evolved very differently. And I love it. I love what you could call "vindaloo Britishness". It's a mixed-up thing. You hear it in British music, and you taste it in British food. This purity notion is nonsense, and I cherish that (Cooke: n.p.n.).

His trademark Dutch wax is, he says, a metaphor for interdependence and thus, perhaps, a metaphor for city life as well: 'We all pinch from one another. We take what we like, and in doing so, we are, whether we like it or not joined together in one great and vibrant web' (Cooke 2010).

References

Atha, C. (November 1998). 'Diary of a Victorian Dandy', *Artists Newsletter Magazine*, p. 18.

Bhabha, H. K. (1994). *The Location of Culture*. London: Routledge.

Cooke, R. (2010). Yinka Shonibare's *Nelson's Ship in a Bottle*. *The Observer*, http://www.yinkashonibarembe.com/resources/content/articles/40/61/OBSERVER%202010.pdf, p. 6. Accessed 22 November 2012.

Davidson, B. (1961). *The African slave trade: Precolonial history from 1450-1850*. Boston: Little, Brown & Company.

Diawara, M. (ed.) (2004). *Independence Cha Cha: The Art of Yinka Shonibare*. Museum Boijmans Van Beuningen Rotterdam: NAi Publishers.

Fanon, F. (1967). *Black Skin, White Masks* (trans. C. L. Markmann). New York: Grove Press.

Fisher, J. (2000). 'Yinka Shonibare: Camden Arts Centre, London', *Artforum International*, 39: 1, p. 186.

Gilroy, P. (2001). *Against race: Imagining political culture beyond the color line*. Cambridge, MA: Harvard University Press.

———— (2002). *The Black Atlantic: Modernity and double consciousness*. Cambridge, MA: Harvard University Press.

Hall, S., & Jacques, M. (eds) (1989). *New Times: the changing face of politics in the 1990s*. London: Lawrence & Wishart.

Halliburton, R. (1 February 1999). 'Why Mr Darcy You're Black', *The Independent Weekly*.

Hynes, N., & Picton, J. (2001). 'Yinka Shonibare: Re-dressing history', *African Arts*, autumn, pp. 60–73.

Kent, R., Hobbs, R. C., & Downey, A. (2008). *Yinka Shonibare, MBE. Exhibition Companion to the first retrospective at the Museum of Contemporary Art and the Brooklyn Museum of Art*. New York: Museum of Contemporary Art and the Brooklyn Museum of Art.

Maxwell, R. (2003). 'Sari to Sarong: 500 years of Indian and Indonesian textile exchange, a National Gallery of Australia Exhibition', *Textile Fibre Forum [Textile and Fibre Arts of Australia]*, 70, p. 56.

Oguibe, O. (1999). 'Finding A Place: Nigerian Artists in the Contemporary Art World', *Art Journal*, 58: 2, pp. 31–41.

Rall, D. N. (1 July 2010). *Costume & conquest: The impacts of European interventions on garments and textiles [unpublished]*. Paper presented at the Popular Culture Australasia–New Zealand [PopCAANZ], Sydney.

Relph, M., & Irwin, R. (2010). *African wax print: A textile journey*. London: African Fabric Co.

Said, E. (1993). *Culture and imperialism*. New York: Knopf.

Shonibare, Y. (2012). 'Yinka Shonibare, MBE'. http://www.yinkashonibarembe.com/. Accessed 25 August 2009.

Smith, W. D. (2002). *Consumption and the making of respectability, 1600–1800*. London: Routledge.

Spée, M. (1982). *Traditional and modern batik* (trans. I. Diefenbach). Kenthurst, NSW: Kangaroo Press.

Tulloch, C. (2004). *Black Style*. London: V&A Publications.

Notes

1 Another reason why the year 2000 can be identified as a point of explosion for Shonibare is that the 1990s had brought with it a significant shrinkage of the world with the development of the Internet as a world-wide, civilian resource. With much of the world networked at the turn of the millennium and the emergence of broadband for increased speed of access, the ethos of being a 'citizen of the world' became available to those living outside the developed world.

2 See http://www.nationalgallery.org.uk/about-us/press-and-media/press-and-media/press-releases/scratch-the-surface.

Chapter 9

Costume and conquest: Introducing a proximity framework for post-war impacts on textile and fashion

Denise N. Rall

Introduction

Changes in regime have often dictated changes in costume. These alterations in clothing are usually arbitrary, but are put into place to serve a variety of purposes. Such changes are often incorporated into the indigenous culture as 'native' practice. Two examples suffice: the first occurred after the Manchu takeover of the Ming dynasty in China in 1644. The Manchu leader Dorgan, as a way of enforcing his power, had all Chinese men shave their foreheads and wear their hair in a long, single plait down their back (Spence 1990: 39–40). At the same time, long, loose-fitting robes were replaced with high, tight-fitting collars on shorter jackets. In turn, these imposed changes became associated with the stereotypical 'Chinaman' portrayed in early western cinema (Dong 2007). With one costume change, the centuries-old Chinese civilization with a wealth of sartorial tradition was distilled into a single costume, enacted in the mid-17th century.

A second example offers a similar perspective on the patchwork nature of so-called indigenous dress. In this event, a shipload of British bowler hats, named after the Southwark firm of feltmakers (Baclawski 1995), was bound for Argentina. But due to unfavourable weather, the boat reputedly foundered on the coast of Ecuador. Rather than fulfilling its destined function as a 'best hat' for the middle-class businessmen of Buenos Aires, the bowler was adopted by the Ecuadorian village women as part of their national costume, where it remains today. Even though other versions of this story persist, it supports the point (see Miller 1993).

These two incidents clearly indicate how the label of 'indigenous' becomes compromised and fragmented as everyday clothing is reconfigured following the dictates of ascendant cultural practices through military conquest or trade. Above, the Chinese plait and the English bowler hat demonstrate how conquest – in battle or in trade – becomes embedded within local fabrics and practices. The change in costume remains as evidence, and that very process allows for the construction of a *textile narrative* (Costello & Rall 2013) that continues to circulate through the cultural economy of garment design and construction. Some anthropologists have recently specialized in evaluating the impacts of military invasion on 'post war' cultures, although none have taken up the specific problem of addressing the subsequent changes in textile and clothing (Culbertson 2006).

Case 1: Textile and clothing in Peru

The brutal side of empire can be found anywhere in the world, in particular, Africa, North America, Central and South Americas, and throughout the Asia Pacific region. As a consequence of European invasion most native peoples experience changes in their dress. A salient example comes from the Spanish invasion of the Inkan[1] empire. John V. Murra notes in 'Cloth and its function in the Inka state', that, as decoded from archaeological remains, the empire was constructed and maintained on the production, use and trading in textiles (1989: 275–302). From this, the rise and subsequent fall of the Inkan empire provides an exemplar for how culture practices became embedded in cloth, and what transpires when those practices are disrupted by military and commercial interventions.

The Inkan empire came to dominate an enormous part of South America, estimated at over one million square kilometres. In a similar fashion to other of the so-called pre-Columbian empires in the Americas, the rise of the Inkas was swift. In just less than 100 years they achieved dominance over the local Indian populations, who had previously clustered in autonomous clans abetted by inaccessibility of the rugged terrain (Mann 2005: 69–75).

The Inkan rulers, from their capital near the present-day Cusco were served by a well-organized bureaucracy, an excellent road system, and a common language, along with a large populace which flourished without deprivation. This empire was increased through the re-settlement of outsiders into previously established villages, maintaining their own distinctive culture and dress, although all were required to communicate in *Runa Sumi*. Through internal conflict, and later the Spanish incursion, this massive enterprise was demolished after about 100 years.

Following a series of bitter internal battles among Inkan factions, the victor Atawallpa was defeated at Cajamarca by the Spaniard Francisco Pizarro with 168 men and 62 horses in 1532 (Mann 2005). Note that what is often omitted from the dramatic retelling is that the Spaniards also had four cannons, along with their muskets. With further insult, Pizarro's army suffered not a single casualty. This remains one of the most terrible defeats of a highly civilized indigenous peoples by a foreign conqueror, known to history by their Spanish name, *conquistadors*. The Spanish were only one of the major European colonizers (e.g., British, French, Portuguese, Dutch and Belgian) and later, joined by the European Americans; but the name remains.

As many historians now agree, history has a slightly more complicated tale to tell (Denevan 1976; Dobyns 1983, 2004; Dobyns & Doughty 1976; Lovell 1992). Today, scholars concur that the Inkas lost their empire through a combination of inbreeding, infighting among lords for turf, and the top-down organization of its military generals, as well as the royal lineage based on inter-marriage between brothers and sisters (Mann 2005: 86). Further, the Europeans were never so successful as when spreading epidemic diseases. Prior to Pizarro's attack, smallpox was brought by early explorers and the resultant losses were devastating among those in the small, top-heavy ruling class (see Mann 2005: 86–92; citing Dobyns and others). After invasion, subsequent waves of smallpox, typhus, influenza, diphtheria and measles arrived from visiting Europeans travelling from remote settlements elsewhere, and were spread by explorers, soldiers, traders, government officials and missionaries. Dobyns and others have concluded that epidemics probably killed nine out of ten of the local population (Cook & Lovell 1992; Dobyns 1983).

The multiple vectors of destruction are somewhat immaterial – of primary importance here is the story behind costume and conquest.

Locating the marks of conquest

In the case of the Inkas, it is not so easy to trace the marks of conquest because of the patchwork nature of the various incursions. The first incursion was the subjugation of the previous indigenous populations by the invading Inkas. After many civil wars and territorial disputes, the Inkas finally held the large land mass for which they are known today, symbolized by their most famous temple at Machu Picchu. The second incursion, described above, was by the Spaniards in 1532. To distinguish these two conquests, Edward Luttwak's (1976) seminal study of ancient Rome delineated two types of empires: *territorial* and *hegemonic*:

> Territorial empires directly occupy territories with their armies, throw out the old rulers, and annex the land. In hegemonic empires, the internal affairs of conquered areas remain in the hands of their original rulers, who become vassals. Territorial empires are tightly controlled but costly to maintain; hegemonic empires are inexpensive to maintain, because the original local rulers incur the costs of administration, but the loose tie[s] … encourage rebellion. Every conquest-minded state is a mixture of both … (Mann 2005: 71, citing Luttwak 1976).

This typology explains the differences between the Inkan conquest of native Peruvians and subsequent Spanish and Portuguese conquests in the Americas. The Inkas built a *hegemonic* empire, which retained local customs, including weaving, but enforced other hierarchies, particularly the forced adoption of a common language. Therefore, the indigenous populace varied greatly from district to district, and the archaeology indicates that people maintained distinct patterning in their clothing (Tidball 1969). Further, the technology of textile continued as part of their way of life, much more than was simply necessary to produce clothing and blankets. In contrast, the Spanish invasion was to establish a territorial empire, with its subsequent impact on all aspects of Inkan life, including textiles and clothing.

The first example of how textile was embedded in cultural practice is the use of knotted cords for record-keeping (Locke 1923; Quilter & Urton 2002). The use of the *khipu* (or *quipu*), or the knot-record, is the only knot-based form of human literacy that has been located in the archaeological record. For a long time, they were assumed to be meaningless, as scholars could not decipher them. Initially, these knotted ropes challenged Spanish assumptions about written records, and they were later burned as idolatrous objects, leaving only six hundred remnants for present-day scholars to decode (Mann 2005: 345). Today, it is understood that the *khipu* had a number of functions, comprising record- and bookkeeping, and possibly storytelling. Recently, Gary Urton has worked out a decoding system based on various computer models that suggest the knotting system could provide more than twice the number of 'information units' offered in the Egyptian hieroglyphs (see the Khipu Database Project from Urton & Brezine 2009).

Both pre- and post-Inkans wore elaborate outfits woven and stitched with both cotton and wool. They used spun fibres in their knotted record-keeping; overall, fibre was absolutely central to the Andean way of life. Their metallurgy was adapted to produce ornaments not weapons, for which 'they preferred fibre' (Mann 2005). Therefore, boats were built of knotted reeds, and weapons were constructed from woven slings designed to toss rocks. Even their soldiers wore armour of densely overlapping bits of textiles, woven as finely as 500 threads per inch (Leuchtman 1993: 254–59).

Further commentary will be offered in a later section, 'Textile and clothing: the micro-level of analysis'.

Case 2: Lamine Kouyaté and XULY.Bët

An example provided by contemporary fashion is that of designers such as Lamine Kouyaté. As Victoria Rovine reports, Kouyaté from the mid-1990s began to connect 'the cutting edge of fashion' with 'the frayed edges of the past', further, with a 'suggestion that [his] garments might also contain a broad cultural critique from the perspective of Africa and other non-Western locales' (2005: 215).

Lamine Badian Kouyaté was born in Mali, but due to upheavals in the capital, his family relocated to Paris when he was 14, then to Dakar in Senegal when he was 16, where he remained until he was 24, before moving back to France to study architecture and then fashion design, thereafter moving to Paris. His brand, XULY.Bët was named for a term derived from Senegalese slang, roughly translated as 'voyeur'. This idiom allowed him to peel back 'the exterior to reveal the often uneven surfaces layered beneath' which he emphasized in his use of recycled garments as well as 'his presentation style of exposing the seams and past histories of his garments' (Rovine 2010: 742). Various techniques were employed to expose 'past histories', including the dissection and re-use of flea-market clothing, turning used garments inside out, and retaining their original labels, over which he placed his own brand marks (Rovine 2010: 742).

In 1993, his models strode the catwalk wearing Band-Aids on their faces and bodies. Kouyaté explained the bandages as traces of the struggles these bodies have endured: 'People have gone through the jungle of life and these are to cover the scars where they need to be bandaged up' (Spindler 1993: 13). Victoria Rovine continues, 'XULY.Bët's recycled garments might also be read as subversive, or at least as an astute testing of the limits and the logic of the fashion system. Kouyaté reshapes the detritus of Paris, a Western economic and political center and former seat of colonial power in Mali and Senegal' (2005: 226). Here, Africa is viewed as a place forced to make use of the leftovers from the West, even in fashion. Kouyaté's approach uses the refuse of the colonizers as a point of departure – for a defiant, postcolonial refurbishment. Previously, Richard Wilk has written that fashion must resist the historical narrative of colonialism, and reject terms like 'primitive, backward, and underdeveloped' (1990: 84).

As Wilk suggests, one can resist colonialization by stepping outside its system: 'only when people obtain and consume objects outside the flow of colonial time do they challenge and resist the social order of the colonial system' (Wilk 1990: 89). Kouyaté's garments reinvent the 'detritus' of western second-hand clothing, to step outside of colonial time, 'to create garments that are global in their references and distinctly contemporary in style'. He then employs his garments as 'allusions to the work of identity production in a globally oriented culture' suggesting 'that the old and the new, the Western and the Africa, are in a perpetual state of flux' (Rovine 2005: 227). The illumination at the end of this process is a re-working of past cultural invasions. This process opens up the opportunity to allow contemporary African-European fashion to write its own cultural narrative; what Kopytoff names the 'cultural biography' of things (Kopytoff 1986: 90). Kouyaté's re-fashioning of second-hand garments allows him (and others) to re-write the story of historical conflict, to give clothing a new 'cultural biography' – even if the new storytelling includes the wearing of bandages as witness to invasions of the past.

Far from voyeurism, Kouyaté's fashion design resonates as an exorcism of the postcolonial.

Framing post-conquest textile and fashion

The previous chapter's discussion of the textile artworks of British-Nigerian Yinka Shonibare, along with the two case studies cited above – the Spanish conquest of Peru, followed by Rovine's study of Lamine Kouyaté – have described how conflict becomes embedded, and also resisted, in textile and costume. These are very different stories, but they each explore the conflict between indigenous practice as it faces dominant aspects of western aesthetics. The Peruvian example provides a classic study of the impacts of European invasion, while the example of the African designer reinterprets colonialism not only as an Africa vs the West conflict, but within the flow of globalized commodities.

As evidence from the archaeological record appeared, researchers were led to re-evaluate the role that textile and design played in establishing cultural dominance. Over forty years ago, anthropologists began to analyse how cultures interact with textiles and clothing (Cordwell & Schwartz 1973). Identity, gender, status and wealth have always been expressed through clothing and adornment. Breaking down these elements into coherent systems of meaning have varied between approaches offered in the sociology of fashion (Kawamura 2007), material culture (Küchler & Miller 2005), history and fashion theory (Vincent 2009), art history (Hollander 1993), interpretive analyses (Wilson [1985] 2003), and literary criticism, such as the semiotic work of Roland Barthes (1983). Recently, eco-criticism has come to the fore in fashion theory (Brown 2010). Dedicated academic journals, such as the series *Critical Studies in Fashion & Beauty* from Intellect Ltd, have carried this discussion forward (2011–present). Here, the present volume explores the issues of identity, gender, military fashion, along with military conquest and colonization by religion and commerce as they intersect with fashion and textile.

This chapter now begins to explore the reasoning to develop an analytical framework to deal with such disparate elements. It starts with a set of cultural practices that engage in the production of textiles and clothing, of necessity, from strictly indigenous sources (wool, cotton, linen, fur, etc.). At the next level, decisions are made about the use of garments, as clothing and adornment attain status and come under various systems of control. The 'lace tax' in Great Britain is an oft-cited example (Vincent 2009: 28–30). At the highest level, fashion becomes globalized, and widely (but unevenly) distributed throughout the world. At the extreme, clothing and garments are no longer tied to local practice, but to a globalized market – even the poorest people in the world recognize the 'swoosh' trademark of Nike either from the original design or from replicas. In the modern age (see below) attire has become a way for individuals to express themselves in society by making a 'personal choice', however much that choice has been influenced by market forces.

Such a framework is difficult to locate, as the elements are so diverse. There is the necessity to seek a large-scale framework to provide the appropriate measures for analysis. It is also important that this scale can work across, and between, cultures. Further, this scale can offer the opportunity for mobility between levels.

A tiered proximity analysis: Micro, meso, macro

Joseph A. Schumpeter (1883–1950) was an economic theorist who sought to develop an underpinning for economics through the democratic capitalist, rather than Marxist, traditions. While at Harvard University in the 1930s, he differentiated his work from other strictly mathematical economists and developed a set of theories which led to the new field called evolutionary economics (Dopfer & Potts 2008). However, as his micro-meso-macro framework easily explains multiple levels of social interactions, it was adopted by many social scientists. In parallel to these seminal economic theories the social ecological model was developed and employed by those in the field of psychology and child development (Bronfenbrenner 1979).

This model of a tiered ranking of proximity between the elements under discussion – textiles, clothing, society – is key to this study of fashion and the military, because it facilitates the comparison of many types of simultaneous interactions over multiple levels.

An example of such an analysis at work is that of the anthropologist David Hakken, who very successfully laid out his study of social relations in cyberspace (Hakken 1999: 8–9).

The micro-level implies the closest level of relations, involving direct interaction between individuals. At the meso-level, the interaction was at the group level: communities interacting with each other, such as e-democracy campaigns, and so on. Finally, Hakken considered the macro-level of relations, such as how nations interact with one another, taking into account that the Internet is a transnational phenomenon. Hakken's overall concern was the promotion of true democracy. In other fields, sociologists have often used this type of proximal framework to explicate a number of social phenomena, as outlined on the Applied Sociology website.[2]

Textile and clothing: The micro-level of analysis

Naturally, the micro-level reflects a closeness in social relations. In the first instance, this includes the closeness of the textile, as product, to the textile producer. On the surface, this is classical Marxism, but there are further nuances to be examined here. The closeness of the product to the primary producer could be signficant, but it is the close proximity of the relationship between textile production, the textiles as products, and the local 'way of life' – i.e., cultural significance – which matters here. The Inkan empire is rather an extreme example, in that power within the empire was legitimized through furnishing and controlling vast warehouses of textiles (Murra 1989, as above). Likewise, textiles were employed to maintain the empire's written records (see Figure 1).

Many experts have commented on the physical and cultural durability of weaving methods associated with pre-Inka Peru. Andean weaving retains the legacy of previous civilizations (Bauer 2001). In fact, their weaving methods were developed and refined to the point where the familiar four-stick weaving that is practised throughout the Americas (today, often for tourist goods) can be traced to pre-Inkan artefacts (Tidball 1969). The anachronistic traces of local practice in weaving goes further: today's tourists prefer textiles with 'authentic' or pre-colonial patterning (Anon. n.d.).

The argument here is that the Inkan empire and its peoples held a micro-relationship to their textile production, as the textiles themselves underlined all aspects of their cultural practices and institutions: government, religion, trade and commerce, and record-keeping. Of course, textiles were used for garments – civilian, ceremonial, royal and military. Again, the stress is not on closeness of the producer-production relationship, but rather on the proximity of textile and weaving to every aspect of the indigenous culture.

To comprehend the changes on costume imposed by the Spanish conquest, the discussion needs to evaluate the role of missionaries and clerical workers. Indeed, almost all of the source documents concerning the native Indian and Inkan ways of life were provided by clerics associated with the Roman Catholic church. However, the two worked hand in hand: as noted above, when the Spanish bookkeepers challenged the record keeping of the local scribes, as these were deemed 'idolatrous', the scribes lost their indigenous means of recording numbers.

Textile and clothing: The meso-level of analysis

The meso-level takes us a step further away from immediate local practice. Any interaction that brings distance into the equation (distance being definitively postcolonial) 'opens up' an opportunity for intervention. Institutions of all kinds, whether educational, governmental, religious or military, force the participants to act in ways that benefit the institution rather than the individual. The meso-level offers the platform from which an outside cultural practice becomes the 'new norm.' In regards to clothing, once those practices are disrupted due to internal or external conflict, changes come to the wardrobe, but also to the very fabric (sic) of society (Küchler & Miller 2005).

As Jones and Stallybrass comment:

> We need to understand the animatedness of clothes, their ability to "pick up" subjects, to mold and shape them both physically and socially – to constitute subjects through their power as material memories … clothing is a worn world: a world of social relations put upon the wearer's body (2000: 2–3).

Indeed, the Spanish imposed their own 'world of social relations' after invasion, as former traditions in the society were destabilized. Indigenous weaving practices were generally maintained on the local level, but the colour, shape and style of the clothing reveals significant variation. Robert Harrold notes that while local weaving continued the traditional Inkan designs and colours, skirts changed to black. The adoption of black is an unusual colour in the Andes, but 'the use of black has been attributed to mourning for the last Inca ruler' ([1988] 1999: 242). In the countryside, skirts were mid-calf in length, allowing for easier movement when working the land, and lifting the skirt from soil and mud (see Figure 1).

A clear example of post-missionary clothing is shown in a photograph, dated 1934, from the French collection *Ethnic Style: History and Fashion* (Geoffroy-Schneiter 2001: 128). Here, a peasant woman of the Combapatan Indians wears an almost floor-length skirt, following the requirement to add 'Christian decency' to her dress. The peplum, shawl collar and deep cuffs appear in the abbreviated jacket, similar in appearance to the tight-waisted, short jacket of a riding habit (Arnold 1999). Overall, with the exception of the woven details, the effect is that of a 'civilized' style of western dress that became associated with women on the edge of an established frontier (Hansen 2010: 156). Likewise, the hat maintains a broad brim, but rounded in the crown, and ornamented with a bow tied in the hat-band. To conclude, while the style of dress is significantly western in appearance, the shawl retains two significant details that tie it to the Inkan or pre-Inkan period. The shawl itself is worn slightly over one shoulder, with a deep triangle shape that resembles the ubiquitous Central and South American poncho. Further, the fine detail of the woven or crocheted edging on both shawl and cuffs recalls the style of pre-conquest weaving work (see Figure 2).

Niall Ferguson, in his comprehensive book *Civilization: The West and the Rest*, notes the following:

Figure 1: Illustration by Phillada Legg, from Harrold, R., & Legg, P. ([1999] 1988). *Folk Costumes of the World*. London: Octopus Publishing. p. 242.

Figure 2: Example of post-missionary clothing worn by a peasant woman of the Combapatan Indians, 1934, from Geoffroy-Schneiter, B. (2001). *Ethnic Style: History and Fashion* (trans. D. Dusinberre). New York: Assouline Publishing. p. 128.

In the mountains of the Andes, the Quechua women still wear their brightly coloured dresses and shawls and their little felt hats, pinned at jaunty angles and covered with tribal insignia. Except that these are not traditional Quechua clothes at all. The dresses, shawls and hats are in fact of Andalusian origin and were imposed by the Spanish Viceroy Francisco de Toledo in 1572, in the wake of Túpac Amuru's defeat … what Quechuan women wear nowadays is a combination of these earlier garments with the clothes they were ordered to wear by their Spanish masters (2011: 197).

Therefore, the meso-level provides the pathway through which invasive cultural institutions are embedded in the construction and appearance of local garments. And more significant than the production and decoration of garments from traditional or non-traditional methods is the imposition of westernized social relations embedded in particular forms of dress.

An Andean woman would have no practical use for a European style of 'riding coat' (see Figure 2)[3], as the steepness of the mountain pathways necessitated travel by foot, with loads carried by llamas. Horses were introduced by the Spanish, but they were difficult to use in the highlands, as they could not navigate the mountain roads (Mann 2005: 85). So the imposition of western-style clothing was an ornamental layer that served no purpose, other than to show the wearer's obedience to conventions that were shaped by the religious and social values of the Spanish.

Examples of useless adaptations abound, particularly as to styles of clothing. However, anachronisms remain from the micro-level, too. The patterns and colours of traditional Andean weaving retains the legacies of previous civilizations: while somewhat reduced, the weaving still shows textile work at the micro-level, indicating a close proximity to traditional methods. Note that an interdigitation takes place, where remnants of indigenous practice are embedded in the colonizers' clothing (see Figure 2). As demonstrated above, artists and designers such as Yinka Shonibare and Lamine Badian Kouyaté would later problematize these vestigial remnants in their work.

Textile and clothing: Slippages at meso-level

On the meso-level, as indicated above, it becomes evident that foreign institutions have imposed their own traditions on local practice. But this is rarely a straightforward exercise. As Yinka Shonibare and Lamine Kouyaté suggest, there is often resistance, such as the wearing of black for the lost Inkan empire. Jones and Stallybrass continue this argument that clothing 'materializes identity' but, 'clothes are detachable, [in] that they can move from body to body. That is precisely their danger and their value: they are bearers of identity ... even as they confuse social categories' (2000: 5).

To cement their conquest of Peru the Spanish encouraged rapid intermarriage between the native Indians, Europeans and Africans (who were brought to the colony as slaves), and this ultimately led to a caste system (Root 2010: 470). As Charles Mann reports, the Spanish fear of the increasing population of 'mixed' peoples included sartorial policies:

> In the second half of the sixteenth century, Spanish governments began restricting mixed people, forbidding them from carrying weapons, becoming priests, practicing prestigious trades (silk making, glove making, needle making) and serving in most government positions ...
> *This also became codified in clothing.* Afro-European women were not allowed to wear Indians clothes. Afro-European women were not allowed to wear Spanish-style

gold jewelry or the elegant embroidered cloaks called *mantas* ... (Mann 2011: 316, emphasis added).

Note that the prestigious occupations, besides government service, all centred on textiles and garment-making, so silk, gloves, and even needles were restricted. This salient example demonstrates slippages in the meso-level. First, the Spanish invaders imposed western-style dress on the Indians, in order to produce a 'civilizing' effect. That, along with encouraged interbreeding, significantly altered the social relations between clothing and those clothed. After a short period, perhaps less than a decade, this 'civilizing' of costume became viewed as a threat to Spanish dominion. Therefore, the meso-level adjusted to a new set of social relations – that of distancing the mixed peoples from their conquerors, rather than the earlier attempts to narrow the gap between them.

Textile and clothing: The macro-level of analysis

At first glance, the macro-level of analysis is part and parcel of the process of globalization. Today, most people wear textiles and garments that have no close proximity to their producers – excepting elite home-made garments (Griffen 2003). In 2003, Betsy Greer coined the term *craftivism* (Greer 2007 and elsewhere) in protest about globalization, as well as inequities in a number of timely issues including health care for victims of AIDS, environmental policies, multi-national corporations and child labour, and so forth (Rall & Costello 2010: 91–92). The precepts of eco-fashion, and eco-criticism of fashion, argue that the fashion system must be rebuilt to remain an ethical exercise (Tseëlon 2011). These critiques are important, but this discussion of conquest and its impacts suggest that other factors come into play.

Roland Barthes, in *The Fashion System*, grounds this system in the necessity of 'proposing a model' that will 'circulate Fashion broadly as a *meaning*' (1983: 10, emphasis original). As has been fully explored by Ferguson (see the chapter entitled 'Consumption'), fashion has indeed circulated, to the degree that 'most people around the world dress in much the same way: the same jeans, the same sneakers, the same T-shirts' (2011: 197). That this matches global trends in worldwide consumption of the same manufactured goods is an argument easily made.[4] But other considerations should not be left out of the picture. Virginia Postrel makes much the same argument about the interconnectedness amongst as she states in the subtitle of her book, 'commerce, culture and consciousness' (2003). However, Postrel then builds the case for a chosen aesthetic control: 'the more our bodies become subject to design ... the more responsibility we face not only for who we are and how we act but for how we appear' (Lehrman, citing Postrel 2003). Here lies part of the groundwork to present a macro-level of clothing and textile: a place where meaning is negotiated, not *outside* of commerce but from an aesthetic narrative that coalesces beyond clothing as permeated with a particular time and place.

In her seminal essay, *The modernization of fashion*, Anne Hollander carefully builds the argument for re-grounding the system of fashion as an aesthetic system. It is important to quote her argument at length:

> The conscious modernization of fashion has required reviving the ancient idea that clothes are as fundamentally interesting as art itself, even from a wholly formal and not just a social point of view ... there are non-modern societies for which this has always been true, where dress is the chief art, using living bodies in conjunction with other media, perhaps none of them cloth, to create meaningful and perfectly integrated artifacts out of individuals. But if dress were going to be seen as ... aesthetically serious for modern society, then changeable, dynamic form in fashion would have to acquire an authority like that of form in modern art with an analogous prestige.
>
> The route to such prestige lay through the increasingly important realm of modern design. With the advance of modern aesthetic ideals during the last two centuries ... [design] began to seem less like merely providing trivial ornaments or practical tools, and more like finding an authentic medium for personal aesthetic expression, even for *collective moral expression* (Hollander 1992: 27, emphasis added).

There could be many objections to her argument, in particular, the use of the word 'modern' which Hollander firmly ties first to formal, then social, semi- and post-industrial practices. This is a careful construction of how to reconstitute solid ground under the seductive, 'anything goes' dilemma which fashion currently debates (Horyn 2011). This search for a collective aesthetic then gains momentum:

> With the establishment of serious interest in design, the way was even further opened for an aesthetics of mass production ... suitable to modern democratic ideas, and consequently suitable to modern dress ... part of a generally profitable and differently creative scheme of commercial design and even industrial production, without losing its aesthetic honor. The attractiveness of pure form in clothes, like that in cars or telephones, could determine their success in the marketplace (Hollander 1992: 27–28).

As with her later work, *Sex and Suits* (1994), Hollander tells the tale of the modern men's suit as the signal demonstration of modernization in clothing, starting after the 12th century, where 'men followed the path first indicated by fitted armor, continuing to articulate the body' (1992: 29). This increase in tailoring became widespread in 'post-Napoleanic Europe and the young United States' as the suit took on a formal simplicity, based on 'proportionate measurements, which permitted its multiple production with no loss of integrity (1992: 31). The military plays its part – in the US, ready-to-wear began with pre-cut garments, cut in hundreds to be made up for uniforms during the war of 1812 (Hollander 1992: 31). These pre-cut manufacturing processes were then employed in clothing the civilian populations.

In Hollander's analysis, women's clothing took longer to modernize, but it eventually happened, as, 'the key to classic modern design for female dress was seen to lie in the Neoclassic method of masculine tailoring, the creation of an intelligible bodily envelope out of inventively cut fabric shapes, something that revealed its own structure along with that of the body' (1992: 33). As above, the story of fitted garments includes the story of war as the technical innovations from British tailors were used to serve the ready-made garment industry (1992: 31). Her argument continues as the narrative of fashion is circumvented with 'the manifold expressive material of a postmodern world' (1992: 33). So, Hollander acknowledges postmodernism but states emphatically that the tailored suit, as a formal and social structure, is embedded in social conventions, and will continue its popularity in the 21st century despite resistance and interventions.

Conclusion

This final chapter has proposed that conquest – both military and commercial – has engendered changes in costume and the meaning and use of clothing. These changes are present in the multiple narratives that in turn comprise these three layers of meaning in textile and fashion. Therefore it is important to evaluate these social and material changes within a coherent framework, in this case the micro-meso-macro proximity analysis borrowed from methods in applied sociology. This analytical framework employs these three levels, to measure the proximate distances between textiles, clothing and fashion, and the society they inhabit. Working with a proximity system is the pivotal key to this chapter on war and fashion because it can compare various types of simultaneous interactions over multiple levels, taking in both an indigenous and globalized framework for how conflict changes costume – in the past and undoubtedly, in the future.

This volume concludes with the Afterword which comments on the 'military look' and its impact on contemporary fashion.

References

Anon. (n.d.). 'Peru: History & Culture (1998–2007)', http://www.geographia.com/peru/peruhistory. html. Accessed 1 April 2008.

Arnold, J. (1999). 'Dashing amazons: The development of women's riding dress c. 1500–1900', in A. de la Haye & E. Wilson (eds), *Defining dress: Dress as object, meaning and identity*, pp. 10–29. Manchester, UK: Manchester University Press.

Baclawski, K. (1995). *The guide to historic costume*. London: B.T. Batsford.

Barthes, R. (1983). *The Fashion System* (trans. M. Ward & R. Howard). New York: Hill and Wang.

Bauer, A. J. (2001). *Goods, power, history: Latin America's material culture*. Cambridge: Cambridge University Press.

Bronfenbrenner, U. (1979). *The Ecology of Human Development: Experiments by Nature and Design*. Cambridge, MA: Harvard University Press.

Brown, S. (2010). *Ecofashion*. UK: Lawrence King.

Cook, N. D., & Lovell, W. G. (eds) (1992). *'Secret judgements of god': Old world disease in colonial Spanish America*. Norman, OK: University of Oklahoma Press.

Cordwell, J. M. & Schwarz R. A. (eds) (1973). *The fabrics of culture: the anthropology of clothing and adornment*. Chicago: International Congress of Anthropological and Ethnological Sciences.

Costello, M., & Rall, D. N. (2013). 'Making memories on cloth, or Miss Liberty's Pinafore – A collaboration in textile narrative', *Australasian Journal of Popular Culture*, 2: 2, pp. 197–209.

Culbertson, R. (2006). 'War and the nature of ultimate things: An essay on the study of post-war cultures', in V. Sanford & A. Angel-Ajani (eds), *Engaged observer: Anthropology, advocacy and activism*, pp. 60–74. New Brunswick, NJ: Rutgers University Press.

Denevan, W. M. (ed.) (1976). *The native populations of the Americas in 1492*. Madison, WI: University of Wisconsin Press.

Dobyns, H. F. (1983). *Their number became thinned: Native American population dynamics in Eastern North America*. Knoxville, TN: University of Tennessee Press.

——— (2004). 'Statement', in W. G. Lowell, et al., (1941), 'In search of Native America', *Journal of the Southwest*, 46, pp. 443–47.

Dobyns, H. F., & Doughty, P. L. (1976). *Peru: A cultural history*. New York: Oxford University Press.

Dong, A. (2007). *Hollywood Chinese: The Chinese in American feature films*. Arthur Dong, Center for Asian American Media (CAAM); DeepFocus Productions Inc.

Dopfer, K., & Potts, J. (2008). *The General Theory of Economic Evolution*. London: Routledge.

Ferguson, N. (2011). *Civilization: The west and the rest*. London: Penguin.

Geoffroy-Schneiter, B. (2001). *Ethnic Style: History and Fashion* (trans. D. Dusinberre). New York: Assouline Publishing.

Greer, B. (2007). Definition of 'craftivism', in *Encyclopedia of Activism and Social Justice*. New Haven: Yale University Press.

Griffen, M. (18 May 2003). 'Knitting girl', *Sunday Life*, pp. 23–26.

Hakken, D. (1999). *Cyborgs@Cyberspace?: An ethnographer looks to the future*. New York: Routledge.

Hansen, K. T. (2010). 'Colonialism and imperialism', in V. Steele (ed.), *The Berg companion to fashion*, pp. 155–159. Oxford: Berg.

Harrold, R., & Legg, P. ([1988] 1999). *Folk Costumes of the World*. London: Octopus Publishing.

Hollander, A. (1992). 'The modernization of fashion', *Design Quarterly*, winter, pp. 27–33.

——— (1993). *Seeing through clothes*. New York: Viking Press.

——— (1994). *Sex and suits*. New York: Alfred A. Knopf.

Horyn, C. (17 April 2011). 'Sailing blindly', *The New York Times*, p. 4.

Jones, A. R., & Stallybrass, P. (2000). *Renaissance Clothing and the Materials of Memory*. Cambridge: Cambridge University Press.

Kawamura, Y. (2007). *Fashion-ology*. Oxford: Berg.

Kopytoff, I. (1986). 'The cultural biography of things: Commoditization as process', in A. Appadurai (ed.), *The social life of things: Commodities in cultural perspective*, pp. 64–94. Cambridge: Cambridge University Press.

Küchler, S., & Miller, D. (eds) (2005). *Clothing as Material Culture*. Oxford: Berg.

Lehrman, K. (2003). 'Does It Come in Chrome?', *New York Times* Book Review [online] 16 November. http://www.nytimes.com/2003/11/16/books/does-it-come-in-chrome.html. Accessed 30 November 2012.

Leuchtman, H. (1993). 'Technologies and power: The Andean case', in E. H. Boone (ed.), *Configurations of power: Holistic anthropology in theory and practice*, pp. 244–80. Ithaca: NY: Cornell University Press.

Locke, L. L. (1923). *The ancient Quipu or Peruvian knot record*. New York: American Museum of Natural History.

Lovell, W. G. (1992). '"Heavy shadows and black night": Disease and depopulation in colonial Spanish America', *AAAG*, 82, pp. 426–43.

Luttwak, E. N. (1976). *The grand strategy of the roman empire from the First century A.D. to the Third*. Baltimore, MD: Johns Hopkins University Press.

Mann, C. C. (2005). *1491: New revelations of the Americas before Columbus*. New York: Knopf.

——— (2011). *1493: Uncovering the New World Columbus created*. New York: Knopf Doubleday.

Miller, F. R. (1993). *The man in the bowler hat: His history and iconography*. Chapel Hill, NC: University of North Carolina Press.

Murra, J. V. (1989). 'Cloth and its function in the Inka state', in A. Weiner & J. Schneider (eds), *Cloth and human experience*, pp. 275–302. Washington, D.C.: Smithsonian University Press.

Postrel, V. (2003). *The substance of style: How the rise of aesthetic value is remaking commerce, culture, and consciousness*. New York: HarperCollins.

Quilter, J., & Urton, G. (2002). *Narrative threads: Accounting and recounting in Andean khipu*. Austin, TX: University of Texas Press.

Rall, D. N., & Costello, M. (2010). 'Women, craft and protest – Yesterday and today', *Australian Folklore: A Yearly Journal of Folklore Studies*, 25, pp. 79–96.

Root, R. A. (2010). 'Latin American fashion', in V. Steele (ed.), *The Berg companion to fashion*, pp. 469–72. Oxford: Berg.

Rovine, V. L. (2005). 'Working the edge: XULY.Bët's recycled clothing', in H. Clark & A. Palmer (eds), *Old Clothes, New Looks: Second hand fashion*, pp. 215–27. Oxford: Berg.

——— (2010). 'XULY Bët' in V. Steele (ed.), *The Berg companion to fashion*, pp. 741–42. Oxford: Berg.

Spence, J. (1990). *The search for modern China*. New York: W.W. Norton.

Spindler, A. M. (2 May 1993). 'Prince of Pieces', *The New York Times*, pp. 1, 13.

Tidball, H. (1969). *Peru: Textiles* (Shuttlecraft Guild Monograph 25). Freeland, Washington: HTH Publishers.

Tseëlon, E. (2011). 'Introduction: A critique of the ethical fashion paradigm', *Critical Studies in Fashion and Beauty*, 2: 1 & 2, pp. 3–68.

Tseëlon, E., Gonzáles, A. M., & Kaiser, S. (eds) (2011–present). *Critical Studies in Fashion and Beauty*. Bristol: Intellect Ltd.

Urton, G., & Brezine, C. (9 September 2009). Khipu Database Project. khipukamayuq.fas. harrvard.edu. Accessed 18 November 2012.

Vincent, S. J. (2009). *The anatomy of fashion: Dressing the body from the Renaissance to today*. Oxford: Berg.

Wilk, R. (1990). 'Consumer goods as a dialogue about development', *Cultural History,* 7, pp. 79–100.

Wilson, E. ([1985] 2003). *Adorned in Dreams: Fashion and Modernity.* London: Virago.

Zalopany, C. (20 November 2011). 'Trigger fingers', *The New York Times Style Magazine,* p. 13.

Notes

1   Records in the *Runa Sumi* language, the adopted common language of the Empire reconfigures the spelling as Inka rather than the Spanish word, Inca. The Spanish called this language Quechua. These spelling changes are reflected in recent scholarship (Mann, 2005: 66).

2   See the website appliedsoc.org.

3   Copyright for this photo, attributed to Martin Chambi (1934) is undetermined after a diligent search. Should you own copyright to this photograph please notify the book publisher.

4   Naomi Klein speaks of the 'homogenizing effect of what the Indian physicist Vandana Shiva calls "the mono-culture" – it is in effect, *mono-multiculturalism*' (Klein 2001: 130, emphasis added).

Afterword

The military in contemporary fashion

Denise N. Rall

The linkages between war, textile and fashion have a long historical past, and the cycles of fashion will continue to 'roll out the [gun] barrel' (sic) as long as the merchandise continues to sell. In February 2010, *Vogue* (Australia) offered the following advice:

Calling all fashion cadets: it's time to get in line.

Order number one: wear a touch of the military this season, as inspired by the myriad of army-style looks on the runway ... the season's colour palette was equally inspired by all things martial: "Beige and cream colours dominated the runways, as did a touch of army green".

As Jane Jasper of Sydney boutique Land's End says: "Khaki is a great colour to wear because it captures a tough mood ... put a khaki T-shirt under last season's jacket for an instant style update."

... but which camp to join? One side ... conjured up glamazon, edgy army girls clad in ripped jeans and T-shirts and jackets adorned with mesh and graphic colour. The other were clean, structured looks ... (2010: 35–36).

The options for military chic in the 'first camp' included clothing and footwear under subcategories including 'Soldier on', 'Boot camp', 'Tactical response', and 'Jungle warfare' to name a few. In the second 'camp', that of lean structured lines, items were offered under subcategories like 'Line up' and 'Body armour'. Boots, belts and buttons were all quite evidently on display.

This is not to say that the cruelties of conquest have not affected current trends in high fashion too. The animal rights movement and its impact on the hunting and wearing of furs is the most prominent, or outspoken, of the various anti-cruelty movements. Some of today's most important designers with international profiles – Stella McCartney comes immediately to mind – refuse to employ any animal products in their work.

Highlighting the cause against cruelty to humans, on the other hand, has centred on the globalization of clothing production, and the politics of sweatshops and children's rights. These are very worthy causes and high fashion has played a significant role in publicizing the issues, even though the production of clothing, in fashion as elsewhere, remains focused on the 'bottom line.'

Individual designers occasionally find that they must simply 'do something' or, perhaps, *be seen to do something,* about military atrocities. In 2011, jewellery designers Peter Thum and John Zapolski opened a new collaboration called Founderie 47, to reduce Africa's 'estimated 20 million assault weapons by turning the metal into jewelry':

> Working with the Mines Advisory Group, the company has helped remove more than 5,000 AK-47s [automatic machine rifles] from Congo. Designed with the jeweler Philip Changi, each steel and gold signet ring ... finances the demolition of 75 more guns and is etched with the serial number of the weapon it once was (Zalopany 2011).

It is evident that this effort, while commendable, will have very little impact on reducing the numbers of assault weapons, whether in Africa or elsewhere in the world. A ring made with 75 rifles with an estimated 20 million weapons still in play serves to demonstrate the futility of reducing the world's weaponry through a fashion statement.

In summary: where can fashion go in a world of conflict?

This discussion of the many issues surrounding the intersection of war, the military and the theory and practice of textiles has produced more questions than answers. There are many further avenues for exploration: with the ravages of ongoing conflicts in the 21st century, can fashion studies take its place in the examination of war within popular culture? This could link the study of textiles and fashion to an area of investigation that some theorists have named post-war studies.

However, it is important for textile and fashion academics to continue their critique of the military and its presence in popular trends in clothing. Currently, artists are beginning to take notice; particularly interesting are the new discussions around the concept of 'camouflage'. Recently, the Canadian War Museum offered an exhibition entitled: *Camouflage – From battlefield to catwalk*[1], the title clearly acknowledging the relationship between war and fashion (2009–2010).

Further, since 9/11 the topic of war has become intimately linked to trends in popular culture, especially among New Yorkers that are associated with the fashion industry. This became evident in a recent release of high fashion photography entitled *Eleven* from Philip-Lorca diCordia and his publishing partner Dennis Freedman, of the New York women's fashion daily *W*. During the book launch, diCordia was interviewed about the book, and about fashion, in an article that suggests that the artwork presented here becomes 'focused past fashion'[2]:

> It is strange that the cover of the book is of the World Trade Center and the first image in the book is Cairo on fire. All that we're hearing now about what has happened in Egypt under Mubarak was happening then. If I was absolving my conscience of something, it was to suggest that not everything is perfect, and fashion isn't just about clothes and beautiful people.

If this volume has a single conclusion, it is this: war, textile and fashion are incontrovertibly linked.

Denise N. Rall, Editor

Notes

1   See http://www.warmuseum.ca/event/camouflage-from-battlefield-to-catwalk/ An earlier exhibition about camouflage was also held at the Imperial War Museum in London in 2007.
2   See http://tmagazine.blogs.nytimes.com/2011/02/11/artifacts-philip-lorca-dicorcias-perfect-eleven/?_r=0.

Contributors

Prudence Black

Dr Prudence Black is an ARC Postdoctoral Fellow. Black completed her Ph.D. in the Department of Gender and Cultural Studies at the University of Sydney in 2009. Prudence has taught courses in the areas of cultural studies, fashion, industrial design, design history and theory at the University of Sydney, the University of Technology, Sydney and the University of New South Wales. As well as her academic roles she has worked at the Powerhouse Museum and the Australian Museum as a curator and researcher for exhibitions about Australian popular culture, fashion, design and Indigenous culture. She has published mainly in the areas of design, modernism, fashion and popular culture. Current research projects include a study of occupational dress for disadvantaged and incarcerated women re-entering the workforce, intimacy and affect in home dressmaking, and the industrial and gendered history of flight attendants in Australia. She is a member of the Gender and Modernity Research Group and the Australian Fashion Studies Network. Black has held consultancies with the Centre for Olympic Studies, University of NSW, Department of Foreign Affairs and Trade, Australian Museum Business Services and Global Campus Management. She is currently a host of the annual meeting of the Cultural Studies Association of Australasia. Her recent book, *The Flight Attendant's Shoe* (NewSouth Books, 2011) is a design and cultural history that uses the flight attendants' uniforms to chart the links between the Australian fashion and textile industry and versions of Australian nationalism, militarism, cosmopolitanism, and the corporate world.

Annita Boyd

Dr Annita Boyd is a lecturer in the School of Humanities at Griffith University in Brisbane, Australia, teaching in Screen Studies and Cultural Sociology. Her research interests include the intersection of fashion theory with film and television, and its uptake in various sites of popular culture. She has written on the representation and consumption of branded prestige handbags, the costumes of Little Edie (Bouvier Beale) of *Grey Gardens* fame, but also has an interest in Victorian fashion and the forgotten histories of Australian women. Her article, 'The Private and Public Life of Nellie Stewart's Bangle' is forthcoming in *The Journal of Popular Romance Studies*, and focuses on the hidden story behind the widespread craze for a plain gold bangle.

Jane Chapman

Jane Chapman is Professor of Communications at Lincoln University, visiting fellow at Wolfson College and the Centre of South Asian Studies, Cambridge University, and an adjunct professor at Macquarie University, Australia. She is the author of eight books and numerous academic articles and book chapters within the field of journalism, media history and literary journalism, specializing comparatively in France, India, Britain and Australia. Jane trained as a historian at University College London, Cambridge, and the LSE, where she obtained a doctorate in French social movements during the 1920s. She is currently a research leader for a grant project entitled 'Comics and the World Wars – a Cultural Record', funded by the Arts and Humanities Research Council (AHRC) in the United Kingdom.

Jennifer Craik

Jennifer Craik is Research Professor in the School of Fashion and Textiles at RMIT University, Melbourne; and Commissioning Editor of the Australia New Zealand School of Government ANU E-Press series, Canberra, Australia. Research interests include interdisciplinary approaches to the study of fashion and dress, contemporary culture, cultural and media policy, cultural tourism, and arts funding. Publications include *The Face of Fashion: Cultural Studies in Fashion* (London and New York: Routledge, 1993), *Uniforms Exposed: From Conformity to Transgression* (Oxford and New York: Berg Publishers, 2005), and *Fashion: The Key Concepts* (Oxford and New York: Berg Publishers, 2009). *The Fashion Studies Book* (London & New York: Routledge) co-authored with Dr Sharon Peoples is in press.

Richard Gehrmann

Richard Gehrmann is a Senior Lecturer at the University of Southern Queensland where he teaches international relations and history. His recent publications have addressed the migration dimensions of intercountry adoption, Australian soldiers in colonial India, and war and culture in contemporary Afghanistan. He is interested in the fields of cultural history, and war and society. Current research projects include the representation of recent conflicts in film, White African migrant identity, and the military relationship between Australia and India during the colonial era. As an Australian Army Reservist he served in Iraq in 2006–07, and in the Mentoring and Reconstruction Task Force in Afghanistan in 2008–09.

Davinia Gregory

Davinia Gregory is a part-time Lecturer in the Creative Arts and Fine Arts programmes at Bath Spa University. Her MA is from the Royal College of Art and Victoria & Albert Museum. Currently, her teaching appointments include Kingston University (Design History), University for the Creative Arts (Fashion Theory), the Victoria & Albert Museum (Twentieth-Century Design History) and the Musée du Louvre (Art History) as well as Bath Spa

University. Her research includes projects which examine and combine twentieth-century city planning, redevelopment and lived experience with the effect of decolonization and subsequent multiculturalism on the material cultures of Britain and its former colonies. Her projects span the fields of visual culture, architectural and social history, cultural geography and post-colonial studies.

Kylee Micajah Hartman-Warren

Kylee M. Hartman-Warren is a Ph.D. candidate in Film and Digital Image at the University of Sydney, Australia. She is the current Vice President (Community) at Sydney University Postgraduate Representative Association (SUPRA), and an International Officer at Council of Australian Postgraduate Associations (CAPA). Kylee has been involved with student representation much of her academic career, and she began her time at SUPRA as its Director of Student Publications in July 2010. Before attending the University of Sydney, Kylee spent time in the United States working as a sustainability coordinator, and volunteered for both political campaigns and environmental organizations. Her experience includes volunteer work for Rowe Sanctuary, and the American Museum of Natural History, as well as internships under a photographer for National Geographic, and for the Bosque Del Apache Sandhill Crane Festival. Kylee started studying film and digital image when she began documenting crane migration in 2008. Kylee graduated from Reed College where she studied philosophy and classics.

Amanda Laugesen

Dr Amanda Laugesen is currently with the Australian National University, Canberra, ACT, Australia. She completed her Ph.D. in the History Program at the ANU in 2000, and subsequently worked as a research editor at the Australian National Dictionary Centre, ANU, as well as undertaking teaching in the History Department. She produced two lexical monographs while working at the ANDC, as well as working on a number of other projects relating to the history of Australian English. Amanda was appointed as a Lecturer in History at the University of Southern Queensland in 2004, and Lecturer in History and American Studies in 2006. She returned to Canberra at the end of 2008. Laugesen's research has included publications in the areas of historical memory, the history of reading, libraries and publishing, cultural history and lexicography. Her most recent book, *Boredom is the Enemy: the Intellectual and Imaginative Lives of Australian Soldiers at War* (Ashgate, 2011), is a study of Australian soldiers' experiences of education and entertainment during wartime. Currently, she serves as Director of the Australian National Dictionary Centre.

Denise N. Rall

Dr Denise N. Rall is an adjunct lecturer in the School of Arts & Social Sciences at Southern Cross University in Lismore, NSW. She holds a Ph.D. in Internet Studies from Southern Cross University, and her thesis explored Internet studies programmes at the Oxford Internet

Institute, the University of Minnesota, and Curtin University in Western Australia. Rall also holds an MA in Comparative Literature from the University of Wisconsin, where her focus was the German romantic novel. In 2009, after completing a course in Costume, she began making costumed-mannequin textile sculptures and wearable art. Her work has been exhibited around Australia, including the School of Fashion and Textile at RMIT, Melbourne, and in the Rocks, Sydney, as well as in the United States. Her most recent publications include 'What would Kant think?' a study of search engine logics (Emerald 2012) and 'Making memories on cloth, or *Miss Liberty's Pinafore*: A collaboration in textile narrative' with Dr Moya Costello, published in the *Australasian Journal of Popular Culture* (Intellect 2013). Her collaborations include an event called 'Wear the Wild Words' – an evening of poetry where her wearble artworks were modelled by students and academics from the Creative writing programme at Southern Cross University. She currently serves as Secretary of the Popular Culture Association of Australia-New Zealand (PopCAANZ).

Heather Smith

Heather Smith lectures in public relations at the University of Southern Queensland and is the owner/managing director of a Queensland based public relations consultancy. She is currently researching the construct of the brand of the muscled military body, and regional challenges facing modern public relations professionals. She has extensive experience in public relations, media and marketing across numerous sectors including education, local and state government, finance, energy, natural resources and not-for-profit.

Joanne Turney

Dr Jo Turney is the subject specialist for contextual studies and the course leader for the MA Investigating Fashion Design at Bath Spa University. She is the author of *The Culture of Knitting* (Berg 2009) and the contributing editor of *Fashion and Crime: Dressing for deviance* (I.B. Tauris 2013) as well as other books and papers relating to everyday textiles and dress. She is also the editor of the journal *Clothing Cultures* published by Intellect. She is interested in the material culture of contemporary life and likes cats.